FROM HUMAN SENTIENCE TO DRAMA

FROM HUMAN
SENTIENCE TO DRAMA

Principles of Critical Analysis,
Tragic and Comedic

Richard N. Pollard
and Hazel M. (Batzer) Pollard

Ohio University Press: Athens, Ohio

TO OUR PARENTS
JOHN AND SUSIE POLLARD
FRED AND AGNES BATZER

PREFACE

Because over the centuries critical commentary has so pro-
liferated, approaches to artistic interpretation have become so
many, theories and hypotheses of artistic and critical purpose
have so multiplied, and critical vocabulary has become so vari-
ously used as to create confusion in meaningful interpretative
evaluation, we are attempting to enunciate a principle of artistic
impulse and descriptive analysis that will make use of a new
critical vocabulary (contextually defined); base interpretation
on the common sentient apprehensions of the impressions of
experiences of man in the world that is his—genetically, environmentally, topically, universally, and conceptually; delineate the impulsive sources of artistic inclination; and establish
procedural approaches to a common sense interpretation of
artistry and its experience-meaning origins in the state of man
as a sentient creature in Nature determined only by the unique
experience offered by Nature as the common denominator (the
universally apprehensible impulse of experiential impression)
of man, individually and collectively. We do not attempt to differentiate that experience in terms of religious, philosophical,
or scientific points of view; rather, we wish to allow the reader
to apprehend the principle in the broadest sense amenable to
the label he attaches to our referential base, *Nature*. This view,
of course, includes physical, mental, emotional, spiritual, and

behavioral states of and in Nature as responsive parts of any concept significant to the reader; and it excludes none of the bents toward which his particularized leanings might direct him. We ask only that we be allowed *Nature* as a communal assumption (the reader may wish to substitute *God, divine inspiration, evolution, racial memory,* or some other term in its stead) upon which to establish our essential premise as motive, inspiration, and genesis of sentient apprehension and its expressionable impressions of natural impulses of experience-meaning in the re-creative processes of art.

The Natural Ethic-Aesthetic excludes none of the generic types of substantial forms from consideration, but we have chosen to limit our discussion in this work primarily to *tragedy* (as either a natural or a topically determined phenomenon illustrative of the principle) and secondarily to *comedy* (as an essential corollary derivative of the same impulses) without attempting value judgments on the superiority or inferiority of these or any other artistic media. Indeed, the principle applies equally well (in our experience) to any art form: architecture, tragedy, comedy, tragicomedy, dramatic romance, epic, metaphysical poetry, painting, music, sculpture, or any other expression in substantial form of man's apprehensive re-creation or reincarnation of experience-meaning. But because the principle we enunciate is descriptive, synthesizing, and assimilative, we find it impossible to define except in the total effect of the work itself (which is its own descriptive function), or to elucidate without formulaic prescriptive definition (which is precisely what we wish to avoid), all the possible applications of the principle within the scope of one volume. This makes the work merely a suggestive preface to other works by providing a principle of approach deriving its essential premise from the Natural Ethic-Aesthetic and establishing a means of analysis and interpretative apprehension of artistic experience-meaning that avoids the formulaic saws of prescriptive criticism.

To achieve the present work, we have pooled a century of sentience, nine decades of intense study, and half a century of teaching experience. Some may object to the absence of footnotes, bibliography, and other scholarly paraphernalia (we admit that we have read countless books and articles approaching our subject); but the essential material of this study comes from experience that can not be attributed to any particular authority. If specific debt is owed, perhaps we should give credit to Nature and to our fathers whose roots in the soil and fidelity to that Nature of which they were so much working parts implicitly impressed our focal and perspective apprehensions of the ethical and aesthetic principles inherent in Nature that (both consequently and subsequently) we found essentially evidenced in the re-creative functioning of experience-meaning in the works of great art. Our secondary sources would then be, of necessity, the works of a host of philosophers, artists, critics, scholars, and doers of work essential to survival, whom we have appreciated and learned from to derive our own experience-meaning of Nature and of the nature of art as its expressive derivative.

Richard N. & Hazel M. Pollard

CONTENTS

I

THE SENTIENT IMPULSE

A MULTIPLICITY OF WORLDS INTERFUSE TO MAKE UP THE Nature that is the habitat of that Johnny-come-lately, that late bloomer, that sentient creature who is the epitome of the willful doing, making, thinking, emoting, fantasy creating, god-worshiping, behaviorally conditioned, memory-preserving part of Nature called man. Another multiplicity of worlds make up the experimenting, curious, error-prone, physical, mental, emotional, spiritual, and behavioral nature that is man's in his role as a fallible determiner of his own place in the scheme of Nature's substance, form, and movement. Man alone, of all Nature's parts, records his experiences in forms of suggestion and associational imagery and perpetuates their meanings from one generation to another by means of translation of experience into substantial representational forms; and man alone is capable of an ethical and aesthetic extension of experience-meaning through intellectual progression and intuitive apprehension into work of such contextual integrity that a similar experience-meaning may be transmitted from one generation to another or from one place or time to another. Man alone, of all the parts of Nature, evidences the ability, capacity, and inclination to

1

apprehend in his own nature and in the nature of Nature of which he is a part, the comedy, tragedy, and apathy to which he is subjected and to retain these conditions by means of art.

Two worlds, specifically, interfuse to make up the world that is man's: the world outside man and the world within man. The world outside man is made of a number of worlds: the whole natural universe; the supranatural world, or that which transcends the natural world or is beyond the natural world; the world of the cultural milieu of time, place, and people; the immediate public world of man; and the immediate private and personal world of man. Each man lives in all worlds that are outside himself; and, while living in them as he does, he lives in the world that is within himself. The totality of these worlds outside himself and within himself makes up the condition that is his in the world that is his. The world within man particularizes him: his human nature with the unique sensitivity to and perceptivity of experiences that are his and the receptivity that makes those experiences a part of him determine what he is both individually and collectively. For each particular man, the condition that is his is a condition, finally, of his own apprehension.

Through his prehistory and history, man has known but partially and inaccurately the world that actually is or may be, naturally or supranaturally. He has constructed and continues to construct what for him is his natural world out of the perceptual data he has of that world; he has constructed and continues to construct a supranatural world, or a world in and about and beyond his natural world, out of perceptual data that seem inexplicable according to laws of natural process. How accurately and completely man individually or collectively, isolatedly or cumulatively, through history, has constructed his natural and supranatural worlds depends upon how accurate and complete have been the perceptual data he has used in constructing those worlds. But however accurate or inaccurate, complete or incomplete, these worlds are, for him they are the

2

facts of the world outside him and the facts of the world within him. For the particular man, these do not necessarily remain the facts that they seem; instead, they are what they are for him by the way he sees them, by the way he knows them at any specific moment of awareness. His nature and his experience determine how he sees and knows the condition that is his world. And the condition of the world that is his works to make his nature and experience what they are. Out of the natural and supranatural worlds of man, out of his inner and outer worlds, man creates another world, an institutional world to regularize the nature of his existence and his ways of living at any particular time. The institutional world is a manifestation of man's long anthropological cultural evolution. Institutions usually have their beginnings in the needs of man in some early time of his history, or even in his prehistory. The ancient beginnings of most of man's institutional conditions and the imperceptible changing that may have marked their evolution from their beginnings to what they are at any specific time may make them seem to have a particular authority and sanctity and inviolability rooted in tradition. These institutional conditions may change, however, in accord with man's knowledge, illusions, and delusions about his world and his experience in that world. Though the immediate public and private institutional worlds involve man with seemingly more real influence and concern than do the larger natural and supranatural worlds in which he in his immediate world has his setting, those worlds make up the juxtaposed and interfused conditions and needs that require his development of the institutional world. Man's public and private worlds, as well as his natural and supranatural worlds, impose implicit and explicit contractual obligations on him in his relation to all other men in his private and public worlds and in his relation to whatever supernatural power there may be for him. These contractual obligations are implicit in the quality or nature of the natural and supranatural conditions of man's

3

world and in the relationship of those conditions. They are explicit in the consequences of action determined by the natural and supranatural conditions or by arbitrary or artificial institutionalizing of natural or supranatural conditions. Whatever the contractual obligations, they bind man to others in his world and they bind others to him. The bonds may be internal and spiritual, and they may be external and formal. The intricate and intimate relationship that they may make may be integrally organic. They may make man one with humanity; they may make all humanity one in localized and unlocalized time and place.

Man, in his general nature and through the process of his cultural evolution, has come to recognize three substantial conditions in the complexity of his world: presentient, sentient, and postsentient; in his individual nature, however, he may reject one or more of these conditions or qualify their natures by his particular understanding, belief, prejudice, ignorance, or knowledge. But whatever the conditions he accepts or rejects, his world is the world he creates out of those conditions; and the world he rejects will impose obligations on him as will the world he accepts. For both collective man and individual man, there may be no contractual obligations except in terms of positions which provide alternatives or choices. For either collective man or individual man there may be acceptance or rejection of obligations arbitrarily imposed. For neither collective man nor individual man will all obligations remain constant or invariable. But for all sentient men there are three invariable, physical certainties that are the absolute facts of sentient being: birth, death, and the variable interim between these extremes. Because man has no control over his own birth or the conditions precedent to his birth or the conditions subsequent to his birth but precedent to his sentient state, he is subject to an inviolable natural contract emanating from the condition of Nature herself. His physical being; his sex; his particularities of race, including perhaps his racial memory; his origins; his setting in time and place; and all qualities of parental heritage are determined in the presentient state at the moment of conception. The natural or elemental contract of the presentient state before birth involves man in all conditions subject to natural law, the subconscious condition subject to later conjecture, and the amorphous condition of the atavistic or natural influence and the animistic or supranatural influence. The presentient state between birth and sentience involves man in conditions wherein he is subject to and sensitive to environmental conditioning but wherein he remains precognitive. In the presentient state all conditions are outside man's consciousness and outside his exercise of any control by his own will or through the process of abstract thought.

Two qualities of the natural contract have been achieved totally and irrevocably by conception and birth. The third quality of the natural contract is achieved with sentient cognition which is requisite to functioning within the second contract: the sophisticated or institutional contract. No moral judgment is implied in the natural contract, and only with specific, topical conditions in the institutional contract; moral judgment is implied or defined arbitrarily in the supernatural contract. The state of the sophisticated or institutional contract is the sentient state. The sentient state involves all conditions of consciousness; the quality of acceptance, qualification, or rejection of particular conditions or circumstances; the creative condition, including the creation of institutions and loyalties; the speculative condition, wherein man envisions conditions other than they seem to be in reality; and all conditions developed by man himself in order to regularize the nature of his existence. In the sentient state the condition of man is both natural and institutional: he is still subject to inherited or natural qualities, but in addition he is subject to the sophistication of his environment. In the sentient state man's sensitivity to and perceptivity of conditions evolve and develop, and as he becomes capable of reason and exercise of reason he is enabled to create through thought and imagination new conditions that exceed the conditions of the natural contract. Man who does not achieve sentience may be subject to the institutional contract, but only sentient man may function in it and exercise influence over it, or shape it to fit his own needs and the needs of others. In the sentient state of the sophisticated or institutional contract, man is in essential control of conditions. His basic obligation to the terms of the contract is to fill the space between sentience and death, even though that space be filled with only the single act of suicide. All men are obliged to fill that space; they may fill it in different manners under the influence of different external and internal conditions, but all must fill it. In this one respect all are alike, and all have the same elemental obligation: to fill the space between sentience and death. That elemental obligation establishes an identity among all men, collective man. The degree of each man's involvement with the obligation in relation to other men will depend on the conditions that influence individual man: his own thinking and experience, the nature of his institutional control, and his acceptance, qualification, or rejection of personal, private, or institutional prescriptions. In the sentient state man is subject to topical conventions, mores, laws, and institutions; these provide the external conditions of his existence. His responses to those conditions, based on the perceptions and sensitivity and receptivity of both his natural and his institutional contract and on his internal conditions, will evidence his participation in the sophisticated or institutional contract. The sentient state involves the conditions of regularization and control. Because the sentient state is the state of awareness or consciousness of conditions, it is the pre-eminent state in the development of tragedy, comedy, and apathy, the conditions of man's consciously recognized existence.

In his sentient state man creates a conjectural state involving an existence beyond physical, conscious reality, outside the realm of invariable concrete evidence, but imposed upon man's consciousness by institutional tradition and by individual belief. That state, beyond the conditions of evidential sentience, beyond the sentient state closed by death, is the postsentient or unconscious state. In terms of physical reality it is conjectural, though in terms of man's beliefs it is as real and it exercises as much influence as do the conditions of man's physical existence. The postsentient state involves all the conditions concerning man's beliefs, his preternatural experience, his abstract concern for problematic solutions, his hopes and fears stemming from uncertainty about existence following the close of the sentient state, and conditions inexplicable by natural contracts. Within the postsentient state functions the supernatural contract focusing attention on such amorphic conditions, in terms of physical reality, as man's identification with Nature, with spiritual being, with total oblivion. The supernatural or conjectural contract of the postsentient state may be paradisaic, nirvanic, reincarnative, deific, theistic, pantheistic, or atheistic. It may be viewed as the cessation of all attributes relating to phenomenal existence and the total loss of identity. It may, in the speculations of some men, revert to the presentient and to a cyclic continuation of the processes of birth, life, death sequences. But whatever the qualities of conditions of the postsentient state may be, for individual man and for men of similar views, those qualities and conditions are as real and as influential as the facts of the natural universe in the shaping of the conditions that comprise the world of man.

Three states comprise the world of man: the presentient, the sentient, and the postsentient. In man's awareness of conditions making up his world, these states may be subconscious, conscious, or unconscious. The conditions themselves are natural, sophisticated, and supernatural. Man's contractual obligations to these conditions are elemental, institutional, or conjectural. An evolutionary process controls the progression of states, awarenesses, conditions, and contracts; but the evolutionary process itself is modified and differentiated by the imagination and creativity of man himself as he sees himself in relation to the conditions that comprise his world and as he creates new conditions by assimilating and synthesizing his impressions of his world. The conditions created by man out of his reasoning about, sensitivity to, and perception of the conditions of his world may, in unique man's being, exceed any previous set of conditions: natural, sophisticated, or supernatural. Man may bring into being a new world, the world of his own creativity, peopled by his own generation of identities and subjected to the conditions of his own imagination.

Man, in varying degrees and circumstances and subject to a variety of conditions and actions and impulses, is a creative creature. His sentience, his emotions, his fanciful nature, his beliefs, his speculative capacity, his imagination, and his inadequacies in seeing, feeling, sensing, and interpreting the whole of the reality of the complex accumulation of conditions that comprise his world, may cause him to create or establish within his own being a world that is not a photographic or phonographic representation of the world that exists in physical reality, discernible alike to all other men. That is not to say that the world created by individual man is not a real world, that it is not a world in which every characteristic is not a believable representation of reality and in which every character is not as true to life as any flesh and blood creature of the physical world. Man's individual world may be as genuine a representation as a photograph, yet it may have none of the identical qualities or conditions of the photographic representation of the world.

Man is a repository of thoughts, impressions, sensuous interpretations, dreams, fancies and fantasies, beliefs, prejudices, and emotional responses: in short, a microcosmic world in himself that may be and probably is unlike any other world but not necessarily alien to or different from any other world. For example, a man sees and knows two people, two separate, distinct, uniquely complex human beings. Man interprets their characters; gains specific sensory impressions of their physical forms; infers particular qualities of their moral, mental, and spiritual natures; senses certain states of emotion in each; and develops his own understanding of what their total human nature suggests and evidences. These impressions, conscious and subconscious, fragmented and totaled, suggested and evidenced, become for man the sums, separately, of the reality of his two subjects. These impressions are deposited in his own nature and there transformed and altered by his beliefs, understandings, prejudices, and limitations imposed by his physical, mental, emotional, spiritual, and behavioral fallibility. These impressions may lie fallow in the repository of man's nature, or they may become the substance of creativity when activated by impulse or imagination. If the impressions become activated and sort from their repository separately and descriptively, they are apt to bear little resemblance to the total complexity of their original sources; but they may, individually and separately, be as true a representation of a being in real life as any other individual, separate representation, though their exact counterparts may not be found anywhere in the physical universe. The impressions may also become mixed and juxtaposed in their repository, and in the mixing of natures and characteristics and forms a marriage may occur that may produce progeny so unlike either parent impression that when it sorts descriptively from its repository, no trace of its heritage will be discernible, though it may be as real, descriptively, as any real creature described. In such manner conditions may become other than what they seem in physical reality, and a whole new set of conditions may develop to create the world of man as it exists for him.

II

THE TRAGIC IMPULSE

TRAGEDY IN ITS ESSENTIAL FORM IS THE EFFECT CREATED when a juxtaposition or combination of conditions, or an alteration within a condition, activates a tragic impulse which educes and evokes responsive awareness of painful consequences deriving from particular circumstances within the conditions or condition of man's world. Though man may remain passively unreceptive and unresponsive to conditions that exist, he may, when the tragic impulse is activated, become aware of implications in those conditions that will demand suffering if he responds responsibly to the consequences of action stirred by the tragic impulse. He may also be caused to suffer by the tragic impulse and its consequences even though he never quite becomes cognizant of the nature of the impulse and its consequences; he may come to experience suffering through imagined conditions and through conditions arising spontaneously outside his range of awareness.

Sentient man, generally, may be sensitive to and perceptive of the conditions of his inner and outer worlds. The intensity of his impressions will be determined by his capacities for sensitivity and perceptivity, by his abilities to be sensitive and perceptive, by his will to be sensitive and perceptive, and by the receptivity of his nature: physically, mentally, emotionally, spiritually, and behaviorally. His receptivity will be determined by his capacity, ability, instinct, inclination, and will to receive the impressions stimulating his perceptivity and sensitivity; his receptivity will give him a potential resource for responsiveness. The intensity and magnitude of his response will be determined by his capacity for responsiveness, his ability to respond, the nature of his instinct to respond, his inclination to respond, his will to respond, and by impulses in his physical, mental, emotional, spiritual, and behavioral states that urge him to respond. His awareness of the import of his response will be determined by his capacity, ability, instinct, inclination, and will to be aware, and by the value judgment he places on the object of his awareness. The intensity, or qualitative degree, of his awareness will be determined by the depth of his understanding; the fineness of his sensitivity; the scope of his perceptivity; the capacity of his receptivity; the profundity of his contemplation; the nature of his psychic experience; the range of his physical, mental, emotional, spiritual, and behavioral powers; the ability to respond; the reasonableness of his decisions; the limits of his logical nature and powers of sequential thought; the extent of control he exercises over his own nature; the influence of the subconscious on his nature; the beliefs he holds dear; and the conventions, mores, obligations, restraints, physical conditions, institutional influences, and value judgments of the world he exists in. The magnitude, or quantitative degree, of his awareness will be determined by the intensity of his response, by the scope of his responsiveness, by the universality of his response, and by the accumulation of conditions relating to his awareness. The universality of response will be determined by applicability of the response outside topical limitations of time and place; by identification of the response with primal, primitive, sophisticated, speculative, or fanciful conditions of awareness; by as-

11

sociation of the response with an evolution of causal motives and effected consequences; and by continuity of the value systems evoking a response.

Tragedy, then, will occur to man when he becomes aware that the conditions of his world have created circumstances demanding personally responsive choice of action wherein the choice can lead only to consequences of inescapable suffering that will require a level of endurance seemingly unbearable. Tragedy is the presence of a dilemma, the choosing of a response demanded by the dilemma, and the suffering occasioned by the consequences of the choice; it is not only being caught between Scylla and Charybdis, it is choosing between Scylla and Charybdis and responding to, resisting, and enduring the consequences inherent in the choice. It is man facing and resisting inscrutable fate and enduring its uncertainty; it is man straining for the unattainable with hope and enduring the despair of failure; it is man being toppled from the pinnacle of bliss into the abyss of denial; it is man daring to meet the implacable and attempting to face it down; it is man realizing his uniqueness in a world antagonistic to individuality; it is man groping painfully for understanding of the conditions of his world; it is man spurning arbitrary and ready-made answers by questioning of conditions prescribed by tradition and convention and opportunism; it is man shaking the bases of the *status quo* of institutionalism with revolutionary ideas and evolutionary ideals and it is man suffering when the values of institutional tradition are threatened or subverted; it is man resisting fanaticism and enduring fanatical reprisal; it is man doing under one law and enduring judgment under another; it is man choosing to endure suffering rather than to renege on principle or succumb to opportunism; it is man causing and enduring pain for himself because of his resistance to impulses inherent in the conditions of his world; it is man alienated from a sense of well-

12

being, of belonging, of freedom and liberty, and of fitting into the external conditions of his world; it is man denied communion with others of his kind and abandoned by all he holds dear: family, friends, god, race; and it is man alone, resisting and enduring his loneliness, suffering his aloneness.

Man suffers tragedy because he is a sentient, feeling creature who resists what is antagonistic to his nature, responds to the impulses to action in the conditions of his world, and endures the pain brought about by the conditions of his world. Man suffers tragedy because he is sensitive to the ambiguous impulses stimulating his responsiveness and demanding his awareness. He suffers tragedy because his sensitive, perceptive faculties recognize painful impulses and because his receptive nature admits the painful impulses into his being and the inner conditions of his world. He suffers tragedy because he has the ability to be aware of the pain in his world and because he has the capacity to respond to the impulse of painful circumstances. Man suffers tragedy because he is curious about the conditions of his world, questions their meaning, and responds to their consequences. Man suffers tragedy because the conditions of his world evolve and alter and because he cannot evolve and alter with them, or because he alters and evolves and the external conditions of his world do not change with him. Man suffers tragedy because he feels that his moral or ethical qualities have suffered outrage, or because his moral or ethical qualities do outrage to the accepted standards of his external world. Man suffers tragedy because he is a creature of unattainable hopes and desires, and because he is not omniscient. Man suffers tragedy because of his frailty in relation to the demands he makes on himself or the demands his world makes on him. He suffers tragedy because his world demands responses he is unwilling or unable to make. Man suffers tragedy because he is man, because he has power to reason, to feel, to sense, to be

13

outraged, to demand, to hope, to fear, to love, to hate, to accept or reject, to dream, to know or to be ignorant, to be individual, to be man in a world of like and different men.

The tragic impulse is an impetus or driving power that inheres in the totality of conditions touching the existence and making up the world of man and that urges or impels a responsive resistance involving the recognition and suffering of pain. The impulse is the essential quality of a condition without which there would be no responsive awareness of the influence of the condition on a receptive being or, by extension and expansion, on the developing of awareness of the qualities of associated conditions. The impulse in conditions making up the world of man is that which absolutely cannot be left out without removing the essential reason for response, for the continuation of response, and for movement or action within a particular condition or affiliated conditions. Consequently, the impulse that moves man to an awareness of suffering and to response to the consequences of suffering is the tragic impulse and the first movement toward tragedy.

The tragic impulse inheres in each and every condition of existence both separately and collectively, but it requires particular associations of circumstances involving a particular or unique man with the particular sensitivity and perceptivity that make him receptive of and responsive to the impulse that inheres in the conditions that constitute his world. The tragic impulse is not invariable or singular, for there may exist in any condition or combination of conditions discordant, contrary, opposite, or antagonistic impulses that could urge varying responses, depending on circumstances and human nature. Particular juxtapositions or combinations of impulses could establish a dilemma requiring a choice (even if the choice be to do nothing). All the conditions that make up the world of man contain the potential tragic impulse. Whenever one condition or set of conditions comes into contact with another, or when-

14

ever a condition contains within itself the qualities capable of urging a response, the tragic impulse has its source of energy, its impetus, its driving power. The tragic impulse may, therefore, become active within a particular condition, spontaneously; or, it may require external stimulation to bring it into the awareness of a sentient being. Whether the power to urge the latent impulse into motion be internal or external, the impulse itself is essential to the development of circumstances capable of creating the pain and the suffering of tragic awareness. But however latent the tragic impulse may be at any particular time under any particular circumstances with any particular man, it may, with or without warning, power a tragedy; and the tragic impulse may exist either subliminally or supraliminally for man before his receptivity of circumstances brings it into his conscious awareness; but its driving or impelling power, arising from the conditions of man's world (and man's own nature and experience are a part of this condition) may, as the person is receptive of it, generate the flow of circumstances from which tragedy may result for him as a consequence of his response to the tragic impulse. How he responds, the degree of the intensity of the response, and the magnitude of the consequences of that response will determine the tragic stature of man.

The impulse to tragedy in the totality of the conditions that touch the existence of man, singularly or universally, inheres in the conditions, particularly or severally or infinitely totally, that make up the universe: the natural and the supernatural; the sensuous, the mental, and the emotional; the conscious and the unconscious; the environmental and the hereditary; the real and the imaginary; the instinctive and the conditioned; the physical and the metaphysical; the rational and the intuitive; the mystical and the spiritual: in sum, all the conditions of the world of man subject sentient man to the potential of the tragic impulse. For to be sentient is to be capable of awareness of that impulse; and to respond to that impulse, whether by accident of

Nature, by choice, or by coercion, is to be exposed to those consequences which may constitute tragedy or result in tragedy. Though all the conditions of man's world contain the potential tragic impulse, not all the conditions of that world need be involved in man's tragedy. Nor does the presence of the tragic impulse in a particular condition necessitate a response that will invariably have tragic consequences, and not all the conditions of the world derive their essential qualities from the tragic impulse alone, for the conditions of the world of man contain, in addition to the tragic impulse, other impulses quite at variance with the tragic impulse.

Though the tragic impulse permeates the world of man and is inherent in the conditions that make up the world of man, and though man is exposed to the potential of tragedy by the fact of his birth, tragedy is not necessarily inevitable; for along with the tragic impulse there is also present a contrary impulse, an impulse antagonistic to the suffering essential to tragedy, an impulse conducive to pleasurable circumstances and to joy. So long as these two impulses maintain a balance, a moderating influence one on the other, man remains in a state of physical, mental, emotional, spiritual, and behavioral equilibrium, knowing neither the pain of tragedy nor the exhilaration of an outstanding joy. The balance between these two impulses, pleasurable and tragic, may be termed well-being or happiness; but an imbalance between these two impulses may create conditions offering either blissful or tragic consequences. If the tragic impulse predominates, tragedy may result; if the pleasurable impulse predominates, joy may result. Man may hope to avoid the suffering implicit in the tragic impulse by a conscious stimulation of its contrary, or he may expect conditions to be such that the tragic impulse may remain submerged or latent and that the pleasurable impulse will take precedence over the tragic impulse; but once the tragic impulse is activated, tragic conditions, circumstances, and consequences will result unless countering

16

impulses are stimulated to nullify the influences of the tragic impulse. The inevitability of tragedy is dependent on the maintaining of its supremacy by the tragic impulse, just as the inevitability of happiness is dependent on the maintaining of its supremacy by the pleasurable impulse.

The aggregate condition of the world of man, in terms of his responsive role in association with the condition, will be constituted of physical, mental, emotional, spiritual, and behavioral parts with varying degrees of complex relationships of the parts to each other. The relationships of the parts will establish the quality of the condition as a whole; but the response of man is not necessarily to the totality of the condition; he may respond to a single, unique part of the condition, or he may respond to a relationship of two or more of the parts, or he may respond to variable arrangements of any or all of the parts with each other. But that which will evoke his response to the condition or to its parts will be the impulses that generate action within his physical, mental, emotional, spiritual, and behavioral natures. His responses, originating in his personal and inner world and creating an expanding and evolving personal and inner world, will constitute a source for other impulses and create the complexities of his private, unique world. That world, as it becomes involved with the conditions of the environmental external world, will create still other impulses, which when activated will demand responsiveness, and establish a relationship between the inner and outer worlds of man; and the relationship so established will contain impulses that will prompt aware responsiveness and create the total condition of the world of man as he may know it.

The impulse to action will arise, usually, from an imbalance in the mixture of the parts constituting the whole, and will consequently create a resistant force deriving from the friction generated by the imbalance. The resistance, then, will create a new condition, provoke an awareness of the constitution of the old condition, or contribute to an evolutionary alteration of the constitution of the old condition. From this resistance new impulses will be generated; and a dynamic evolution of conditions, impulses, circumstances, and consequences will occur, demanding new awarenesses and new responses. But neither pleasure nor pain will result if the impulses within the conditions remain static and demand no resistant responsiveness; for there can be no pleasurable or painful awareness or experience so long as the impulses remain latent or impotent, even though the fusion of man's inner being with the conditions of his external world will provide all the essentials required to establish his participating role in the universe. The mixture of impulses, deriving from the states of man's physical, mental, emotional, spiritual, and behavioral being and inherent in these qualifying conditions of man's world (qualifying because they help to determine the nature of man's response by directing the impulses to particular parts of his responsive being, and because they appeal to particular sensitive and perceptive qualities, and because they influence his will and inclination and receptive capacities) will constitute the temperament of man and of his world and determine whatever responses he makes to his world: inner or external or a combination of the two.

The temperament of man's world is determined for him by the constitution of the conditions of that world, both internal and external, with respect to the mixture or balance of all the parts and qualities and impulses that inhere in or pertain to the conditions of that world. Man is the integral element, the essential part, of his own world, for he creates the reality of his world by his apprehension of it; and all the impulses of his world either emanate from his awareness of conditions and responses to them, or they find a focus in him for the direction and impact of their influence. Man may then be either the protagonist offering resistance to the impulses inherent in his particular conditions, or he may be the antagonist to whom the conditions direct impulses that resist his will, inclination, or understanding. It matters little whether the impulses derive from the conditions of the inner nature of man and find resistance in the external qualities of his existence or if they derive from the external conditions of man's world and find resistance in his inner nature; man remains the focus, both singular and collective, both attractive and repellent, both the resource and the recipient, of the impulses in his world that move him to awareness, response, and action. The inner world of man is his positive pole; his external world is his negative pole; his existence is the animating current moving from pole to pole within the conditions of his world and charged by the impulses in the conditions. But the impulses have the quality of being able to reverse the poles and redirect the current, creating disturbances in the equilibrium of the conditions of man's world and with fluctuating polarities offering possibilities of variable responsiveness, awareness, resistance, and activity. These variations may then lead to either pleasure or pain, depending on the nature of the conditions affecting man and the direction of his responses to the impulses. Because the impulses may be conducive to either pleasure or pain, and because the impulses are multidirectional and multipolar, emanating from a variable multitude of conditions and directed either toward or away from man in infinite directions, the inevitability of either pleasure or pain is qualified by myriad impulses affecting the conditions and by the qualities of man's sensitivity, perceptivity, receptivity, awareness, and responsiveness and by the nature of his will and inclination to resist or accept the consequences of action necessitated by response to the impulses.

Because man, not being omniscient, is fallible in judgment, defective in reasoning, prone to error in prognostication, gullible, susceptible to false impressions, and liable to certain inscrutable qualities of conditions, he is the potential prey of tragedy; but because he is the antagonist to pain and the proponent of pleasure, he may, if conditions permit and his inclination prevails, escape the consequences of the tragic impulse by remaining unaware of conditions that might cause discomfort, displeasure, or disaster, or that might disturb the equilibrium of his sense of well-being or equanimity. He may avoid the consequences of tragedy by refusing or failing to respond to conditions activated by the tragic impulse. He may evade the consequences of tragedy by creating states—physical, mental, emotional, spiritual, or behavioral—that nullify the tragic impulse and nourish the impulse to pleasure. He may vanquish the most painful consequences of tragedy by dulling his sensitivity and perceptivity and by limiting the capacity of his receptivity. He may repudiate the consequences of tragedy by renouncing his contracts with life and by freeing himself from the influence of the tragic impulse. Or he may, by the mere chance of the nature of the conditions of his world, never be exposed to the activated tragic impulse. But he may never be exempt from the potentiality of tragedy that thrives, as impulse, in the conditions of his world, without severing all conscious relationships to that world.

If there be order in the world of man among the myriad conditions affecting and making up that world, that order must derive from the impulses inherent in the conditions and nature of that world and directing the awareness and the responsiveness and the actions of man. It is the impulse that stirs awareness, that prompts responsiveness, and that demands action. It must be the impulse, therefore, either implosive or explosive, that will provide the cohesiveness necessary to establish order or the semblance of order among the conditions of Nature and the world of man. With man as the focus, and with the impulses emanating from him or directed toward him shaping the conditions of his world, the conditions fluctuate in and about him according to the impulses inherent in him and in them—he is himself a condition of his own world. This establishes a variable order, a dynamic order, that ever changes as conditions change and create new impulses. But because man is the source of awareness of the impulses in his world, he is the impressionable unifying principle of that world; for it cannot be his world unless his responsive faculties provide the awarenesses to create impressions of it. And because the impression creating impulses inherent in the conditions of his world and in him cohere to him as their focus or source, he is essential to provide the sentient base on which a humanly oriented order may be established or discerned as a correlative of natural order.

As man responds to the conditions of his natural world and absorbs into his own nature his impressions of those conditions, either consciously or unconsciously impelled by the qualities of his physical, mental, emotional, spiritual, and behavioral states and the responsive impulses inherent in his particular conditions in those states and regulated by his sensitivity, perceptivity, and receptivity and his personally unique will, inclination, or compulsion to respond, he becomes charged with an infinitely unique and infinitely varied and complex accumulation of impressions of conditions and impulses that assimilate, fuse, merge, and synthesize within the personalizing and reconstituting condition of their recipient. The assimilating, fusing, merging, and synthesizing may so alter the impression of any one or any combination of conditions that identification with the originating condition or conditions may become virtually impossible and only vestigial echoes of the originating condition or conditions may remain in the multiformity of new conditions emergent from the synthesis of combinations of impressions and responsive impulses. Because of the variety and complexity of responsive and receptive impulses, never will there be an absolute identity of the emergent condition with the condition that occasioned it, nor will there be an identicalness of response, impression, or emergent condition with that of any other recipient of the originating conditions. The individuality of natures and states of the recipients precludes specific identity, but it does not preclude similarity in the generalized nature of the responses nor in the generalized impressional qualities of the emergent conditions. The minute, the specific, detailed qualities of the emergent conditions will be as varied and as unique as the natures of the responders and the recipients.

Tragedy, as an impression-creating impulse inherent in the states and natures of conditions requiring response for identification, is not in itself a vision or a feeling or a meaning or an awareness. It is rather the experiential apprehension through any or all of the receptive faculties of a sentient being of an inherently disordering, imbalancing potential structured by Nature into the evolutionary balancing and ordering of Nature's parts. There is no predetermination by or in Nature for the emergence of the tragic potential and its presentation of apprehensive reception; rather, since tragedy, or at least the sentient apprehension of it, depends on sentient recognition, there is in Nature an allowance of interacting and interrelating manifestations, emergent from the conflicting impulses of individual and uniquely fallible sentient beings responding either to other fallible manifestations of willful sentient nature or to infallible evolutionary processes of Nature herself, generating the responsive impulses that stimulate the sentient apprehension of suffering. The vision or feeling or meaning or awareness of tragedy is then merely the sentient experiencing of the potential brought to the responsive faculties and re-created in the form of impression-evoking activity. The experience, or the experience-meaning impression, is itself the meaning, the feeling, the vision, and the awareness of suffering. Tragedy is the apprehension of that experience, and it is of consequence only to the sentient being capable of achieving an apprehensive impression of the magnitude and the intensity of the elemental processes of Nature as a whole evolving under the ethical principles of her own perpetuating impulses striving for natural order, or the disruptive

22

impulses of Nature's parts striving for an identity outside the tolerances allowed by Nature's ethic. In either case, suffering is occasioned when a sentient being is caught in the inexorable processes whose only constant is evolutionary motion between the excesses and deficiencies generated by the parts of Nature seeking permanence of identity and being painfully constrained and put in tolerable balance and integral harmony with other parts and with Nature as a whole by the self-perpetuating essence of Nature's self-imposed regenerative ethic-aesthetic.

III

THE TRAGIC CONDITION

THE CONDITIONS OF THE WORLD OF MAN ARE THE ELEMEN-
tal source of all the qualities of his existence; but man does
not function, tragically or otherwise, until he responds to those
conditions. His response to conditions is the primary force impelling motion in the impulse inherent in all the conditions of
man's existence; the secondary force activating the impulse is
the nature of the conditions themselves: the innate qualities
within particular conditions that create friction or conflict of
and by themselves through interfusion and juxtaposition of
circumstances that activate the impulse that educes suffering
merely by association of conditions or by generation of power
to move the impulse within a condition that remains outside
the awareness of man. Because this is so, tragic conditions may
surround man, the impulse to tragic action may be constantly
present in the conditions of his existence, and tragic circumstances may touch his every movement. Yet man is not a tragic
figure, to himself, and he has not suffered tragedy until he is
responsively aware of the import of the conditions and is moved
to suffer responsively by them. Responsiveness is then an essential quality of tragedy, and awareness of suffering is its es-

sence. Because all men are not equally responsive, and because the intensity of awareness is different for each man, there are different degrees of tragic experience among men, even though, externally, they may be subject to many of the same conditions evoking responses. Both the inner and outer worlds of man subject individual man to the tragic impulse. Only the outer world of man subjects collective man to the tragic impulse that is universally a part of collective man's existence and experience-meaning.

Tragedy, then, as an experience touching the inner nature of particular man, is primarily an individual concern; and only secondarily, as an experiential movement touching also the outer nature of man in general as well as particular man, is it a public or collective concern. Tragedy is essentially private; but its effects, as they touch conditions involving other men, may establish circumstances and impulses that alter the conditions surrounding and influencing other men, and, as a result of their impact on collective man, take on the nature of public concern. But it is individual responsiveness to and individual awareness of conditions involving suffering that establish a tragedy that is not diluted by collective inclusion or generalized by collective experience. The particular and ultimate intensity of tragedy can touch only one man at a time at its peak because individual differences in responsiveness and awareness specify individual reaction; for, try as he may to become identical to any other man, individual man is so subject to the conditions of his own world that total identification with the conditions of another's world is virtually impossible. The individuality of responsiveness and awareness conditions the tragic experience and establishes the degree of intensity of the tragedy. The individuality of sensitivity, perceptivity, and receptivity establishes the capacity and ability and will and inclination of unique man to discern the tragic implications in the circumstances and impulses that make up his unique world and to respond to the impressions that are his alone in relation to the impulses that command awareness. The individuality of response and awareness establishes the uniqueness of tragedy, but the primary contracts with existence establish its universality. Only the individual man can feel completely the pain that is uniquely his; vicarious pain may demand sympathetic response, and the imagination may create intense pain, but the reality of pain is uniquely the experience of the person suffering it either in physical reality or in rarely achieved total empathetic reality. Substitutionary suffering quite well may be a degree of tragic experience, and for some it may be the only available experience, but the totality of tragedy demands immediate and personal responsiveness to uniquely felt and experienced suffering. Only by responding to his own pain and enduring its consequences may man come to a full understanding of what he himself is in relation to the circumstances, conditions, and impulses that have caused his pain. This is not to say that there might not exist men of such empathetic powers of sensitivity, perceptivity, receptivity, responsiveness, and awareness that identification with another is possible to such a degree as to bring about a transference of total experience, one to another. It is also quite probable that men of such powers, or even lesser powers, are capable of experiencing, responsively and with awareness, implications of consequences that will escape a sufferer with more limited capacities, abilities, and inclinations to respond. It is also possible that imagination stirred by vicarious experience may create awareness of and responsiveness to pain greater than that actually experienced in reality. Comparatively, however, given identical powers, an actual sufferer will suffer to a greater degree than a vicarious sufferer because his experience with the particular condition will be fuller. Personal involvement with particular qualities of suffering may, however, dull man's responses to other qualities, or even make him unaware of other qualities of the same experience; and one who is not a participant in the actual suffering experience may be aware, both objectively and subjectively, of qualities that have remained outside the consciousness of the actual sufferer and respond to those qualities of experience with greater intensity of feeling and awareness of the total experience than does the sufferer himself.

Sentient beings are usually aware of the suffering of others, and that awareness helps to establish the nature of the conditions of their own worlds. The contracts with life itself, both explicit and implicit, provide a source for that awareness, though sheltered man may never come to realize the existence of the latent impulse conducive to tragic suffering in conditions external to his own world. Indeed, he may never know that tragic suffering exists latently below the level of his own consciousness or outside the ken of his awareness of the conditions of his own world. But generally, to a degree, man is aware of the potential of suffering in both himself and in others and in the conditions that exist both for himself and for others. Ordinary powers of observance reveal many possibilities and some probabilities for tragic suffering. Greater powers reveal more possibilities and probabilities. The man of exceptional sensitivity, perceptivity, and receptivity will be most aware of the potential for tragic suffering, not only for himself but also for others. Man's identification with others may create an aware realization of the suffering experienced by others; empathy may so associate particularly receptive man with the conditions experienced by others that he may re-create their suffering in his own being to such an extent that their sufferings become his sufferings. Possibly this is so even to the extreme wherein man loses his own identity and becomes so involved in the nature and personality and condition of another that nothing remains of his own individuality, and he suffers the pain of another even to the extent of dying the other's death. Sympathy and understanding and pity may also contribute to an association of conditions and feelings that

27

will emphasize an awareness of the suffering of others and demand a response from sympathetic man. Particular man may, through the application of his own understanding of conditions and his awareness of his own suffering to similar conditions involving another, induce responsive awareness. A comparison of known qualities of conditions, circumstances, consequences, and impulses may reveal pain-causing potentialities in the conditions of others. A sense of moral or ethical obligation might well command aware response. Intuition and premonition may reveal the suffering of others, and psychic powers may be potentially one of the strongest activators of the impulse for responsive awareness. The suffering of others may be felt or sensed by man of responsive nature. The invasion of the privacy of others might also reveal conditions of suffering and demand responsive awareness. Spiritual affinity, physical contact, mental action, emotional involvement, and behavioral association all contribute to man's source of awareness of the suffering experienced by others. The degree of his awareness is established by the limits of his receptivity, and his response is controlled by his capacity, ability, will, and inclination to respond.

Man is aware of suffering, the conditions producing suffering, the impulse that moves man to suffer, circumstances derived from suffering and involved in suffering, and the consequences of suffering. Man, generally, gains this awareness through real experience, by vicarious participation, or by empathetic association. Though he responds with different levels of intensity, because awareness is achieved to different degrees by individual men, each man responds within the limits imposed by the conditions of his inner and outer worlds, the condition that is his in the world that is his. Man's response to the suffering of others and to his own suffering falls anywhere between two extremes: total altruism or total egocentricity. But because most men feel some degree of contractual obligation to that from which they spring—the human condition identifies man with other men—

the responsive concern occasioned by the awareness of suffering as a part of the condition of the world of man will evoke a response from most men that tempers egocentricity with altruism and complements altruism with self-concern. Egocentricity will, therefore, find in the suffering of another a threat to self, a disturbance of equanimity, a violation of serenity. Man is threatened by what he sees others afflicted with; generally, he suffers because they suffer (unless he is capable of divorcing himself completely from the world of man, and that in itself could establish a tragic condition of suffering), excepting, of course, the alienatory capabilities of his nature or the qualifying conditions of his impulses toward identification. Escape from the realities of the world of man and its conditions probably requires a particular substitutive condition wherein the impulse to suffer is still present but submerged in the protective mechanism of his responsive nature or conditioned by his awareness that he himself may not be the direct object of threat to equanimity.

Because man is threatened or senses threat, he responds either overtly or suppressively. He may manifest guilt for the conditions that evidence threat; he may recoil from the conditions; he may actively look for a means to alleviate the conditions; but he will rarely remain impassive before them. When man does remain passive, when he rejects responsibility to respond, when he deliberately (or unconsciously) disassociates himself from the conditions that cause suffering, he in a sense negates or nullifies the contract with life that requires participation in the act of living, of filling the space between birth and death. The ultimate nullification of the contract, the ultimate rejection of the conditions of life, the ultimate disassociative act would be suicide. That in itself could, however, be the expression of a supreme awareness of the conditions of man's world and an active response to those conditions. Associative guilt may derive from many causal sources: a sense of the depravity of man; a recognition of the responsibility of collective man for the development of all conditions not of natural origin that touch the existence of man; a sense that mankind itself is guilty when one man violates the collective harmony; a sense of the failure of man to control natural conditions that contribute to the suffering by man; a feeling of obligation to participate with other men in the conditions that demand painful awarenesses; sympathetic identification and association; fanatic reasoning about individual authority, responsibility, infallibility, and ability; failure to recognize individual limits to capacity; feeling that individual man has been negligent in his responsibilities: practically all of man's feelings and attitudes could contribute to a sense of guilt for conditions conducive to painful consequences. Generally speaking, the more man feels himself threatened personally, the more sense of guilt he has, unless, of course, he is capable of shifting all responsibility onto others. At the two extremes, total guilt and total innocence, are found the societal aberrants: the fanatic zealots, the selfish and the selfless crusaders, certain martyrs, and all the extremists of moral or immoral excesses.

Just as there is a certain ambiguity inherent in the impulses in the conditions of life—man may respond in two directions, positively or negatively, with acceptance or rejection, or with passivity, and his responses are often inexplicable in terms of evidence or reason—there is inherent ambiguity in the responsive awareness evidenced by most men, and in the actions they perform resulting from the impulse to action found in the conditions because the complex nature of the impulse often demands contrary responses or it may be obscure or equivocal in its prompting of awareness or its demands for action. The very complexity of man's world, both inner and outer conditions of that world, and the complexities of man's collective and individual natures demand a variable complexity of responses. The variety of response, the individual characteristics of each response, the consequential significance of each response add to the complexity of each condition or circumstance created as a result of response and action. The result is a differentiated condition for each individual responding to a particular circumstance, but, at the same time, a complex universality for the collective unity of man subjected to a community of conditions, a similarity of circumstances, a parallelism of impulses, and an identity of natural sources of being and natural termination of being.

Man, generally, with few exceptions, is naturally antagonistic to pain. Even the presentient being and the nonsentient being respond to pain and discomfort. The responses are varied because sensitivity to pain varies and because the capacities, abilities, inclinations, and will for endurance of pain vary. But most animate beings respond to pain, even if the response is only an instinctive recoil. Some few, however, relish pain in themselves; some others delight in inflicting pain, either on themselves or on others. These are, however, aberrants from natural antipathy toward pain.

Pain, as an essential of tragedy, has its source in the impulse that activates the conditions of man's world and focuses man's awareness on the particular pain-producing circumstances of those conditions. The general states of pain inhere in the conditions of man's nature: physical, mental, emotional, spiritual, and behavioral. These states—physical, mental, emotional, spiritual, and behavioral—may differentiate the conditions or circumstances of pain and induce a particular kind of suffering limited to the immediate nature of the state, physical, mental, emotional, spiritual, and behavioral. They may also limit responsiveness to or awareness of the conditions of that particular state by focusing the attention of the sufferer on a single state. The more intense suffering of pain, however, will involve the identification of suffering with all the states of pain. Combinations of states, one intensifying another, will be conducive to development of conditions of greater tragic significance than will conditions involving only one state of pain. The intensification of suffering, the intensification of awareness of suffering, the intensification of response to that awareness, and the intensification of the realization of the import of the consequences of suffering will be instrumental in establishing the magnitude of a tragic experience. The intensity and magnitude of the tragic experiences or circumstances will, in turn, delineate the limits of tragedy.

Awareness of the implications of the states of pain involves the sentient contract. To differentiate the state of physical pain from the other states of pain, it is necessary to limit consideration of physical pain to those experiences of pain involving the corporeal body and the sensorial response to pain-producing stimuli; the isolation of the state of physical pain and the recognition of its presence in the corporeal body is primarily a matter of sentient awareness. The assumption is, that in terms of tragic suffering, that for tragic pain to occur, there must be more than a merely instinctive response to the presence of pain and that the enduring of the pain must be conscious before tragedy may result for the sufferer of pain. Though physical pain may be felt by nonsentient beings, the nonsentient being is incapable of associating the state of pain with the conditions producing the pain and then differentiating the consequential circumstances deriving from sentient awareness. This is not to say that physical pain is limited entirely to the sentient contract, for it is obvious that the natural conditions of man, the determination of the nature of his physical being and the development of his nervous system occurred prior to sentience during the period of the presentient contract. Also, this is not to say that mental, emotional, spiritual, and behavioral states of pain do not at times manifest themselves in physical suffering, and that consideration of the postsentient contract might not produce a physical suffering. Certainly, as an example, some physical pain-seekers, particularly those of religious beliefs demanding self-infliction of pain as a purification ritual, may be involved in the demands of the postsentient contract. Many persons may regard painful physical affliction as divine infliction; and, depending on the personal point of view, this could involve any of the contracts man has with his world. But, whatever the natural contract demanding physical pain, the sentient contract is primary in the recognition of consequences and in the establishment of awareness that may produce tragedy. Even the infliction of physical pain as a means of inducing nonphysical responses—physical pain to create a moment of awareness between consciousness and unconsciousness wherein normal sensorial responses become nonfunctional and psychic phenomena appear as the only reality—involves the sentient contract, and certainly the communication of information about the pain-produced psychic experiences to a nonpsychic being requires sentient consideration of symbols, parallels, analogies, associations, and patterns of sentiently communicative devices.

Physical pain completely divorced from the other states of awareness of pain would be non-tragic pain because there would be no realization of cause-effect relationships or of consequential results shaping and altering the conditions of man's world if there were no referents in other states of pain to which it could be related. But physical pain, even pain artificially created by drugs, hypnosis, or other pain-producing agents not part of the natural organism of man himself, is real pain as far as its sufferer is concerned; and it may be an ingredient of some tragic experiences if responsive awareness of its import is present in the consciousness of its sufferer. Though physical pain may be more susceptible to localization than the other states of pain, it is no more real than the other states of pain, and it may be of less consequence in tragic experience than mental, emotional, spiritual, or behavioral states of pain. As a matter of fact, it would seem that the conditions of life more often than not exact a suffering from man that is more intense the more it is removed from the physical nature of pain. And physical pain must be accompanied by other conditions before it, of itself, may become a tragic determinant; for pain, by itself, may be a natural condition of life, and until it is related to an alteration of conditions through the impulse that generates it, and until it has a specific relationship to a cause of suffering and to consequences that must be endured, and until there is a conscious responsive awareness of its causing a distinct change in the conditions of man's world, it is little more than a slight disturbance of the conditions of life and no more than a minor contribution to the tragic experience. Pain, to be of great consequence in the tragic experience and to establish the highest realization of tragedy, must do more than disturb the serenity of its sufferer; it must stagger the equilibrium of the conditions of the world that surround man and establish his place in the world of men, and it must overwhelm man's sense of inner-world well-being. The greatest tragedy will exhibit suffering of the greatest intensity and magnitude, and that suffering will be so great that it would be unendurable for anyone without the greatest capacity for endurance. But that endurance, in great tragedy, must not stem from insensitivity, lack of perceptivity, or failure of receptivity. It must be felt, greatly. It must be endured, without passivity, greatly. It must be responded to, greatly. It must alter conditions, greatly. It must incite the greatest struggle man is capable of waging with the conditions of his world, and it must arouse the greatest awareness, responsively, of man's place in his world. And that responsive awareness must tax the limits of man's capacities, abilities, inclination, will, sensitivity, perceptivity, receptivity, and responsiveness. The direst suffering is not tragedy if its alleviation is facile or its consequences negligible; it is not great tragedy if it does not try the limits of man's endurance and his will to resist.

The great tragedy must stagger imagination but not credibility; and for it to occur, man must have the inclination and the will to endure suffering, but he must struggle against the conditions of the world that cause his suffering in order to establish and insure those qualities of his world that seem to be threatened or that, evidenced by his suffering, seem to be undergoing an unfortunate transformation. He must have the inclination and will to attempt to preserve the values of the world that is his or to improve the values of that world for himself and for others, or he must have the inclination and will to alter those values when they no longer function properly in his world, even though his inclination and will lead him to conditions of unendurable suffering, of unbearable consequences, of insurmountable crises. And for great tragedy to occur, his struggle must be of monumental stature. No petty railing against fate or against the conditions or the impulses that activate the conditions will be sufficient to establish tragedy of any great consequence. There must be action and struggle, either overt or covert, responsively, before tragic experiences may develop; and there must be awareness of the significance of the response and its implications before tragedy may occur as an observable reality. Coincidentally with or subsequent to the awareness of tragedy, there must be a recognition of consequences and a realization of their impact on the world of the sufferer; for in most tragedies, even though the initial impact of tragic awareness may be instantaneous, there is a continuation of circumstances, a creation of new impulses, a growing awareness or recognition of complementing and complicating conditions, and a diffusion of implications that affect the entire world, inner and outer, of the person suffering tragedy. Great tragedy is dynamic; it grows and evolves and engulfs its subject; and great tragedy does not end until it has tested the limits of the nature and endurance of its subject.

The state of mental suffering involves the three contracts with the conditions of man's world: presentient, sentient, and postsentient. Man's consideration of and concern for the presentient and postsentient conditions stimulate the impulse that generates mental activity, which, if it is centered about doubt, worry, fear, uncertainty, displeasure, or dejection, might cause mental suffering, though the suffering itself would probably be in terms of sentience. The postsentient contract may involve man in the anguish of previsioned suffering, particularly in anguished premeditative concern about pain after death. It may also involve painful mental suffering relating to fear of the future, dejection about trends indicated by present circumstances, uncertainty about the fulfillment of hopes or dreams, or worry over that which has not yet come to pass. The presentient contract will involve the mental state of suffering in doubts about origins and natural capacities, uncertainty about presentient conditions and their relation to present time, fear that inherited characteristics will have an unhappy effect, dejection because happenstance of birth does not contribute everything deemed necessary for serene existence, displeasure with heritage, and worry about the past shaping an unpleasant future. The pre- and postsentient contracts involve suffering only in a speculative manner in the mental state, but that suffering may involve conditions of great tragic significance because that which the mind conceives takes on a reality of its own in the shaping of the conditions of man's world; and mental preconceptions and prejudices often take precedence over evidential realities opposed to them. Tradition and habit, often developed through familial association and derived from presentient conditions, may create conflicts within present conditions opposing them and result in suffering for man caught between demands of custom and contemporary reality. Mental suffering is no less painful if it is based on faulty reasoning than it is if reasoning is valid. It is no less suffering if its source is speculation than it is if its source is physically observable.

The state of mental suffering is related, however, more to the sentient contract than to the presentient or postsentient. It is sentiently known experience, or experience that is contemporary and immediate, that most readily lends itself to mental analysis and reason, though all of the conditions of environmental exposure, all the conditions of spiritual belief or disbelief, all the conditions of physical reality, all the conditions of emotional response, and all the conditions of speculative origin, ultimately may be subjected to examination in the sentient mental state. Mental suffering may, as may any of the other states of pain, be so intense that it obliterates the sense of other pain. It may, and the other states of pain may, lessen man's awareness of other pain or intensify other pain to a degree not apparent when only one state of pain is present if it conjoins with another state or other states. The state of mental suffering may find its expression in many conditions and circumstances: regret, remorse, grief, loneliness, fear, insecurity, misunderstanding, guilt, disillusion, discord, and hatred are a few, though they probably will be associated as intimately with other states of pain as they are with mental suffering. Mental suffering racks the mind and creates circumstances of discord between man and his comprehension of the rightness of the conditions of his world. The impulse that activates the state of mental suffering provides a force to create a mental disequilibrium or a disturbance of the smooth flow of serene thought. It poses dilemmas to man and necessitates the activity of choice-making. It demands the taking of sides, the resistance of contrary influences and impulses, and the endurance of consequences of choice. Mental suffering may take the form of mental fatigue wherein the necessity of decision-making, choice-making, or activity-planning becomes so burdensome that actual discomfort results. Mental suffering may become so intense that it obliterates the functioning of the mind; prompts escape into madness or mental aberration; causes withdrawal into comatose states; excites violent responses of varying degrees; disturbs physical, emotional, spiritual, or behavioral functions; heightens or lessens any other responsive awareness; pushes man into examination of the conditions of his world; drives to extremes of action or brakes to inaction: in short, it may influence any or all of the activities of man related to mental determination, cognition, perception, reception, awareness, inclination, will, or response. It may establish negative or positive responses of any degree, intensity, or magnitude, depending on the sensitivity, perceptivity, receptivity, inclination, and will of man and on the capacities and abilities he has to determine his influence on the conditions of his world and their influence on him.

Because man is a creature of physical, mental, emotional, spiritual, and behavioral states, he must act in relation to those states, even though his action may be negative or minimal in relation to any one state or combination of states. To be wholly man, he must function in all these states of man. In actuality, it is unusual for man not to do so, though his inclination and will may often establish a lack of balance or equilibrium among the states. The qualifying influences of one state on another may intensify man's responsiveness to the conditions of that state, or they may lessen an undue intensity by bringing into play considerations that would not be present without the interaction of states. The interrelation of states may also create conditions that were not present in an isolated state and bring into being both conflicting and complementary circumstances to alter man's perception of his world; and because man does not normally respond from a single isolated state, his response will vary according to the degree of application of the qualifying influences of the other states in determining the conditions of his world as he feels and sees and knows them.

To respond emotionally without mental control would be to use less than the potential establishing man as unique, and would create conditions not truly representative of man's total nature and capacity. To respond mentally without emotional complement would be to create a mechanical indifference to beauty, love, hate, or any of the qualities that contribute to man's societal relationships or to man's aesthetic nature and development. To respond physically without control or conditioning by the other qualities of his being would be to establish man as sub-animal in relation to the conditions of his world. To respond only spiritually would be to negate all the other qualities of man's nature and establish abstraction or immaterial vision as the only reality, contrary to the other evidenced qualities of man's nature. To respond only behaviorally would be to minimize all that is not observable in behavior, unless, of course, behavioral psychology were to be taken from the realm of science and placed in the realm of theoretical speculative philosophy. But whether or not behavior is the study of all the conditions of man's world, the behavioral state will be treated here as observable science, and observable behavior will be regarded as only one quality, albeit an important quality, of man's total world. That total world of man, composed of the interfused states of man's responsiveness, will be greater and more complex than would be the world that consists only of the sum of its separate parts, and it will be greater and more complex than the world of any organism that does not evidence responsive natures including all five of the states. One state may enhance the others; the commingling of responsive states may intensify the qualities of each, separately or collectively, and create an intricate complexity of qualities that make up the world of man, differentiating, qualifying, intensifying, and determining the conditions of that world as he is sensitive to it, perceptive of it, and responsive to it.

The awareness of man is not whole when it fails to take into account all the states of his world in the interfused, complex nature of their influence on him and his surroundings, or when an imbalance of those states creates disproportionate responses to conditions. But to respond totally to all the complexities of man's world would require superhuman qualities of sensitivity, perceptivity, awareness, receptivity, and responsiveness. To respond to less than the total (because of limited sensitivity, perceptivity, awareness, receptivity, and responsive capacities, abilities, inclinations, and will) would be to establish less than the potential for total involvement in the world of man and thereby create lesser degrees of tragic experience.

Moral and ethical suffering, as viewed from the main focus on self, is a sub-state of the all inclusive, overwhelmingly complex conditions of the world of man and Nature. The essential nature of this sub-state is rooted in the physical, mental, emotional, spiritual, and behavioral states that make up the world of man and derive topically from man but universally from Nature; it can be communicated thoroughly and effectively only in relation to states wherein it has its source and in terms of the impulses that motivate it into action and create consequential suffering as a result of the conflicts that have been generated by a whimsy of happenstance bringing together discordant conditions, by mental activity, by emotional responsiveness, by spiritual inclination, by physical awareness, by psychological reaction, or by any combination of these states and the qualifications placed upon them by the impulses creating activity among them within the conditions of man's world. To limit consideration of man's tragedies to those circumstances that reveal topically defined moral or ethical consequences would be comparable to limiting sensory impressions to the sense of smell. This is not to say that moral and ethical considerations are not usually inherent in the conditions of conflict and suffering of man and that moral and ethical considerations are not usually stimulated by the impulses within the conditions, but that morality and ethics are variable according to time and place and institutional values, and their consequences are variable. What they generate and what they are generated by vary. There is no necessary universality in topical moral or ethical expression, and a view or vision of man's condition in his world that is based on any particular topical moral or ethical principle as a controlling or activating force will be so limited in scope and range that consideration of man's condition will be a simplification or fragment of his world. Man is a complex creature, and the conditions that are his are complex. To define him in terms of topical reference or arbitrary values is to treat him as something less than he is. Man, individually and collectively, is aware and responds differently according to conditions and circumstances and impulses as they affect his inner and outer worlds and as they are seen in new lights according to alteration of conditions and circumstances and according to the goading to action by the impulse in the conditions of his world. No one value system, no one view defined by a system, may delineate all that he is in the particular, unique world that is his. Man's moral and ethical natures derive from his psychological conditioning, from his spiritual traditions and beliefs, from his emotional responses, from his physical appetites, from his instinctive responses to the conditions of his natural world, from the mores and conventions imposed upon him by his institutional world, and by the operation of his own mental processes and his self-defined philosophy of life. To treat the tragedies of man as though they were matters of only moral or ethical significance would be to skim the surface of man's nature and the conditions that make him what he is as evidenced by his acceptance or rejection of, by his resistance to and endurance of, the impulse that becomes manifest in his responsive actions, and by his attitude toward the consequences of those actions in relation to all the states of his being. The moral and ethical qualities so derived from evidenced responsiveness or failure to respond or degree of response will be part of the nature of man as he is in relation to both his inner and outer worlds. The theoretical or hypothetical or arbitrary values of an observer, the particular moral or ethical views or conventions or visions of an observer,

41

will have little significance in establishing a fullness of realization to the meaning of a fusion of states and the resulting creation of whole conditions and their influences on the inner and outer worlds of a man actively responding to the impulses in his own total world and establishing consequences for himself. The arbitrary moral or ethical views of persons not directly concerned with the immediate situation or circumstance or impulse (the views of those observing rather than of those participating) should not determine the significance of actions or of the consequential results of actions; but rather the participant himself should evidence the moral or ethical values derived from the conditions and the impulses to action and the awareness of consequences in his own world. This is not to say that an artist, re-creating, imitating, or interpreting actions and conditions, will not structure conditions and consequences to create a presentation of his own moral or ethical views; it is to say that the moral and ethical views of a noninvolved observer should not be superimposed on the conditions as a formula for critical appraisal and evaluation and analysis. The critical analysis of life and its conditions should be disciplined by the life and its conditions, not by a theory or view or wish of the critic, no matter how valid the theory or view or wish might be in relation to the critic himself.

The post- and presentient states of spiritual suffering are brought to aware responsiveness in the sentient mental state, often through the influences of interfused and juxtaposed physical, emotional, and behavioral conditions. Man may suffer spiritual pain when he questions his identity in relation to the spiritual forces he senses and the beliefs that are a part of his own world. When conditions force him to decide upon a course of action that is not sanctioned by his beliefs, or when a new awareness of conditions makes him distrustful of his beliefs, or when reason demands a particular course of action contrary to his previous beliefs, man may be forced to suffer by the impulse activated by the dilemma posed by the dichotomy of spiritual nature and the conditions of reality. Reason may demand a particular responsiveness contrary to spiritual inclination; the result may be either spiritual or mental suffering. The impulse of emotional responsiveness may be at variance with either reason or spiritual sense of well-being; suffering will result. The impulses in man's psychological conditioning, and the imposed dilemma of accepting, qualifying, or resisting spiritual responsiveness in contrast to behaviorally acceptable or institutionally required responses may cause intense spiritual suffering. Impulses prompting physical responses to the conditions of the world may be opposed by a sense of spiritual obligation that is violated by the demands of physical response, and suffering will result. Any impulse inherent in any of the states of man's condition may, under a particular set of circumstances, threaten man's sense of spiritual well-being and create spiritual suffering. If man senses a threat to his condition in the hereafter—paradisiacal, nirvanic, infernal, reincarnative, obliterative—he may suffer spiritually. Any sense of disillusion concerning beliefs, any sense of guilt occasioned by violation of spiritual feelings, any sense of disharmony with the spiritual universe, any sense of spiritual insecurity, outrage, remorse, or regret will create spiritual pain and produce a state of spiritual suffering within the conditions of man's world. Forces operating outside the range of man's physical awareness; discordant acts of Nature; alterations in customarily recognizable identities; unexplainable happenstances in real or imagined conditions; accidents of unknown cause or origin; attribution of super-real qualities to inadequately known identities, conditions, or impulses; seeming illogicality of occurrences; sense of predestined happenings; sense of ill-fatedness; irrational coincidences: any or all of these, and more, may well contribute to man's spiritual condition and to his exposure to the impulses of spiritual suffering.

Though spiritual suffering may be intensified by interfusion with the other states of suffering, it is not essential in all cases for there to be a recognition of interrelations of states to establish an awareness of spiritual suffering that is not consciously attributable to any state or whose effects have no discernible relationships to any other states. A sufferer may or may not know, consciously, the cause or effect of his suffering at any given moment of his suffering, and he may never know how close tragedy is to him even though he may be surrounded by latently tragic impulses and conditions for his entire existence without those impulses or conditions ever coming within the ken of his comprehension or awareness. In such cases man remains statically a potential tragic figure; he may even be seen by observers as a tragic figure; but tragedy does not explode into reality for him until he at least senses—physically, mentally, emotionally, spiritually, or behaviorally—the presence of the impulse that prompts his suffering. The power of his gods, a sense of the inscrutability of Fate, and the destination of his existence may not be consciously realized by man, but any one of them may plunge man into a turmoil of conditions that may engulf him and cause him intense suffering. The intricacies of commingled conditions may hide specific causes of suffering from man and make him insensitive to relative qualities of various states of potential suffering, and inveterate beliefs may make man imperceptive in distinguishing particular relationships with other states, but his receptive capacities will still provide a potential reservoir of tragic impulses. When these impulses become active, and when man responds, even instinctively or intuitively, tragic circumstances may evolve and eventually, or suddenly, envelop man and envenom the conditions of his world. Spiritual inversion, loss of faith, alteration of habitual spiritual concepts, conversion, moral aversion: these may all contribute to the activation of the tragic impulse and the impulse to suffering in the conditions of man's world.

Man's psychic nature may also be a potential source of conditions and impulses conducive to spiritual suffering and to psychological suffering: psychological when seemingly psychic phenomena may be attributed to natural responses or conditioning or observable behavioral characteristics; spiritual when seemingly psychic phenomena demonstrate no recognizable influences of material, physical, mental, sensorial, or scientifically testable sources. Unexplainable miracles, spiritualistic visitations, ghostly appearances, poltergeistic disturbances, witchcraft powers, natural phenomena occurring as seeming answers to prayers or incantations, unnatural trance states, premonitions, divination, clairvoyance, transnatural memory or affinity, spiritual transfiguration, magic, ritualistic exaltation, and any supranatural occurrences or occult experiences—when believed in or when exciting a response—may be as much a part of man's spiritual state as his god or gods are and will be as much a part of the conditions of his world as are the natural or physical conditions. The spiritual state will contain the impulses leading to potential suffering just as will any of the other states. Ritualistic suffering—flagellation, fasting, mortification, maceration, crucifixion, martyrdom, scourging, scarification, and other forms of infliction of pain for religious purposes—may originate in the spiritual state, but it may also originate in the behavioral state. Whatever the source, ritualistic suffering will also be associated with the states of physical, mental, and emotional suffering once there is a conscious awareness of pain.

For tragedy to occur at the human level, not only must there be an awareness of the presence of suffering—whether instinctive awareness, cognizant awareness, behavioral awareness, mental awareness, physical awareness, or simply primal recognition of pain—there must also be conscious responsiveness to the impulse that produces the pain, whether or not the specific particularities of the impulse can be isolated within the condition producing the pain or attributed to a particular state of pain. For pain to have a genuinely tragic effect, its suffering must be borne by responsively aware man; he must endure the suffering though his natural inclination will be to avoid pain through whatever means are available to him and by whatever devices his ingenuity can create to alleviate it. He must offer resistance to his suffering and the causes of his suffering because normal man is antagonistic to pain by nature of physical aversion, mental reservation, emotional dislike, spiritual distaste, and behavioral antipathy. But for great tragic consequences to develop he cannot succumb to his suffering without offering resistance, and he must have no illusions about the consequences as they relate to him and the conditions of his world. The means of endurance and resistance will derive from the same states that produce the suffering; the physical, mental, emotional, spiritual, and behavioral states that produce the suffering also produce the antagonism against suffering that is the impulse prompting resistance and endurance. One state may so temper and control and complement another that suffering may become tolerable. For example, the excess-mean-deficiency tolerance discussed in Chapter VI may offer adequate control of the mental state to make spiritual pain bearable by rationalizing away its impulses or by substituting mental conditions that are nonproductive of painful consequences for the spiritual condition that produces the spiritual suffering. Likewise, any of the other states may be brought into contention with a state producing pain and so alter conditions and impulses that the original state of pain is no longer predominant or in control of the conditions. Influences of other states may so ameliorate the condition of spiritual pain, with or without diminishing the consequences to the spiritual state and the resultant responsiveness by man to the impulse that generates the pain or to the conditions that emerge from the state of awareness, that an entirely new set of conditions and circumstances will prevail, and an entirely new impulse will be generated, all containing the potential for tragedy. But suffering merely for the sake of suffering, or enduring pain merely for the sake of endurance, would not be conducive to the establishment of great tragedy. The suffering must be borne for causes or effects other than for its own sake. There is no merit to suffering unless it is conducive to something or creates something or contributes to something other than to its own topically ego-centered perpetuation.

Man's resistance toward conditions of his world is in itself a pain producer because resistance generates friction, and friction—physical, mental, emotional, spiritual, and behavioral—activates the tragic impulse to create a degree of suffering within the states of man's being. To be born is to be exposed to potential suffering, to the pain-producing states of man's existence and to the tragic impulses inherent in the conditions of man's world. To live is to expand the exposure to the tragic impulse however latent it may be at any particular moment. Man may hope to avoid pain, the natural antagonist to serenity, and some few do, totally; but most men—men of principle and action, men searching for self-identity and men aware of the conditions of their worlds, men sensitive to life and responsive to its demands—most men meet pain and suffer its consequences. Some endure it, and some succumb to it. Some resist it, and some few show a predilection for it and invite it. Some greet it with aware responsiveness, and some are able to avoid it or blunt their responsiveness to it. But man, individually or collectively, is subject to pain-producing impulses and conditions; and the Nature-derived states of suffering are not selective, in any particular degree or object, in their choices of sufferers. The natural states of suffering do not take into account the moral or ethical natures of their victims; they have no consciences in themselves save in their adherence to the principles of the natural ethic-aesthetic mean-tolerance rule (discussed in Chapter VI); they have no compunctions concerning sex, age, or condition; they have no regard for social position, race, religion, economic status, level of learning, or happenstance of birth. The states of suffering are nonselective in terms of germinal impulses; they make no arbitrary distinctions between good or bad, rich or poor, ugly or beautiful, moral or immoral, ethical or unethical. The natural states of suffering recognize no time or place; they are not topical except when they derive from sentiently defined time-environment focuses and perspectives; they are universally present in Nature. They respect no conventions or mores or standards or institutions in their primally natural states; they may touch any particular man; they may touch all men. The states of suffering, in themselves, are natural conditions without consciousness, conscience, or personality. They cannot by themselves select or respect, distinguish or recognize, because they have no faculties for recognition, distinction, respect, or selection. They are natural states without consciousness, and value judgments require consciousness for attribution. Though natural selection does occur in Nature through ecological interdependency, there is no consciously sentient appraisal of humanly derived moral or ethical values operative in the selection; adaptability, functionality, and utility are the bases of natural selection; and capacity and ability and inclination and will to resist and endure are the most essential qualities of adaptability, functionality, and utility in their most natural, primally impulsive states in Nature. Values or value judgments that are artificially or institutionally imposed or superimposed, according to the eccentricities of conventions of time and place, have no intrinsic worth in relation to the impulses that activate the states of suffering within the conditions of the natural world. Because the states of suffering themselves make no value judgments, the "bad" man may be subjected to the same impulse to suffer as the "good" man, and the resultant consequences may be as tragic for the one as for the other. If suffering is an essential ingredient of tragedy, then tragedy—in the conditions of the world of man in his natural state—cannot be limited to men of particular birth or morals or ethics or social stations because the states that induce suffering can make no selection from among arbitrary, institutional definitions of status, position, or value. Indeed, the "goodness" of a man may well activate the impulse that will create tragic suffering within particular conditions, and the "badness" of a man may likewise activate the same or a similar impulse in the same or similar conditions and create a similar degree of tragic awareness and suffering.

The states of suffering take no account of the designations of "hero" or "non-hero"; they merely establish pain as a requisite quality, in potential, of the conditions of man's world; and that quality requires only responsiveness to activate the tragic impulse. Tragedy itself, as a condition of man's world, conscience-less and unconscious, is neither moral nor immoral, good nor bad, heroic nor non-heroic, ethical nor unethical except in terms of Nature's own ethic-aesthetic perspective. Tragedy is a condition of sentient man's world; its goodness or badness, its heroism or its cowardice, its morality or its immorality, are values —positive or negative or indifferent—attributed to it by an observer or by any particular participant in it ascribing its qualities in terms of topical associations; tragedy may provide a basis for a value judgment, but it does not have intrinsic value qualities within itself as an impulse motivational force generating universally acceptable values, nor does it make value judgments of its object or subject. Neither good nor bad of itself, tragedy depends on man's interpretation of it through his powers of sensitivity, perceptivity, receptivity, awareness, inclination, and will for establishing inferentially relative values to it. But those values are only relative; and they are man's values by arbitrary, institutional, personal, topical definition, and not by naturally innate qualities of the condition or impulse of tragedy itself; and they relate to sentiently recognized tragedy only as man relates them to it, finitely and arbitrarily.

Values are derived from conditions by inference and implication and through responsiveness to the conditions and awarenesses of their import; or values are arbitrarily related to conditions by definition or by attribution of extrinsic qualities to the intrinsic nature of an impulse, condition, or circumstance. Values are quite generally arbitrary and personal and topical; what is "good" for one time or place or person may quite well be "bad" for another. Tragedy, too, is personal; what may be tragic for one may be blissful for another; for the conditions demand a different responsiveness from each man, and the derived values are different for each man.

Even the terms *heroic* and *non-heroic* are subject to topical definition, making ambiguous any consideration of tragedy or tragic conditions that depends on heroic qualities in a protagonist. Within the conditions of his world, the actions of man may violate all the conventions and mores of the society of which he is a part; he may be labeled as "evil" or "unheroic" or "subversive" or "unethical" or simply as "bad" if his actions or attitudes fail to meet the approval of his contemporary institutions or of other men, or if he fails to establish—through force, coercion, or persuasion—his own ideals, attitudes, or actions as a new societal convention. But once his society accepts, pays homage to, or adopts the qualities previously considered evil or bad or subversive or unheroic or unethical, his actions become good, ethical, honorable, or heroic, by definition. Rebellion is subversive or evil until it is successful; then it becomes heroic and good, for success too often defines goodness or badness, heroism or cowardice, without consideration of motive or cause or effect, but only in terms of topical utility or practicality; successful rebellion against the *status quo*, for all practical purposes, as evidenced by historical precedent, provides its own license to define its own means, ends, methods, and consequences in its own terms of goodness or badness; and by historical precedent, unsuccessful rebellion against the *status quo* is by its failure, whether committed by an individual or by a mass of men, arbitrarily defined as evil by whatever individual or institution that has defended itself successfully against rebellion or prevailed against alteration of the *status quo*. The rightness or wrongness, the morality or immorality, the goodness or badness of action and attitude is, in the human condition of Nature, within the topical prerogatives of the successful for definition, especially when success carries with it the power to enforce its own ideals and attitudes. Though the loser may never accept the conditions and attitudes and ideals of the winner as moral or ethical or right, he is invariably subjected to them if he continues to exist under the establishment of their institutional structure. And if he persists in his attempt to follow his own conscience or ideals or attitudes in violation of the new *status quo* established by the winner, if he appears to be a threat to that *status quo*, he is apt to suffer tragic consequences no matter how moral or ethical or good his conscience and ideals and attitudes are from his own point of view, the point of view of the previous condition, or the point of view of an uninvolved observer.

Emotions generally involve a psychic reaction, which is primarily associated with the spiritual state, and a physical reaction, primarily associated with the physical state, so they cannot be disassociated entirely from either of these states. The spiritual state is here considered as pertaining not only to extraphysical or corporeal condition but also to that condition of response which seems to rise above or go beyond mental abstraction. The relationship of the emotions to the state of suffering activated by the tragic impulse in the conditions of man's world is ultimately a subjective experiencing of feelings responding to conditions and circumstances or derived from conditions in response to an impulse that excites feelings. The emotional state of suffering probably has the widest range of affective influences on tragic experiences of the five states of suffering because man is a creature of emotion, and his most immediate responses to impulses are either instinctively physical or immediately behavioral, either of which excite emotional reactional responsiveness in man whenever feelings are involved. The emotional state is closely related to man's sensitivity, perceptivity, receptivity, inclination, and will, particularly in those circumstances involving personal responsiveness and demanding personal perception of phenomenal reality or illusory phenomena under conditions commanding impulses of responsive-feeling reactions of the greatest diversity in relation to the object of feeling. Although the emotional state is concerned in the main with the disposition of feelings, it is not divorced from the mental state, for it depends on the mental state for the control of its expression, and it relies on the behavioral state for the evidencing of its psychological dispositioning of responsive feelings.

Emotions are specific responses to specifically activated impulses in the conditions of man's natural world; perhaps the lowest levels of these responses are the general feelings of man as he reacts almost indifferently to the general tenor of his existence. Many responsive feelings at this level are not much more than habitual exercises of routine and have little more import in creating or stimulating involvement with other than a mundane acceptance of conditions than do the natural responses of lower animals. Man is a creature with animal functions, but he is also a creature with a particularized functional responsiveness that sets him apart from other animals, especially in the degrees of responsiveness stimulated within the mental, emotional, spiritual, and behavioral states, and in the aesthetic nature he possesses as a result of his more specialized capacities of sensitivity, perceptivity, receptivity, inclination, and will and his responsive judgments of the beautiful and his capabilities to define conditions and impulses in terms of value judgments.

To suffer responsively as man, as distinguished from other forms of life, there must be a responsiveness that elevates man above other life, and one of the qualities that so elevates man is the intensity of his emotional responsiveness, as well as of his mental, spiritual, and behavioral responsiveness. Another such *man* quality is the level of differentiation and recognition of impulses and responses. With the differentiation of responses and impulses there may come an intensification of feelings that will qualify them by degrees to the levels of emotions or passions. When a creature is capable of differentiating his feelings; when those feelings reach a level of emotional responsiveness and that responsiveness may be intensified into passions; when the abstract relationship of the passions to the impulses and conditions may be judged by the creature experiencing them; when the emotions and passions may be subjected to moral, aesthetic, and ethical appraisal; and when the intellect may control, condition, and qualify responsive disposition of feelings: man, as a sentient creature capable of experiencing tragedy, has evolved to a level of complexity wherein the state of emotional suffering is of major importance in the tragic conditions of his world.

The state of emotional suffering is associated with man's nature in the three contracts man has with life: the presentient, the sentient, and the postsentient. Therefore, it is also related to, and is often indistinguishable from, the other states of suffering to which man may be subjected. Indeed, emotional suffering, when viewed by an observer apart from the actual sufferer, may seem to be or be identical to another state of suffering, so closely related is the expression of emotion to the responsive nature of man reacting to stimulating impulses emanating from conditions productive of other kinds of pain. Actually, the state of emotional suffering is often less apparent to the observer than are the other states of suffering, either because the observer cannot always discern the emotional impulses in conditions not experienced by himself or because he cannot with certainty differentiate among the impulses conducive to other states without actually experiencing the pain himself. Even the sufferer may not always be totally aware of the real nature of his pain, and he may attribute a particular response to a source quite apart from the impulse generating his pain.

Because the emotions and the passions are usually experiences of the inner world of man and because their experiencing is often of such a private nature that they are shielded from public recognition by a natural reticence on the part of the sufferer to reveal himself in what is probably man's most intimately vulnerable state, his emotions, man is likely to disguise his emotional responsiveness whenever possible. Because man is naturally antagonistic to pain and because emotional response is generally considered personal and private, he may fear to suffer public recognition of his emotions—the attitudes of men often make the revelation of emotion or passion a matter for ridicule —and because he hesitates to put himself in a vulnerable possition that exposes him to pain, man is generally antipathetic concerning anything that might make him the object of ridicule or place him in a position in which his responses might be misunderstood, considered excessive, or viewed as a weakness of his nature. The revelation of inner, emotional pain might well subject man to even greater pain—the pain of embarrassment, outrage, or frustration. A consequence of emotional reticence may be the intensifying of pain through loneliness, the suffering alone of the frustration of unrevealed or unshared pain. Sometimes the revelation of emotional frustration may eliminate the cause of pain or quiet the impulse that generates the pain. Misunderstanding, either on the part of the sufferer or by a participant in the emotional experience, may cause emotional suffering. Such suffering may be avoided or voided by revelation. But man, in his hesitancy to reveal himself or his private inner world, subjects himself to the potential tragedy of intense private suffering.

Emotive response may then work in two directions: it may

be the release of pent feelings or passions, providing relief to a sufferer in the emotional state; or it may be the expression that will expose man to even greater suffering. The impulses that stir man to responsiveness permeate the conditions of man's world, and those impulses may activate emotive responses ranging from an ultimate of ecstasy to an abyss of despair, subjecting man to a gamut of emotional experiences with an infinite variety of pains and pleasures. Egocentric emotional suffering may plunge man into the depths of woe and cause him to wallow in self-pity, or it may elevate man to the heights of transcendent glory. Altruistic emotional suffering may thrust man into a chaos of externally imposed painful conditions, or it may provide new human relationships conducive to great happiness. Altruistic emotional responsiveness may induce a sympathetic condition wherein man may enter into the emotional experiences of another and share both the pleasure and the pain of the emotional association. Emotional satisfaction is the protagonist of happiness. Emotional dissatisfaction is the antagonist of happiness, and emotional dissatisfaction may provide agonizing emotional suffering.

In the emotional state of suffering, as the sufferer agonizes, new painful circumstances are usually born, altering the conditions of man's world or creating new conditions demanding further and different responses and eliciting suffering related to the other states of pain. This state creates a sequential and simultaneous evolution of painful impulses each actuating another, an intensifying of painful experiences, and an accumulating of painful conditions. As the sufferer assimilates these conditions, evolving and intensifying and accumulating, through his particular capacities of sensitivity, perceptivity, and receptivity, and as he synthesizes them and responds to them within the limits of his inclination and will, the consequences of his responsiveness result in actions stimulated by the impulses within the conditions. These actions may be either outward expressions of reaction to the conditions or inner turmoil evoked by the impulses themselves. The actions may be overt or covert or dormant, depending on the nature of the responder. Some emotional responses may not be expressible, and their recognition by either an observer or the responder himself may depend on analysis of the attitude or bearing of the responder, or on the manifestation of the response as evidenced by whatever action the responder engages in as a result of the impulse to act. Because emotional responsiveness is conditioned by the physical, mental, spiritual, and behavioral states of man, and because these states differentiate man uniquely and individually, emotional responses vary according to the nature of individual man. It then becomes next to impossible to predict the precise nature of any emotional response; and action and its consequences become the evidential record of the nature of man, his personality, and his character.

Because of the complexities of the relationships among the states and conditions and impulses of man, and the individuality of man's responsiveness, each man is a unique creature within the confines of the conditions and impulses of his unique world. Each man is then the subject of his own world and the shaper of that world; each man is the object of the impulses that animate his responses to the conditions of his world; and each man is uniquely complex in the totality of his responsive qualities. There is no undeviating determinism controlling the responsive natures of all men alike, save the variable determinism of the ecological ethic of Nature, because each man is the unique individual representative of his own world even though his world has conditions created by association with the unique worlds of other men and has similarities to the worlds of other men. And these associations and similarities, infinitely complex in the unique natures of their separate entities, become even more complicated in the conjoining, commingling, juxtaposing congruency of multiple human relationships; and any prediction of specific responsiveness emanating from the associative conditions will be, at best, so highly speculative and fallible as to qualify only as an extremely weak guess. Responsive action (either inner and observed and felt by the responder alone, or overt and capable of being observed and interpreted by someone other than the responder) becomes the source of evidence which may establish the major share of man's knowledge of himself in relation to the conditions of his world, or which may give another person a view of man's position in relation to the conditions and impulses that provoke him to responsive action. But unique man may remain an enigma both to himself and to others. He may never come to a conscious literal understanding of himself or of the conditions that make him what he is; and he may never reveal enough of himself to an outsider to give that outsider anything other than a cursory and partial impression of his real nature or even an erroneous impression of his real nature. By the same token, man may reveal, through responsive action, qualities and characteristics that will allow an outsider to judge and interpret objectively, even though there may be persistent attempts, either conscious or unconscious, to conceal any identification of man's real nature; and the understanding derived from such objective observation may be more thorough than any understanding of himself that man may develop. But subjective analysis may also reveal traits of character and personality and mind and spirit and understanding that never become objectively apparent either to man himself or to an observer. Because of the complexity of man's nature and the conditions and impulses of his world, it is often impossible not to be mistaken in an interpretation of the meaning of man's responses: a friendly gesture may be misunderstood and interpreted as anything from an antagonistic act to an extreme of passionate response. Misunderstanding and misinterpretation may also result because of man's tendency to prejudge or to judge in terms of his limited knowledge and understanding alone. Ignorance and partial knowledge are not only the greatest contributors to misinterpretation and misunderstanding, they are also a major source of pain in all the states of suffering.

The tragic impulse is present, and tragedy may result from the conditions of man's world, whenever the feelings, emotions, or passions of man are elicited in response to the qualities of the conditions of his world and whenever the state of emotional suffering results from man's responsiveness. The state of emotional suffering may be directed inward and establish tragic circumstances and consequences for the sufferer himself, or it may be directed outward and engulf another in its consequences. The object of a response may be as affected by the response, in the shaping of conditions and the creation of impulses, as the person making the response, and the conditions of the worlds of both the object and the responder will be altered by the response. This alteration may in turn generate a new impulse conducive to tragic suffering for either, or for both.

In the state of emotional suffering feelings are apt to be of the least consequence in establishing tragic consequences because feelings are often undifferentiated and may be quite unidentifiable. In man's emotionally responsive nature, feelings may be below the surface of conscious perception and quite outside the range of mental awareness. The impulses generating feelings may well be imperceptible, either to the person experiencing the feelings or to an observer. There may be a vagueness in feeling responses that, within themselves, defies recognition and develops no intensity; this very vagueness, however, may create enough discomfort or unease to agitate the impulse within a condition and to provide the motion generating responsiveness to another state of suffering. Feelings may provide the impulse that will alter conditions to an extent that will demand a high level of responsiveness: the excitement or agitation of emotion. If the emotional reaction intensifies to a degree wherein it exercises a controlling influence over the responsive

58

nature of man, or wherein it is so powerful that man becomes subject to its dictates, it may well qualify as a passion. This would suggest that the passions are the elicitors of the most intense responses in the state of emotional suffering, and that the passions may well be the chief contributors to the highest level of tragic experience. The emotions, so long as they remain within the responsive condition effectively controllable by reason, will usually find expression as zeal or enthusiasm in relation to an object or cause exciting interest, admiration, or devotion. But at times, though reason may lead to zeal or enthusiasm, zeal or enthusiasm may exceed the bounds of reasonableness and may contribute to disastrous errors in judgment or unreasonable or rash action, especially when passion proves itself stronger than reason. Impulses developing such responses might well establish tragic conditions evoking intense emotional suffering. Zeal and enthusiasm, as well as other passionate responses, often blind the responder to other conditions and impulses that may make man a victim of external forces beyond his immediate awareness or may subject him to internal conditions causing unfortunate errors in judgment, over-zealousness, frenzy, or excesses in any number or kind of responsive situations. Overpowering emotions or passions may also elicit impulsive action that might result in accident or error demanding suffering as a response. Zeal for a cause might well drive man to heights, or depths, of realization or accomplishment where he would find himself completely alone and vulnerable to all those painproducing conditions that are most intense when suffered uniquely and individually. Zeal or enthusiasm, as well as accident, may place man in positions of leadership or authority demanding decisions and responses capable of producing painful consequences both to himself and to others. The intensity of emotional experience, as well as the intensity of experiences of the other states of man's nature, will most certainly help to establish the degree and magnitude of tragedy if man responds with awareness to the impulse generating the painful conditions and circumstances and endures the consequences of his responsive awareness. Refusal to recognize the consequences, inability to respond to the consequences, ignorance of either the impulse or its consequences, apathy toward the conditions created, and escape from the consequences would all tend to negate or minimize the degree and magnitude of tragedy.

That is not to say that man may not resist the tragic impulse, rail against his misfortune, attempt to assuage his pain or ameliorate the conditions that cause his suffering, or correct the consequences of his actions and still not suffer tragedy. Indeed, the very resistance he offers to the conditions, to the suffering, to the impulse to respond, to the awareness he has, to the consequences of his responsiveness may be the creation of his tragedy; and perhaps the greatest tragedy would be an impasse: the coming together of such powerful will and inclination and resolve to resist that nothing can supplant them with circumstances and conditions that pose insurmountable obstacles to man's serenity—a position in which man neither succumbs nor triumphs but is totally aware of that position in relation to its causes and effects. Such a situation could possibly create the ultimate in tragedy with no fall, no moral or ethical implications, no defeat, no failure, only the elemental power of resistance and endurance opposed to the elemental forces demanding resistance and endurance in response. Man caught in circumstances beyond his ability to triumph, circumstances posing insuperable obstacles, insoluble problems, and insufferable conditions, might, in desperation or as a matter of principle or because of stubbornness or because of ignorance of the consequences or because of the challenge offered or because no escape seems possible, resist and endure states of suffering unique in human experience. And the responses he offers, resistance and endurance, together with whatever physical, mental, emotional, spiritual, or behavioral reactions he makes, may create an awareness of self that supersedes any previously perceived identification of self with the conditions making up the world of man, either public or private, and set in motion forces focusing on the unique man with such intensity and magnitude that he becomes engulfed, both as responsive receiver and as responsive emitter, by the flow of irreconcilable impulses that overwhelm him in either a tragic or a serene state. On the other hand, man's responsiveness may range away from total awareness, through an indeterminate number of intermediate stages or levels of awareness, toward a total absence of awareness of the import of the circumstances; and awareness of the conditions or of the responses made to them may be outside the ken of either the responder or an observer. Depending on his nature and inclination at any particular moment, man may respond overtly or not. He may be aware, whereas an observer may not, of the states of suffering he is in or the experiences he is having. The conditions of awareness may be reversed, however, and the observer may be more cognizant of conditions, circumstances, and consequences than the initial responder. Within the range of awareness of either, however, may come the recognition of the tragic impulse and the resultant responses. If the observer alone is aware of the implications of tragic impulses operating within the conditions of another's world, the tragedy will be substitutive or vicarious. If, however, the responder is himself aware, the tragedy will be personal. The personal tragedy may never be recognized by an outside observer, for man may choose or be compelled to suffer in silence and never give external evidence of his awareness. Consequently, tragedy in man's world may be intimate, personal, and introspective when the conditions, impulses, circumstances, and consequences all operate to create a responsive awareness in man of his own situation in relation to all the states of suffering involved in the particular evocative experience. On the other hand, though man may be completely submerged in tragic conditions, circumstances, impulses, or consequences, without responsive awareness he is not experiencing tragedy in the sense that it has experience-meaning for him. An observer, who recognizes the tragic implications of the conditions, impulses, circumstances, or consequences, though not experiencing the actuality of tragedy, may discern its imminence. The immanence of the tragic impulse, when discernible to an observer, may create an expectation of tragedy, but tragedy itself will probably occur in its most painful experiencing only in actuality, not in its expectative consideration.

Tragedy itself will remain latent until it is experienced in actuality and its consequences are subjected to responsive awareness by its sufferer himself. That is to say that genuine tragedy in the world of man and under the conditions of that world and the laws of Nature involves actual and particular experience more than it involves speculation, expectation, or imagination; though to rule out those qualities as contributors to degrees of tragedy, tragic experience, and experience-meaning would be to reduce man's sensitivity, perceptivity, receptivity, responsiveness, and awareness to considerations of less import than they evidence in the totality of man's capacity and ability to experience and to respond. The immanence of tragic impulses is not the experience of tragedy; the imminence of tragic awareness is not the experience of tragedy; the expectation of tragic circumstances is not the experience of tragedy; responsive awareness of the tragic impulse and the enduring of its consequences is tragedy. An observer, however aware he may be of the conditions, impulses, circumstances, or consequences of tragedy as they surround another, is the subject of tragedy only vicariously, sympathetically, or empathetically; he is not the real figure of tragedy or the experience-meaning of tragic impulses, conditions, circumstances, consequences, or impacts. Man may be a tragic figure to an observer whenever an observer recognizes the presence of the tragic qualifications, but he is not a figure of tragedy to himself until he is himself aware of his situation as a tragic figure; nor is the observer a tragic figure until he participates in the tragic experience afforded by the conditions and develops his own aware sense of the participatory experience-meaning, and tragedy does not occur to either before that awareness becomes functional.

The recognition of tragic conditions, impulses, circumstances, and consequences may be retrospective, immediate, or prospective; and that recognition may lead to an awareness of tragedy functioning within the world and nature of man at any moment. But the mere recognition of tragic conditions, impulses, circumstances, and consequences is not enough to establish tragedy. For tragedy to occur there must be responsiveness to the conditions and impulses contributing to the suffering of tragedy. As man reviews the past conditions of his world, he may become aware of tragic implications in those conditions and conclude that they are the cause of his tragedy or that they may have the potential to lead him to tragedy. Retrospectively, in this case, he may arrive at an awareness of the past that may demand a responsiveness involving suffering. He may also retrospectively discover in the past conditions of his world the cause of his suffering and respond to them with a new awareness that may be defined as tragedy. Analytical retrospection may not only reveal the cause of present conditions, it may also supply the insight necessary to cope with present conditions and to anticipate future conditions. Analytical retrospection will be more closely associated with the mental state than it will with the other states of suffering, but it may also be extremely conducive to the development of conditions wherein the tragic impulse will activate emotional responsiveness. Here again, the qualities of one state will have a direct bearing on the recognition of the nature of another state and will influence the degree and direction of the responsiveness of man to the conditions emanating from that state. The resultant conditions, impulses, circumstances, and consequences will occasion a *mélange* of responses practically indistinguishable as direct derivatives of any one specific state. The mixing of conditions and responses creates an extremely complex world, but retrospection provides bases for comparison through which man may establish means to judge present and future conditions and derive an awareness of values based on experiential evidence. Though the values so derived will be subjected to emotional qualification, their primary emergence will be from intellectual consideration, and the responses to them will be tempered by all the conditions that function within Nature and the world of man. Retrospection will also give man the means to judge tradition, to recognize it and to accept, reject, or alter it to suit the purposes of his immediate and prospective worlds. Retrospection will depend upon the memory of man, his capability to retain knowledge, images, and impressions—consciously or unconsciously—from experiences of the past, and art will function as the primary medium of memory retention. That memory will not only be qualified by past perceptivity, sensitivity, and receptivity, but also by past will and inclination and instinct to retain. It will depend on man's present capacity for recall and on his will and inclination to recall. The verity of impressions of recalled conditions will depend upon the thoroughness of the recall and upon the degree of alteration of impressions of conditions through the evolutionary processes of growth and development in the functioning of the person engaged in the retrospective process. The nature of the recalled conditions will also have undergone alteration through the degrees and levels of sensitivity toward and perceptivity of experience, through the processes of assimilation within the states and conditions of man's receptive capacity, and through the natural evolutionary processes of synthesis within the nature of individual man. In retrospect, the conditions, impulses, circumstances, and consequences will not often be identical to what they seemed initially; but their influences will most certainly contribute to the shaping, qualifying, and complementing of the conditions of man's immediate world. The retrospective lack of total identification with past experience will be occasioned by man's natural inclination to submerge certain feelings and responses in protective forgetfulness, to retain only particularly salient characteristics of an experience in the memory, either actual or artistic, to respond to only parts of an experience either in the actual experiencing or in retrospective re-creation, to depend primarily on emotion as the impulse to activate the memory process, to exaggerate or minimize the importance of recalled experience, to push certain responsive feelings into the subconscious and to retain only particular impressions of feelings in the conscious mind.

Psychologically, some of the submerged feelings and subconsciously retained feelings may often be brought to surface consciousness and be made to play a part in the conscious development of new conditions. More often than not, however, they remain in the subconscious and exert a conditioning influence of which man is quite unaware. Occasionally, forgotten impressions, scenes, and fragments of past experience will spring seemingly unbidden to the conscious mind and create an awareness, not only of the past but also of the present, that will alter, intensify, or complement a present responsive awareness. Retrospective recognition and prospective recognition depend on impulses functioning in the present to stimulate recall or to envision future conditions, impulses, circumstances, and consequences. Retrospection and prospection are, therefore, functions of immediacy in recognition, response, and awareness; but they relate to the past and the future as sources of inspiration or motivation of the impulse that activates them. Although tragedy may spring from past conditions or be envisioned in future conditions, its actual experiencing, other than empathetically or vicariously, will be in the constantly moving but always immediate present, whether it be through recall or through vision. Tragedy, then, of itself, is immediate and present, though its contributing conditions may be either past or present or future, or of any combination of time sequence qualities. Man may experience only the present in actual physical reality; but the conditions of that present reality, moving and evolving, are shaped by the remembered impressions of realities and phantasies of the past and the projections and dreams of the future. The present is an accumulation from the past of all the retained experiences and impressions that have been isolated and stored in the mind and spirit and records of man. Though those experiences and impressions had only a present reality at the moment of their germination, the instant they became the subject of recall or memory or record, they became relegated to the past. That is to say, the past is a moving present with infinite moments of experience and impression subjected to retrospection and building momentary awareness in a present that ceases to exist the instant it takes on the quality of being remembered or subject to recall, but at the same time perpetuates its existence in the continuous evolution of experience and impression that is terminated only with the failure or cessation of sentience. In this sense, immediate recognition is past experience and impression from the moment it occurs, and it functions as the base from which the future derives. But the future is only a continuation of the present and never has an identity of its own save in prospective recognition of qualities and considerations that can be no more than speculation or wish or dream until the reality of experience shifts them into a condition subject to retrospection.

Prospective recognition, an extension of immediate experience and past experience functioning in the present, is determined by man's looking forward to experience and impression that have not yet been in actuality, nor are now evidencing actuality. Prospective recognition may often have tragic consequences and lead to various states of suffering, primarily in the emotional state; because of the uncertainty inherent in hypothetical or theoretical conditions, prospection can rarely foresee all the contingencies, complications, exigencies of fortune, accidents of Nature, miscalculations, alterations of circumstances, or mistakes that will so change conditions as to frustrate expectation, anticipation, hopes, predictions, prophecies, dreams, or prognostications and bring man to the suffering of disenchantment, delusion, disillusion, disappointment, and failure. The failure of man's hopes and dreams of the future is an immediate and powerful source of tragic suffering, and many of man's tragedies derive from the foiling of anticipation. Ambition is one of the most elemental of the prospective impulses, and the expectation of frustrated ambition is one of man's greatest sources of fear, which is often a painful ingredient of tragedy. When man views the future and attaches significant importance to events of the future, he places himself in a vulnerable position. But because vulnerability is not necessarily synonymous with inevitability, man may hope for bliss while at the same time he is aware of the possibility, or even probability, that he will not achieve all that he desires. The uncertainties of the future, either topical or eternal, provide both hopes and fears, both delight and apprehension, both joy and sorrow in the conditions of man's world. Man may hope, even, to conquer the one inevitable, death; but the fear of failure often leads man to tragic suffering. Retrospectively, immediately, and prospectively, man's awareness of and responsiveness to life are complexly associated with man's contracts with existence and with all the conditions of those contracts.

Human behavior capable of being observed, though certainly not alienated from unobservable causes nor disassociated from any or all of the other states of human suffering, is the source of man's awareness of the behavioral state of suffering. Although the state of behavioral suffering may at times be coincidental

with other states of suffering, at times identical with other states
of suffering, or at times the observable behavioral evidence of
the other states of suffering, certain particularities may, at
times, differentiate it from those other states. It is in particularities or peculiarities of differentiation capable of being analyzed,
tested, isolated, and observed in behavior that the state of behavioral suffering will be evidenced as a contribution to the conditions, impulses, circumstances, and consequences of tragic
awareness and response and to the development of tragedy in
the world of man. Perhaps the major emphasis on behavioral
suffering in the tragic condition will fall on subjects ordinarily
relegated to abnormal psychology, but this should not minimize
the relationship of the other branches of psychology to tragedy,
particularly in those conditions wherein the abnormal is only an
intensification or magnification of normal or average behavioral
response. In the sense that the greatest tragedies evidence extraordinary or exceptional awareness and responsiveness, superior
endurance, supernormal resistance, and beyond the average
capacities, abilities, wills, and inclinations, the tendency is to
consider their qualities in terms of abnormality; but supersen-
sitivity, superperceptivity, and superreceptivity (requirements
for monumental or super-tragedy) are not necessarily abnormalities or aberrations except in the sense that they are exceptional or nonaverage in the degree of divergence from the
ordinary, or, in Nature, in their proclivity to creation of the
mutant. There are, however, certain nonnormal qualities and
conditions exhibiting variance from natural behavior that do
not depend on degree of divergence from the normal to require
consideration as abnormalities. Whether the differences are of
degree or of quality, they are still contributors to the conditions
of man's world, and as such they are potential sources of tragic
suffering. Whether or not divergence or variance from the normal or the average is a natural degree of differentiation, an
artificially induced alteration of Nature, a happenstance muta-

tion of characteristics, or a deliberate conditioning of qualities or attitudes, the suffering that may occur may be as intense as that emanating from any other condition and may be as conducive to the development of tragedy as any other suffering.

Among the variances that might not be considered normal because of artificial inducement will be found such conditions as those created by psychedelic—or mind-expanding—drugs, art, diet, or other externally derived stimuli creating nonnormal experiences of fear, anxiety, insight, phantasy, or appetite; hypnotic—or mind-controlling—soporifics, suggestions, mesmeric inductions, spellbinding agents, or surgery or accident tending to alter mental activity; debilitative—or mind-limiting —brainwashing, mental conditioning, drug addiction, alcoholism, or other externally imposed influences tending to limit mental (or other state) responsiveness; psychotherapeutic— or mind-treating—drugs, exercises, surgery, hypnosis, or experiences tending to orient or reorient mental states. Though the primary influences of these agents are on the mental state, the influences are, by no means, limited to the mental state. Indeed, their observable conditions as they are involved in the behavioral state will more often than not be related to physical, spiritual, and emotional experience and expression. Not all so-called abnormal behavior is, however, artificially induced. Hypochondria, kleptomania, schizophrenia, paranoia, psychosomatic illness, insanity, or other mental illness, and other manias, phobias, and mental disorders may result naturally, or they may be artificially induced; but they may all contribute to tragic suffering.

In analysis of the development of the conditions of the world of unique man in his time-place, in Nature, setting, in the consideration of the states of suffering arising from those conditions, and in the emphasis placed upon the tragic impulse inherent in those conditions, it is necessary that the analyst objectify his view and make all judgments in terms of the societal and psychological influences of the time dealt with, rather than in terms of the mores, conventions, and definitions of normality for his own time. What may be considered normal during a particular time or in a particular place may be defined as abnormal at another time or in another place; and the state of behavioral suffering, as well as the other painful states, will often be motivated by societal demands and views that are topically limited to time and place. As an example, lesbianism or homosexuality may pose no problems and evoke no painful circumstances under the conditions of a particular time and place or in a particular societal organization; whereas, at a different time or place or in different societal circumstances, they could evoke the most intense impulses of pain and tragedy. The same qualification should, of course, be obvious in the consideration of attitudes, inclinations, practices, and conventions relating to all of man's activities. Judgment must be limited to the immediate influences and conditions shaping the world of man, excepting, of course, those few conditions and attitudes that are manifestly universal in terms of Nature's ethic-aesthetic principles.

Man is psychologically conditioned by the experiences of his own time and place, real and vicarious; he is a product of his own time and place, topically and retrospectively; the conditions that are his world are his own, and to judge him in terms of influences that lie outside his experience, actually or retrospectively or prospectively or vicariously, is to do him an injustice. To judge him partially—only behaviorally, only spiritually, only mentally, only physically, only emotionally—is to do him an injustice because he is a product of all the influencing conditions of his world, internal and external, and of all the impulses—physical, mental, emotional, spiritual, behavioral—that create his awareness and his responsiveness. And he is subject to the states of suffering emanating from his own world and from no other. Psychologically, status seeking is a major incentive; but status varies with time, place, and circumstance.

70

To judge man in relation to status requirements outside the conditions of his unique world is to do him an injustice, for conditions unassociated with his unique world and its unique status symbols are irrelevant not only in topical context but also in the universal context of Nature and her laws. Some branches of speculative psychology might suggest racial memory or the collective unconscious as determinants of man's nature and his responsiveness, but to neglect the temporal conditions, topical environments, and localized experiences of man as conditioners of man's nature and responsiveness would be to do him an injustice. Man thinks and communicates in terms of symbols, but to suggest that every chance utterance or action has a symbolic significance relative to any particular system, past or present or of universal communality, is to pose a hypothesis quite without sufficient evidential justification, and to judge man only in terms of arbitrarily limiting symbolistic interpretation is to do him an injustice just as interpreting him and his actions only in terms of a particular and limited religious point of view not his own would do him an injustice. Certainly man inherits particular qualities and characteristics and inclinations, but just as obviously he is also a product of his environment and the evolution of his own nature within the confines of Nature. To judge him in terms of heredity only, or of environment only, or of natural evolution only, would be to do him an injustice. Certainly man has characteristics that are similar to those found in other animals, but to interpret him and his nature in terms of his animal nature alone would be to overlook the mental, emotional, spiritual, and behavioral qualities that qualify his animalistic expression and differentiate him from other animals, at least in degree. No deterministic influence, other than birth and death and the inexorable evolutionary forces of Nature, has as yet been unquestionably established as an authentically invariable regulator of man and the conditions of his world. To judge man in terms of a specific determinism alien to the conditions of his

71

nature and Nature would be to do him an injustice. Even if man should concern himself primarily with only one of the natural contracts or naturally deterministic influences, such as death, for the major part of his sentient existence, other conditions would certainly exert some qualifying influence on him, and his nature would not be totally regulated by that one consideration. Even the so-called "death wish" as a preoccupation will rarely be so totally determining as to nullify all other influencing conditions of the life contract and their qualifying roles in the shaping of man's identification with the conditions of Nature and of topical institutionality; and isolation into one specific deterministic quality excluding all other conditioning and qualifying influences would require total control of physical, mental, emotional, spiritual, and behavioral states and all the impulses arising from those states. Such absolute control would be impossible if life itself were to be maintained, and unquestionably life would be virtually impossible to maintain if the "death wish" were the only functioning condition. No one determinism is sufficient to explain the conditions, impulses, circumstances, and consequences of man's existence, at least in the individualistic nature of his noncomputerized personality and responsive states.

As man becomes more sophisticated in his societal relationships, psychological orientation of his responsive impulses by ritualistic exercise to create like acceptance or expression of religious, political, patriotic, moral, ethical, or general conventions may evolve into a technological orientation of man's behavioral functions. Computerized establishment of norms for human behavior, and psychiatric treatment to establish acceptance or expression of those norms, could lead to computerized or mechanical judgments and responsiveness. Under such conditions men might be psychologically programmed to repeat an invariable pattern of responses and lose all variables of physical, mental, emotional, spiritual, and behavioral impulses other than those selected by the computer programmer. If those variables were to be eliminated or subjected to mechanical or technological control, creativity would be destroyed as an individual quality, and the patterned responses of the automaton would result. Man would become a mere production line product, creatively inept, but freed from the tragic conditions of his own creation and from the suffering that life holds for him as a potential in the Nature of naturally evolutionary conditions. Such man would be controllable because his responses could be identified with those of all other men cut from the same mechanical pattern, and his responses would be, under these conditions, quantitative rather than qualitative.

Whenever man becomes a quantitative entity rather than a qualitative entity; whenever his personality and identity are lost in political, national, social, religious, technological, or other mass patterns; whenever his creativity is controlled by externally invariable conditioning or mechanical forces; whenever his spirit and mind and emotions are subjected to arbitrary direction, he becomes something less than a unique human individual and his tragedy is no longer personal and individual, but rather it is communal and impersonal. But the suffering of communal tragedy is still tragic experience, and the group awareness and responsiveness may create conditions and consequences of tremendous tragic import. And any individual variant from a societal or communal norm will most certainly be conducive to the development of tragic impulses within the communal condition whenever there is an awareness on the part of any individual that he is at odds with the *status quo* qualities of the communal organization. Indeed, variation from the communal norm will create an aberration that in itself will be an impulse to tragic suffering either for the aberrant himself or for the group whose qualities he violates. The atypical man usually suffers tragic consequences, and atypical conditions usually establish tragic consequences for any man touched by them. The loss of identity by an individual or by a group will not, in itself, be a tragedy until that individual or group becomes aware of the loss and responds to it. But it may create an awareness of tragic conditions for an observer and be interpreted by him as a tragedy even though the tragic impulse remains latent for the actual participant in the tragic loss. Under these circumstances, the potential of tragedy is not realized by those directly involved in the loss, and indeed there is no tragedy as such for them; but there may be the deepest, most intense pain of aloneness and sense of tragedy for anyone left outside the communal identification. Communal identification itself may create conditions containing painfully tragic impulses whenever man senses that he is losing something of his personal identity through communal association or adherence, and man may suffer intensely because a feeling of loyalty to a societal or communal condition demands that personal interests be abandoned or subjected to the interests of the group. But once again, such a man would be an aberrant from totally inclusive involvement with the group, for particular, individual considerations would be the source of the impulse for his suffering, and he would no longer be a genuine, totally participating, member of the communal identity.

Tragedy may be either individual or communal, personal or impersonal, singular or unexceptional, topical or universal. Its conditions are shaped by the experiences of those involved in it—sympathetically, empathetically, or actually—by observation, association, and assimilation; by responsive awareness; and by recognition of consequences. Individual experiences may help to shape the conditions of a society of which man is a part and provide the impulse that will stimulate tragic suffering for all members of the communal group; or the conditions of the communal group may create experiences for the individual member of its society that will lead to tragic consequences for individual man alone; consequently man may suffer alone with-

74

in the communal group or he may suffer with the group; he may also alienate himself from the suffering of the group even though the group may be in the deepest throes of communal agony, or he may impose his tragedy on the communal group and make it a participant in his agony. Communal agony may also be thrust upon individual man either as a participant or as an observer. Communal tragedy may involve states, religious groups, ethnic groups, political parties, economic associations, or any other union, coalition, organization, or association that unites men with a similarity of interest, location, nature, physical character-istics, or force that draws men together because of common aims, desires, needs, positions, or any other societal motives.

The tragedy evolving from the tragic impulse in communal conditions may involve all the states of tragic suffering of in-dividual man; but communal tragedy, as it affects the whole community with responsive awareness, will depend on a col-lective consciousness of the conditions, impulses, circumstances, and consequences functioning either within the community as painful abrasives on the communal identity or without the com-munity as externally imposed frictions on that same communal identity; it will depend on the collective sensitivity, perceptivity, and receptivity of the communal group; it will depend on the communal will and inclination to resist the impulses that gen-erate its suffering; and it will depend on the communal capacity and ability to endure its suffering. Though a collective con-sciousness may be a requisite for communal tragedy, a collective unconsciousness may be the source of individual tragedy. If the communal group as a whole is collectively unconscious of the conditions, impulses, circumstances, and consequences of events, tragedy will not occur for the group even though the latent potential for tragedy is everywhere. But if one individual man becomes aware or conscious of the effects of the events, he may suffer tragically both for himself and for the whole com-munal group even though the group never grasps the import of the events. Consequently, there may be an intense individual suffering for a subject of communal activity, and tragedy may result for him either because of or in spite of communal association.

Racial memory, if it is a valid quality, would perhaps be the ultimate in communal identification; and, if valid, it may have an intrinsic influence on the development of the conditions of man's world. Obviously there are similarities discernible in the extant evidences of man's evolution of beliefs and expressions that might suggest a continuum of conditioning impulses in an inherited subconscious capacity for retention of natural tendencies and attitudes derived from a common primitive ancestral state. As cultural expressions these tendencies and attitudes possibly have similarities in symbolic referents, but similarity is probably inadequate as evidence for the establishment of racial memory or the collective subconscious as verified scientific truth. This does not, however, eliminate belief in the theory of racial memory as an influence on the conditions of man's world, and consequently as a condition of those arts that employ racial memory or the collective subconscious expression of impression as part of their substance, for man creates the conditions of his world from his beliefs as well as from evidential fact considerations. Other possibilities for explaining similarities in seemingly disassociated cultural phenomena exist and may have as much or more validity than the racial memory hypothesis. One such possibility, and one which may have as much importance in the shaping of the conditions of man's world as the racial memory concept, is the contemporaneity of event theory: similarities in questioning of the unknown, in attitudes toward self and society, in response to environment, and in reaction to conditions occur spontaneously at similar stages of man's cultural evolution and evoke similarities in answers, attitudes, responses, reactions, modes of expression, and symbolic representation. In this sense, natural evolutionary processes occurring within a developing or even a declining social structure could be relatively parallel with the same sort of evolutionary processes developing or declining within another social structure at similar stages of development or decline without contiguity ever occurring. Comparable tendencies with like impulses shaping like responses, similar consequences, parallel conditions, and qualified identities could emerge from conditions of similar nature without the requirements of cyclic succession, contiguous influence, or racial memory; and with similarities evident in the physical, mental, emotional, spiritual, and behavioral natures of man, activated by the impulses that inhere similarly in the conditions of men's worlds and the common setting of Nature, a sameness in the tragic states of men of disparate cultures, times, or places could and do occur. Tragedy arises in similar fashion among different peoples, at different times, and yet it may be identified by like conditions, impulses, responses, and consequences, varied only by the particular identifiable differences in institutional conventions, artificial mores, geographic location, and any other of the merely topical or personal differences that separate individualistic qualities from universal qualities.

Just as pain can seldom be isolated specifically and limited to only one of the tragic states of suffering, so can tragedy not always be limited to a particular, single condition. The impetus for tragedy may, and often does, arise from an impulse within one particular condition; but often that impulse will also activate impulses within associated conditions by a causal-effectual relativity that may attract as much or more awareness than the originating impulse itself does. But usually the awareness generated by the initial impulse to tragedy, even though it provides complications in associated conditions, will of itself produce the dilemma or catastrophe or conflict from which the consequences of tragedy will derive. Each of the related conditions may contain the potential for tragedy, and indeed there may be awareness of the potential for tragedy or the implications of tragic consequence within each of the related conditions and tragic potentiality in either the separate or the conglomerate condition and a potential tragic impulse in the totality of conditions; yet the germinal tragic impulse that ultimately triggers tragedy will usually originate within one condition and then expand and grow until it touches other conditions and activates impulses within them. It may also engulf other conditions and create from them a single responsive awareness that is related to a number of conditions or a mutant condition that is in itself a travesty of Nature and a tragedy to Nature herself and to each of her separate parts. Or a number of isolated impulses may find a focus within a single condition and generate a tragedy derived from multiple awarenesses but evidenced in only a single catastrophic consequence. The impulse to tragedy may be either single or multiple, the conditions may be either single or multiple, the responsive awareness may be either single or multiple, and the consequences may be either single or multiple; but any combination of single or multiple conditions, impulses, awarenesses, responses, and consequences may culminate in tragedy. Singularity or multiplicity, of themselves, will not be the determinants of tragedy, for tragedy may derive from any combination of singularity and multiplicity, and whether or not the qualities germinating the tragedy are single or multiple, the consequences may be devastating to the figure or figures subjected to tragic suffering. A potentially tragic figure may be surrounded by multiple conditions containing latent impulses for tragedy for the entire presentient, sentient, and postsentient periods of his existence, and he may be aware of pain deriving from those conditions for the entire duration of his sentience, but his status as a tragic figure subject to all the impulses of his tragedy will not be confirmed for him or by him until a response, usually generated by a single momentous decision-demanding action, causes him to face up to his suffering-causing dilemma and bear the suffering of the consequences of his action. From the moment his aware responsiveness and his will to endure suffering come into consequent being, focused on the conditions causing his suffering, he is a tragic figure; and from that moment each contributing condition to his tragedy will begin to exercise growingly greater influence on his awareness of consequences, and the intensity of the tragic experience will both expand to influence and include other conditions of his world and establish the magnitude of his tragedy and contract to a sharper focus on the major pain-creating impulse about which his tragedy is centered. Tragedy will continue and endure until a new condition or set of conditions negates the cause of the tragedy or until the suffering subject of the tragedy either triumphs over the pain occasioned by the tragic conditions or until he is defeated by them and becomes unresponsive to them. Consequently, a tragic figure may never know anything but tragedy for the entire duration of his sentience, or his tragedy may be only an instantaneous flash of awareness and catastrophic response in a moment of sentience. The duration of tragedy may encompass any sequence of time between sentience and nonsentience; the intensity of the experiencing of tragedy may wane and increase; the conditions of tragedy may alter and diminish or alter and expand; man's awareness may become dull or it may become more sharply focused; but as sure as he is born, man becomes exposed to the tragic impulses inherent in the conditions of his world and vulnerable to the potential of tragedy. Happily that potential does not always explode into action, and man may escape the consequential effects latent in the conditions of his world.

IV

THE ARTISTIC IMPULSE

ANY SENTIENT HUMAN BEING MAY BE AWARE OF EXPERI-
ences, conditions, impulses, and consequences in the world
of man; he may be cognizant of the complexity of human relationships, and he may have the sensitivity, perceptivity, and
receptivity necessary to a grasp of the implications contained in
the awarenesses he possesses and the responses he makes as a
result of his exposure to the impulses inherent in the conditions
of his particular world and the varied worlds of other men
outside the immediacy of his own participation. Any sentient
human being may possess the physical, mental, emotional, spiritual, and behavioral qualities essential to active participation
in his own world; and he may have the empathetic ability to
merge into the worlds of others. He may have the insights and
understandings to interpret either his particular world or the
more abstruse world outside his immediate experience. He may
have powers to abstract from the conditions of his world and
the world of others the particularities of impulses and the re-
finements of awarenesses and responses that make those worlds
unique. He may have the imagination to project beyond physical
reality and not only discern potential conditions and impulses

and consequences, but he may also create in that imagination a world that does not exist in any actuality other than his imagination. Any sentient human being may and does select from the conditions of his general world and his recognition of conditions of other worlds those experiences of particular import to him; and, depending upon the degrees of his sensitivity and perceptivity, his capacities of receptivity and awareness, and his will and inclination to respond, he fashions a specific world that is uniquely his own. Any sentient human being (within the limits of his capacities, abilities, will, inclination, and compulsion) may express his feelings, understandings, and responses (established within the limits of his sensitivity, perceptivity, receptivity, and awareness) with varying degrees of effectiveness, perspicacity, accuracy, persuasiveness, fidelity, interest, or artistry.

Any sentient human being may be endowed with any one, or any combination, or all of the qualities, capacities, and abilities mentioned above; but each individual sentient human being will have a different endowment, a different perspective, a different quality of expressive ability, and especially a different degree of sensitivity, perceptivity, receptivity, awareness, will, inclination, and compulsion; and each individual sentient human being will have a different degree of responsiveness to the impulses that inhere in the conditions of his world. The average sentient human being will be endowed with varying degrees of average sensitivity, perceptivity, receptivity, and all the other qualities and characteristics that establish uniqueness and individuality of awareness and response. By the same token, the exceptional sentient human being will be endowed with exceptional degrees of these same qualities and characteristics.

But the exceptional sentient human being who is also an artist will also have other qualities and characteristics in varying degrees. He will not only be sensitive, perceptive, receptive, and aware, but he will also have the will, inclination, or compulsion to re-create feelings, impressions, understandings, insights, descriptions, and responses for an audience even if that audience consists only of the artist himself. He will have the ability not only to imitate or interpret the conditions of the world of physical actuality, but he will also have the ability to re-create, with varying degrees of success and effectiveness in selection and delineation, the conditions of that world. He will not only be capable of establishing a semblance of order, his order, among the conditions of the world he imitates or interprets or re-creates; but he will also be capable of discerning and expressing the significance of that order if his abilities and capacities allow for more than a photographic or phonographic re-creation. He will not only be concerned with the fidelity of his imitation or interpretation or re-creation and the integrity of his point of view in relation to his subject, but he will also be able to create stimulation to aesthetic response and apprehension.

The exceptional artist will not only have general artistic ability and capacity, inclination and will and compulsion, sensitivity and perceptivity and receptivity, and awareness and responsiveness; but he will have heightened degrees of these qualities. He will not only be able to re-create an experience effectively with fidelity and integrity; he will be able to re-create that experience with superb skill, uniqueness, imagination, artistic and aesthetic rightness and wholeness. The exceptional artist will not only be able to imitate, interpret, or re-create conditions of the world of physical actuality; he will also be able to create a world that has its exact counterpart only in his imagination but that will have nothing in its conditions and impulses alien to reality or potential reality or an idealized reality, or that will nullify a semblance of actuality or of potential actuality. This is not to say that the artist may not create an imaginative phantasm from the conditions of his world, but that in the perspective of the artist, or the audience, or the character or situation involved in the phantasm, there will be a semblance of credibility or actuality and the conditions and impulses will not exceed the imaginative functional limits of human physical, mental, emotional, spiritual, or behavioral response within the structural framework of the creation as established by the artist. And it may be, in many cases, that what seems to be a phantasm to a reader or viewer or listener is in reality merely a heightened expression or impression of a condition, impulse, or response from actuality intensified by the greater sensitivity, perceptivity, and receptivity of the artist and brought to the audience in a form that is seemingly distorted or exaggerated or esoteric or fantastic. And it may be that many exceptional artists may employ phantasmata or phantasmagoria as devices to emphasize, clarify, or illuminate real conditions and impulses not always readily discernible in actual reality. Trans-actual or supra-real presentation of real conditions with the actual impulses that inhere in them could, in this case, provide a means for founding transcendental or idealistic or impressionistic or expressionistic or surrealistic or mystic arts on the same conditions and impulses that realistic or naturalistic arts are founded on.

Sensitivity, perceptivity, and receptivity give to the artist the means of accumulating, receiving, accepting, and retaining within his physical, mental, emotional, spiritual, and behavioral self his apprehension and awareness of and responsiveness to conditions, impulses, consequences, circumstances, attitudes, feelings, characters, and situations. Sensitivity and perceptivity exercise a stimulatingly selective role in determining the nature, quality, and degree of experiencing that which is accumulated, received, accepted, and retained. Receptivity limits the amount and magnitude of the accumulation, reception, acceptance, and retention of that which is experienced by the artist. The totality of that which is experienced, accumulated, received, accepted, and retained by the artist from his presentient, sentient, and, speculatively, his postsentient states, constitutes the world of the artist. Within his being and controlled by his sensitivity, perceptivity, and receptivity, the conditions and experiences of the artist's world may undergo a transformation through assimilation and synthesis wrought by the impulses of imagination, creativity, thought, emotional stimulation, ethical sense, aesthetic sense, and the happenstance coming together of conditions. The result may be a new world composed of conditions that are themselves transformations of selected conditions and selected parts of conditions synthesized into new wholes and exhibiting variable degrees of identity with the actual experiences from which they are derived. Likewise this new world may be peopled by characters totally unlike any real life counterpart, yet totally credible in lifelikeness. For within the being of the artist, impressions of two or more real life characters may be mated to conceive and create a new character completely unlike either or any of his ancestors, yet truly a child of the creative process of imaginative assimilation and artistic synthesis incarnating a new spirit or reincarnating into new form a uniquely universal being. This process may or may not be a conscious process, and perhaps it may originate in any of the states of man's being: presentient, sentient, or postsentient; and it may derive from any of man's responsive natures: physical, mental, emotional, spiritual, or behavioral; yet the process and its creative result will be the product of the sensitive and perceptive qualities, and the receptive capacities of the artist, and dependent on his will, inclination, and compulsion for artistic expression.

The situations, conditions, characters, and impulses created by the artist become the substance, the materials, of his artistic efforts. The manner in which he structures these materials determines the wholeness of effect, the creative fidelity, the artistic integrity, the aesthetic and ethical rightness, and the evocative empathy of his work of art. His structuring of the materials establishes his affinity to his creation and puts him in rapport with the creative expression of his artistic imagination. When that creative expression finds affinity with an audience through the audience's submitting to the experiencing of the creative expression and coming to know or sense or feel the created conditions, characters, impulses, consequences, and implications as they are structured by the artist, rapport has been established with the audience, and the audience may then re-create for itself the experience embodied in the art form.

The impulse within the conditions of his world that prompts the artist to attempt to produce or reproduce in artistic form the experiencing of actual or vicarious or imaginary conditions which have shaped his being internally and externally and that causes him to attempt to create a new character or reincarnate the spirit of a character, his own or that of someone impressive to him or that which has been created by the assimilating and synthesizing imagination that is his, will, consciously or unconsciously or subconsciously, establish the purpose of the artistic expression. The creative impulse, dependent on the experience and nature and artistic will, inclination, or compulsion of the artist himself and determined by the conditions that make the artist what he is, may take many forms, directions, and attitudes. This creative-impulse-establishing purpose may be didactic, realistic, aesthetic, ethical, pessimistic, or idealistic; or it may derive from any other feeling or point of view or inclination or attitude capable of being experienced within the limits of the conditions of man's world; or it may be composed of any combination of impulses stirring the artist to attempt an expression. The impulse may be brought into action by, from, and through any of the states of man's being: physical, mental, emotional, spiritual, or behavioral; or it may seem to be derived from sheer inspiration without discernible relation to any of the states of man's being. But whatever the artistic purpose may be, it will be the impulse dynamically, generatingly functional in deciding artistic form (poem, play, novel, opera, symphony, ballet, painting, sculpture, or other); in defining the order of arrangement, direction of development, and significance of the conditions, impulses, circumstances, and consequences that are the materials used by the artist; in creatively structuring a coherent whole from the separate but relative impulses to meaning and experience inherent in the materials to provide a focus of attention, both for the artist and for the audience, to effect the artistic harmony, unity, integrity, fidelity, and stature of the work, and, in doing so, determine the experience and meaning of the work in such a way that the audience may respond as the artist may intend and as the work may require and permit or disallow. The audience by its sensitive, perceptive, and receptive submission to the creative expression of the artist may then experience the artist's creation of a world; and from that experience may come an impulse that may be a revelation of conditions to an audience that may provide further impulses evoking re-creative responses within the audience that will be the audience's apprehension of the reincarnated spirits of the characters that people a new world and the re-created conditions and impulses that constitute that world. This apprehension may be the impulse to the audience, depending on its degree of sensitivity and perceptivity and capacity for receptivity and will, inclination, or compulsion to respond re-creatively, impelling it to have the experience which is the meaning of the work of art.

Because the materials or substance of a work of art is composed of the conditions, impulses, circumstances, and consequences of the actual and imaginary, the conscious and the subconscious, world of the artist; because these materials are selected, ordered, and structured within the limits of a particular art form by the artist to establish a particular expression which is his creation of the experience of art; because re-creation of the experience of the work of art by an audience is necessary to establish rapport between the artist and his art, and the audience, and to create a responsive affinity between the work of art and the audience, it is necessary for the artist, as primary creator, to inaugurate the means by which the audience, as secondary creator, may experience the meaning that is the work of art.

The means employed by each individual artist to create the art expression which is the artist's presentation of conditions of his created world to the potential experiencing by an audience and the manner in which the individual artist presents the materials that make up that world of his creation will vary according to the individuality of each individual artist, the uniqueness of his purpose and point of view, the nature of his particular creative impulse, the qualities and circumstances of the conditions selected for his created world, the degrees of his sensitivity and perceptivity in relation to the materials he is using and in relation to his sensing of the potential in an audience to be receptive of and responsive to the experiencing of his presentation, the capacity of his receptivity and the unique ability he has for transferring his understanding or sensing of the nature of the experience to his created world in its presentational form, the nature of the materials themselves demanding a particular presentational form and order of development and structuring to create the cohesiveness necessary to unify the separate parts of conditions and impulses and circumstances and consequences into an artistic whole, and the individuality of his mastery of the tools of his particular art form and his skill in employing those tools.

The manner in which an artist presents the materials of his creation to potential experiencing by an audience will be, largely, a matter of perspectives and focuses. As the artist focuses on selected conditions to satisfy an activated creative impulse, he will discern, objectively or subjectively or intuitively, particularities of functional relationships among the conditions that will establish a contingent evolution of impulses, circumstances, and consequences. Though this evolution may be variable, and though it may have many possibilities as to direction of development or form of development, the purpose of the artist will establish controlling impulses limiting the physical structuring of materials to the perspective of the artist himself. This does not, however, imply that within the physical structuring of the work of art there may not be implications of possibilities of meaning and experience outside the awareness of the artist or beyond the perspective he has of his work as an organic whole; for the contingency of conditions and congruency of impulses within the conditions may compel a focus of attention and create an emphasis not consciously intended by the artist and activate a responsive impulse within the audience that was quite unforeseen by the artist. But if the artist, by the nature of his skill in structuring the materials, succeeds in establishing his focus on the conditions in such a way that the objective on which he focuses becomes the objective on which the audience focuses, and if he structures his materials in such a way that they demand the same perspective from the audience that he has, the effectiveness of presenting his purpose will be established and rapport will be created between the audience and the artist with the work of art providing the focus to compel the affinity of artist and audience as creators and re-creators.

In addition to the focus of the artist and the focus of the audience, externally situated focuses dependent on the view of the artist or of the audience and qualified by the range and clarity of vision of either or both and the degree of sensitivity and perceptivity of either or both and the capacity for receptivity of either or both and the responsive nature of either or both and the awareness of either or both, there will be other focuses. Perhaps the primary focal impulse will be that of a character or characters within the work concentrating attention on a particular condition and becoming aware of a particular activating impulse. Such a focus, demanded by the nature of the conditions within the work and providing the activation of impulses that demand character awareness and response, will per-

88

haps be the most important unifying device of the work of art and will perhaps provide the essential origin of all action developed within the work. The point of focus within the work of art will then become the pivotal center of attention toward and around which responses will concentrate and establish intensity, and from which impulses will emanate and provide relative motion and developmental expansion and establish magnitude. The dual functions of concentration and expansion by the focusing impulse within the works of art will require and permit specific particularities of structure because they inhere within the nature of the materials of the work itself. Because the contingencies of conditions will provide the relative expansion from the focal point and the congruencies of impulses will provide the relative concentration toward the focal point, an internally imposed perspective will develop as a structural quality of the work of art. This internally required and permitted and not disallowed structural perspective may or may not be coincidental with or identical to the externally imposed perspectives of either the artist or the audience. But when there is an absolute affinity between the perspective superimposed by the artist on the totality of materials composing the work of art and the perspective emanating from the contingent and congruent qualities of the materials themselves, an ultimate of rapport between the artist and his work will have been established; and, from the point of view of the artist, his ideal of artistic perfection will have been attained. This particular absolute affinity of perspectives will be achieved, however, only when the artist demonstrates to his own satisfaction a complete control of the materials of his creation, a complete mastery of his means of expression of the materials composing the total work, and a complete efficacy in structuring the materials to establish his focus and perspective as identical to the focus and perspective demanded by the materials themselves with a result that is completely satisfying in terms of the artist's purpose. This hypothetical attainment will, however, establish the perfection of the work of art only when the artist himself is the sole audience. But the moment the audience consists of more than the artist himself he ceases to be the sole possessor of the work of art and ceases to be the sole judge of its effectiveness and perfection. From the moment the work of art becomes the experience of an audience other than the artist himself, an evaluation of its merits becomes most complex and varied; for each member of its audience may become a critic appraising in terms of his own sensitivity, perceptivity, receptivity, awareness, responsiveness, focus, and perspective. Because the individual qualities of sensitivity, perceptivity, receptivity, awareness, responsiveness, focus, and perspective are uniquely varied, it would seem that an absolute identity of critical appraisals would be impossible, and that consequently these qualities would command only varying degrees of effectiveness in critical evaluation. But because the experiencing of the work of art becomes a condition for each member of the audience separately and impulses to responsive awareness are uniquely individual, critical appraisal is subject to both subjective and objective control of responsive impulses, and critical criteria deriving solely from audience responsiveness will either be as individually varied as there are individuals responding, or there will be a compromising of individual focuses and perspectives to establish a common standard for judgment with an arbitrarily defined formula becoming the means of facile and partial appraisal. Of necessity this limits degrees of qualifying judgment to the extent allowed by a compromise between total deficiency in responsive awareness of the experience of the work of art and total submission to the experience of the work of art by an audience with an ultimate capacity for responsive awareness. But if, from the critical point of view of the audience alone, this compromise is not effected, the standard of critical appraisal may be decided and formulated by an individual member of the audience, and his standard may result in arbitrary imposition of a personal view as the major criterion for judgment. If accepted, such a view could dictate critical criteria valid only for the audience that would subscribe to its tenets. It would be limited in applicability only to those qualities designated by and derived from the experience of the critic who establishes the criteria. The result could be a faddist or topically limited formula, deficient in universal applicability and tending to disregard, or define as bad, any quality of art not designated by the formula or not covered by the prejudgment of the critic. It is conceivable that such a formula could, by default or by absence of another view or by acceptance through popular approval of its proponent, become the standard of critical judgment limiting recognition of merit to time, place, culture, language, race, type, form, or any other quality that defaults universality.

If such establishment of critical standards should occur, standards derived solely from the point of view of the audience and without participation by the artist, there would develop the condition wherein the creative impulses that animate the world of the artist would be subjected to control by the responsive impulses of an audience-established criterion that, perhaps, might lack the imagination, the sensitivity, the perceptivity, the receptivity, the submissive responsiveness, and the creative awareness necessary to the re-creative apprehension of art as an experience-meaning. The result could be a dogmatic designation of purpose, focus, and perspective that would preclude the expression of a particular creative impulse and exclude individual mannerisms in the achievement of artistic purpose. It might also create the establishment of arbitrary regulations of art by critics not functioning in the interrelation of artist, work, and audience. Such a condition, though it might standardize certain technical functions of artistry, would probably destroy individual freedom of expression, liberty of choice in selection of conditions and purposes for artistic expression, and unique-

91

ness of artistic achievement. The uniquely creative artist may not function effectively under restraints not emanating from art itself because the creative process derives essentially from impulses within conditions rather than from arbitrary rules and artificial regulations. Though the rules and regulations themselves would be conditions affecting the artist and a potential source of materials for artistic expression, any regulation of their utilization by an agency outside the artist himself and the demands of his purpose, focus, and perspective would limit the impulse that for him would be the impelling force toward creative uniqueness; and any non-artistic agency that might regulate artistic expression or convert artistic expression to its own aims could, in effect, repress creative expression, subvert artistic purpose, distort artistic perspective, controvert artistic focus, and define artistic responsiveness in such a way that the creative artistic impulse would be so burdened with extraneous and non-artistic contributory qualities that creativity would degenerate to imitation and subservience, and artistry would decline to craft and propaganda. Creativity demands freedom, and artistry demands order; but that combination of freedom and order must derive from the nature of the conditions with which the artist works and the impulses that require and permit particularities of artistic expression, not from externally imposed, arbitrary, artificial, or institutional regulation that has as its main purpose the perpetuation of a particular point of view or a topically limiting applicability. And whenever the artist allows the audience to dictate a compromised regulation of his art, whenever he submits to a limitation or externally imposed control of his purpose, whenever he allows topical loyalties to take precedence over universal qualities, whenever he alters his focus to satisfy audience demand or to secure audience approval, whenever he distorts the perspective required by the materials of his art to achieve compliance with contemporaneous mores and conventions, he prostitutes art and he corrupts the nature of artistry. The first loyalty of the artist must be to his art, to creative fidelity, to artistic integrity; and he must not allow the purpose of artistry to be assailed by non-artistic considerations.

But neither should the individual artist or a unique school of artists or a particular art movement become the sole arbiter of artistic taste and quality or the sole judge of artistic purpose, focus, perspective, structure, form, or style; for even though the artist or the art community may be expected to be more knowledgeable concerning the function of art than is the non-art involved general mass of man comprising the audience, and though the individual artist and the art community may be expected to be more sensitive to, perceptive of, receptive of, and responsive to the qualities of art than is the general audience, still the artist or art community is limited to the impulses inherent in the conditions of the immediate world of the artist or of the art community; and the experiences of neither the artist nor the art community are totally universal because of the topical restrictions of time, place, and culture. The artist, as well as other men, is a product of his own time and vicarious experience; and consequently he is ignorant of conditions and impulses that have not touched, either consciously or unconsciously, the states of his being. Neither is the artist nor the art community omniscient; the fallibility of human understanding is as much a weakness of the artist as it is of other men, and infallible awareness and responsiveness is as unachievable by the artist as it is by other men. Indeed, loyalty to a particular art movement or to a particular creative impulse may make the artist less objective in his appraisal of artistry than would be someone not involved in or with art. The artist may be so dedicated to his own unique purpose, focus, and perspective that he cannot be receptive of or responsive to another purpose, focus, or perspective in a constructively critical or artistically valid manner.

Because the artist and the audience may view the function of art with a different perspective and a different focus, the artist externalizing his own purpose and offering it to audience experience from his own unique focus and perspective and with his own unique qualities of structuring and expression and the audience looking for substantiation and perpetuation of its own unique preconceptions of artistic purpose and internalizing as re-creative experience only those qualities of the art expression that coincide with its unique focus and perspective as audience conditioned to expect certain arbitrary standards of structure and expression—the critical functions of both artist and audience may be mutually antagonistic though the critical precepts of either may seem to be unassailable to their proponent. Because both the artist and the audience may arrogate certain proprietary rights in their roles as critics, and because divergences in point of view, purpose, focus, and perspective might create critical vocabularies incomprehensible to each other or establish critical criteria unacceptable to each other, it would seem that neither artist nor audience could be depended on alone to establish a critical purpose, focus, or perspective that would be valid for both or unassailable by either. And because the elimination of either the audience or the artist as qualifiers of critical criteria would by default establish the other as sole authority to define and interpret art, there might come into being a nonobjective, arbitrary, unqualified dictation of artistic intents and principles that would in effect destroy the creatively functional interrelation between artist and audience and establish in its stead a noncreative transmission of authoritarian edicts lacking the stimulating impulses to either artistic creation or re-creative artistic experience. Without a functional relationship between artist and audience and without a mutually respectful attitude each one for the other, art might well degenerate into a stagnant tradition, or perhaps even worse still into a relationship wherein one would function as master and the other as subject in the artist-audience relationship. Because of

94

the dangers to artistry inherent as one-sided impulses in the conditions of the worlds of both the artist and the audience, it would appear that the only neutral basis for the establishment of standards for critical appraisal would be the worlds of the works of art themselves and the impulses and conditions and qualities the works themselves evidence in the transmission of experience-meaning between creative artist and re-creative audience as they derive mutually from a seminal principle inherent only in the ethic-aesthetic of natural phenomena available alike to the experience-meaning of both artist and audience.

The work of art—the creative expression of the artist and the re-creative experience of the audience, the substance of the artist's purpose, focus, and perspective presenting new conditions to the world of the audience and activating impulses to sensitivity, perceptivity, awareness, and responsiveness within the audience—is itself the condition that thrusts artist and audience into a new world association wherein each is an essential and functional part and without which art could not exist as a transmission of experience-meaning. Both the artist and the audience must respond to the conditions and impulses of their own worlds and to the conditions and impulses of their common world, the work of art, to evolve an awareness of the art experience and from that awareness of the meaning of experience derive the means of developing critical criteria valid for each separately and in rapport. The work of art itself is the focal form of substance where the sensitivity of the artist and the sensitivity of the audience merge, where the perceptivity of the artist and the perceptivity of the audience allow a common experience, where the receptivity of the artist and the receptivity of the audience are exposed to the same meaning, where the awareness of each is revealed, where the responsiveness of one tests the capacities, abilities, and effectiveness of the other as creator or re-creator, where the will, inclination, and compulsion of both are engaged, and where the evolutionary processes of interrelating conditions and impulses and awareness and responses prompt the development of criteria for value judgment.

The work of art itself is its own evidence of the conditions and impulses structured into it; and that structuring permits, requires, or disallows the meanings and experiences that are its transmission of whatever values and merits it possesses integrally and inherently as essential impulses evocative of response and awareness. To judge it in terms of superimposed values, of values not natural qualities native to the impulses and conditions of the work itself, of values topically or institutionally derived, would be to judge it in terms not relative to it unless these values are inherent as impulses in the conditions selected by the artist as the materials of his creation stimulating responses and effecting consequences that are permitted and required and not disallowed by the structure of experience-meaning in the work. The presentation of the experience-meaning is the reason for being, the purpose of the work of art. The structuring of the experience-meaning of the work is the creative functional process. The compulsion of the experience-meaning to the stimulation of sensitivity, perceptivity, and receptivity by the audience is its effectiveness. The evocation of audience awareness and response to its experience-meaning is the establishing of its quality and the determining of its intensity and magnitude. The durability of meaning and experience is its universality and its stature in its own world, the world of art. The qualities inherent in a work of art that cause it to perpetuate itself without limitation by, and often in spite of, consideration of time, place, culture, or institutions are the qualities that qualify as criteria for judgment of artistic merit. Art is not only its own justification, but it is also the test of the artist, the audience, and the critic. The work of art is the sole evidence by which the artist may be judged as artistic presenter of experience-meaning, by which the audience may be judged as recipient of the experience-meaning of the work of art, and by which the critic may be judged as an appraiser of the artistic merit of the experience-meaning of the work because whatever does not emanate from or inhere in the work of art itself is extraneous to the qualities of its presentation, to the degrees of intensity and magnitude of its reception, and to the validity of its appraisal.

The work of art is the evidence of the artist's integrity as artist; his probity in the selection and utilization of the materials of his work; his sensitivity to and perceptivity and receptivity of the implications of experience-meanings emanating from the structural fusion of the conditions and impulses that comprise the materials of his work; his skill in structuring those materials to establish and substantiate his purpose as artist in the presentation of the experience-meaning that is the work of art itself; his mastery of the particular tools employed in his particular art medium; his awareness of the consequences of his work as it provides a source for re-creation of experience-meaning by an audience; his responsiveness not only to the impulses that compel him as artist, but also to the impulses inherent in the conditions of his work that demand and permit particularities of expression and to the comprehensive qualities of sensitivity, perceptivity, receptivity, awareness, and responsiveness of his audience; his fidelity to the precepts he has of the purpose, meaning, focus, perspective, quality, and expression of art; his will, inclination, or compulsion to be an artist and subject himself with his work to the scrutiny and feelings of an audience; and finally his ability to transmit, through the medium of his work, the experience-meaning that satisfies his purpose as artist. As the artist functions to create the evidence of his artistry, he also performs to establish that which judges him, establishes his stature as artist, demonstrates his artistic acumen, versatility, and insight, reveals his sensitivity, perceptivity, and receptivity, illuminates his focus and perspective, and tests his awareness and response. Once the artist has transmitted his world of meaning and experience to an audience through the medium of his work, he ceases to be the sole master of those of his qualities that the materials themselves allow—he has never been master of those qualities the materials require—and he becomes subject to evidential judgment by the work itself and to appraisal by the audience and interpretation by the critic. Neither he nor his work remains identically what he or it was for him before its presentation to the vagaries of a world not of his creation. Both he and it have added a new dimension, exposure, and for the artist the world has undergone alteration by the addition of new conditions and new impulses.

But there does remain one constant, one unalterable identity, one self-perpetuator of unchangeable conditions and impulses, focuses and perspectives, qualities and conclusions, meaning and experience, and that is the work of art itself. And though it may be viewed with as many different eyes as there are members of its audience, and though its meanings and experiences may vary with each member of the audience, and though it may be arbitrarily judged and its qualities appraised in as many degrees as there are members of its audience, it is its own evidence of experience-meaning. It remains the same though the individual worlds of which it becomes a condition interfuse it with other conditions to establish a semblance of meaning and experience that is not its actual or total experience-meaning. Ideally the greatest work of art would have the same experience-meaning to all members of its audience; practically, with the variables in audience sensitivity, perceptivity, receptivity, responsiveness, and awareness, there is little likelihood of such achievement. As the work of art perpetuates itself, its meaning and experience, it carries with it the conditions, impulses, circumstances, focuses, and perspectives that make it of consequence not only as an interpretation of the world of the artist set in his own time, place, and culture, but also as a record of those qualities that make perpetuation possible or necessary; and it is those qualities, qualities intrinsically native to the work itself, that provide the sources essential to the derivation of variable and evolutionary bases of standards for judgment of artistic merit. These standards must be variable because the works from which they derive are not of identical natures, conditions, impulses, focuses, or perspectives; and they must be evolutionary because the commingling of qualities from many sources and bases creates new and changing conditions and impulses within the world of appraisal just as changes occur in any other world of man. Though the sources remain constant individually and separately, the juxtaposition of their influences permits, and indeed requires, an evolutionary process in art that precludes an absolute standardization that could result only in stagnation and degeneration. Therefore, the standards derived should be descriptive and not prescriptive; for prescriptive establishment of standards would result in formula, regulation, imitation, and loss of uniqueness and individuality, both in artistic production and artistic appraisal.

The work of art as the test of the artist's skill, capacity, and ability and as evidential judge of the artist's accomplishment stands between the artist and the audience; and as it tests and judges the artist, so it also tests and judges the audience. All that the work is—its form, structure, meaning, and experience —becomes from the moment it is placed before an audience, a test of the audience's sensitivity, perceptivity, receptivity, responsiveness, and awareness; and it, through its cumulative effect upon the conditions and impulses in the worlds of an audience as evidenced by the consequences of audience apprehension of the experience-meaning of the work, judges the abilities, capacities, wills, inclinations, and compulsions of the audience to respond receptively, submissively, re-creatively, and critically to the meaning that is embodied in the experience of the work of art, limited by the judgments, conceptions, and any individual influences of the physical, mental, emotional, spiritual, or behavioral states of the members of the audience.

Because the audience, individually or collectively, must respond and develop its awareness out of the conditions and impulses of its own world, it may not always be equipped by experience, knowledge, will, inclination, compulsion, taste, or attitude to re-create totally the experience-meaning of a work of art that has perpetuated itself from another time, place, or culture. And indeed, an audience may also be out of tune with the artistic trends, forms, subjects, focuses, perspectives, and purposes even of its own time. If an audience is not equipped to respond re-creatively, then the validity of its judgment is questionable at best. But if the work of art itself is of such a topical nature as to preclude anything other than topical consideration of its experience-meaning, then the work of art lacks the means of self-perpetuation as monumental art and may survive only as a curiosity preserved, not by its own qualities, but by the particular interests of a few specialists in oddities or items of historical interest. This does not imply that there is not a great deal of significance to be attached to the works that are preserved by means other than their own self-perpetuating qualities, or that historicity is not important, for it may often be essential to see the universal quality set in its topical conditions in order to grasp the significance or feel the impact of particular focuses or perspectives. It does, however, exclude that which has only an historical interest or evidence of topically limited meaning from the world of great art and from the role of the work of art as test and judge of artistic receptivity. Art must function for and in its own time and place and to satisfy the demands of its own time and place, and part of its function is the preservation of the experience-meaning of its own time and place; but if this be its only purpose and function, art is no more than a topical craft and an historical record. The survivability records of many works, however, with their appeal to the sensitivity, perceptivity, and receptivity of audiences of many times, places, and cultures, and with the evidence of their power to stir the re-creative imagination of man without regard to time or place or culture, and with the self-perpetuating qualities that demonstrate their evocation of responsive awareness of their experience-meaning from audiences of varying times, places, and cultures, would seem to indicate that art has other purposes and functions, and to consider it only in terms of history or curiosity would be to deny the essential nature of real art which preserves and presents universal conditions and impulses of life itself, relevant to all times and places and cultures.

Because the great work of art has the survivability quality, the self-perpetuating quality, the universal quality as an essential of its structural entirety, because that universal quality is apt to be the point of focus of any work that has the survivability quality, and because a human perspective relevant to the point of focus must evolve from the conditions and impulses structured into the work of art to create experience-meaning of a universal nature, the accumulation of great works of art will provide evidential records of universal experience-meaning. Certainly in these records of universals there will also be vast quantities of topical expressions, conditions, impulses, consequences, and interests. It is a function of the scholar to sort the materials in the records and separate the universals from the topicals, to glean from the mass of materials that which has relevance for all time and separate it from that which has only a temporary or limited association with the meaning and experience of life. From scholarly scrutiny should come a panorama of qualities, conditions, impulses, focuses, and perspectives that may be judged as universals because of their recurrence in those works that have evidenced their self-perpetuating abilities to evoke responsive awareness of experience-meaning outside their own topical setting. These universal qualities, qualities evidenced as being held in common beyond time, place, and culture considerations, should then become principles for appraisal of art, the re-creation of the meaning and experience of life. But the principles should be regarded as indicators rather than as rules, for rules could codify, regulate, and prejudge, causing artistic stagnation and unnatural artistic evolution. As indicators these principles would merely provide bases for comparison, a nonregulating, evolving source of criteria for evaluative judgment and a background against which topical qualities would stand out and into which universal qualities would merge, providing by comparison and contrast a means of more than topically limited, faddist, institutionally oriented appraisal of values; and art itself would remain the ultimate source of its own merits and the test and judge not only of its own qualities but also of the artist, the audience, and the critic. The work of art itself would be the means to establish a disciplined orientation toward art through its own demands that consideration of its qualities and merits should focus on it rather than on an externally imposed critical formula. Art, then, has evidencing, testing, judging, and disciplining functions inherent in it because its purpose, focus, perspective, structuring, form, and response-evocative qualities are native to it and to it alone as a condition of its own world and as an activator of re-creative impulses of awareness and responsiveness among the conditions of the worlds of its audiences. If audiences allow themselves to be submissive to the disciplinary functions of the work of art, to be receptive to and aware of the experience-meaning of the work of art, to be responsive to that meaning and that experience, there should be no imposition of topical critical standards not relative to the particular unique work, nor should there be attribution of qualities to the work that do not derive naturally and meaningfully from the work itself.

The foregoing implies freedom from subservience to the past or to tradition, and it is sympathetic toward any soundly disciplined critical theory of any time that takes into account the total effect of a work of art. It requires, however, a recognition of art itself as the vehicle that carries the essential qualities of artistic merit and effectiveness, and it makes the work of art the focus of critical perspective rather than allowing particular critical theories or formulas to usurp the center of attention. Art, as a dynamic expression of experience-meaning, cannot be subservient to anything other than its own principles and purposes without becoming propagandistically oriented or topically utilitarian. When it allows itself to become subservient it becomes static and loses its power to stir imaginatively recreative impulses. But when it construes freedom from subservience as liberty to disregard or deny its sources and its evolutionary development, it promotes an artistic anarchy wherein arbitrary definition becomes the only standard for judgment of merit; for value is attributable only in relation to qualities with which it may be compared; and the only recognizable sources of these qualities, other than arbitrary definition, is in the self-perpetuated merits of the past as they adhere to the ethic-aesthetic principle of the experience-meaning of universal Nature. Subservience to the past would require that art accept the faults of the past as well as the merits of the past and imitate the total quality of the expression and influence of the past; but regard for the past is necessary not only to perpetuate the merits that the past evidences but also to avoid the faults that the past evidences; for progressive artistic evolution requires assimilation of the meritorious qualities and rejection of the faults and imperfections of previous artistic expression of experience-meaning. Denial of the past might well deprive the present of artistic meaning and experience that the present, because of its particular conditions and impulses, is incapable of creating; and rejection of the past might deprive the present of the lessoning in quality, meaning, and experience essential to the creation of an incomparable monument of artistic expression.

But the incomparable monuments of art, though they may be the creation of past genius or rooted in past experience or dependent upon meanings developed in the past, are without time in the sense of past, present, or future experience. They are the contemporary experience of whatever audience is, has been, or will be receptive of them, responsive to them, and aware of their experience-meaning. Their composition may not be contemporaneous in hour or day or year or century designations of time; but they are contemporaneous in event, in condition, in impulse, in meaning, in experience, in circumstance. And it is this contemporaneity that is the firmest evidence of universality and the most compelling reason for utilizing the self-perpetuating qualities of art as bases for principles of critical appraisal. Contemporaneity of event, the similarity of condition and impulses, circumstances and consequences, focuses and perspectives, and awarenesses and responsivenesses, that evolves from the qualities of each culture appearing at similar stages of development, may well be, in its universality, the fundamental impulse in art that gives to monumental art what seems to be a nostalgic tone of reminiscent spirit. And what often seems, in monumental art, to be a foreshadowing of the degeneration of a culture or the collapse of a civilization, may, in reality, be re-creation out of the impulses of artistic sensitivity and perceptivity of an awareness of and responsiveness to conditions of evolutionary consequence in the panorama of shifting focuses and perspectives that characterize individual civilizations. Nostalgia, then, need not be merely a sentimentalizing of the merits of the past; it may be an awareness, intuitive or intellectual or felt, of the consequences of particular conditions and impulses permeating a contemporaneous event and characterized by coincident meaning and experience derived from a retrospective regard for the past or a contemplative concern for an alien, but nonsimultaneous in time, cultural expression. For example, recognition of the primitive may be either retrospective or historical, or it may be immediate and presently experiential. The evidential existence at the same time of cultures of varying degrees of sophistication and development, the evidence of cultural evolution within these coexistent cultures, and the similarities of experience-meaning evidenced in the art expressions of these cultures at similar stages of their evolution would seem to validate a contemporaneity of event hypothesis not only as an historical perspective but also as a present focus. And in art, that which has only a topical reference would be peripheral to the real experience-meaning of the universal in artistic expression. Real art, monumental art, exists contemporaneously in whatever audience awareness of experience it evokes and in whatever audience responsiveness to meaning it impels; the impulses to awareness and responsiveness inherent in the condition of the great art are omnipresent and omnidirectional whenever and wherever an audience exists with sensitivity and perceptivity tuned to the experience of art, and they are omnitemporal and omnificent to whatever audience is receptively capable of responsive awareness to re-creative experience.

Ideally, the experience of a work of art should be the same for all members of its audience including the artist himself; but practically, considering the infinite variables in individual physical, mental, emotional, spiritual, and behavioral states, identical experiencing is virtually impossible. But the omnifariousness of audience sensitivity, perceptivity, receptivity, awareness, and responsiveness does not imply license to invent, by any member of the audience, meanings and experiences not inherent in the work of art or to attribute experience-meanings to the work of art if the work of art itself does not allow or require, by the nature of the conditions structured into it, that particularity of experience-meaning. Just as the impulses that impel awareness, action, and response inhere in the conditions of the world of man, so do they inhere in the work of art which is a re-creation of a world of man, a world created by man the artist responding to the impulses of his world and out of the conditions of that world fashioning a new condition for the world of man the audience. Just as the impulses remain latent in the conditions of the physical universe, so may they remain latent in the work of art that supplies a new condition to the world as an audience unless that audience, with its particularities of sensitivity, perceptivity, receptivity, awareness, responsiveness, will, inclination, and compulsion, submits itself to the experience-meaning structured into the work and undergoes a transformation in its physical, mental, emotional, spiritual, or behavioral states as a result of its exposure to the work of art. And just as the impulses to meaning and experience and the conditions that may activate them and bring them into the responsive awareness of an audience are structured into the work itself, so also are the focus-establishing intensity and the perspective-establishing magnitude structured in the impulses within the conditions composing the work, allowing only particular awarenesses and responses and requiring specific awarenesses and responses from the audience if the audience is to achieve a total, functional experience of the work of art as a condition of its world.

Art is the means of retention of meanings and experiences of the universe insofar as man the artist is capable of grasping, selectively and meaningfully, conditions from the chaos that may surround man and, by the genius of his structuring, capturing that experience-meaning in a form capable of perpetuating it and transmitting it to the physical, mental, emotional, spiritual, and behavioral apprehension of an audience. Creative genius is the power to impose structural order into the mass of materials that compose the work of art, to create a form that most efficaciously presents the experience-meaning of the work, and to master the tools of the particular art form in such a way that a unique transmission of the experience-meaning of the work is effected. The artistic process of structuring order into the conditions composing the work of art does not imply, however, the transmission of impressions suggesting an order that is nonexistent in the conditions that activate the impulse to impel an artistic re-creation of the world of the artist. Art may well re-create the disorder, the chaos, evidenced in conditions of the artist's world, both external and internal; and it may present by distortion a perspective that would render even a well-ordered set of conditions from the external or environmental world unrecognizable to one actually involved in the conditions prior to their re-created transformation. Art may also transmit a focus on conditions, either well-ordered in actuality or without order in actuality, that is not apparent in any experiential response outside the experience-meaning inherent in a work of art. The work of art itself, by the requirements of its unique conditions and by its permissiveness to the will, inclination, and compulsion of the artist, creates its own order and transmits that order to the re-creative potentialities of its audience. Consequently, order is both a matter of predetermination by the artist as he consciously structures experience-meaning into the form demanded by his creative imagination and intellect and a matter of interpretation by the audience as it apprehends the experience-meaning inherent in the structural affinities of the conditions and impulses that compose the work. Explicit functions of the interrelationships of conditions and impulses will be primarily a product of the conscious artistry of the creator of the work as he imposes his focus and perspective on the conditions and impulses comprising the work; and, if he be master of his art, he will so fully develop or formulate structural relationships within his creation as to invalidate audience contention of ambiguity or imprecision. Explicit functions should be entirely within the control of the artist, and their experience-meaning should be apprehended totally and obviously by the audience. But there remains another quality of functional artistic structural order, the implicit functions of the interrelationships of conditions and impulses that determine experience-meanings in and among themselves without the conscious control of the artist. Implicit functions will be primarily a product of the conditions and impulses themselves as they permit and require or disallow an apprehension of suggested, implied, or revealed consequences evolving from particular associations of conditions and impulses creating their own focuses and perspectives, and, consequently, their own experience-meanings which may or may not be consciously controlled or foreseen by the artist as he structures the materials of his creation. The explicit functions of art will challenge the perceptual acumen of the audience; the implicit functions of art will challenge its conceptual acumen; but not until both the explicit and the implicit functions of the work have been apprehended will the experience-meaning of the work of art be functional within the conditions that make up the world of the audience, and then only within the limits prescribed by the sensitivity, perceptivity, receptivity, discernment, discrimination, will, inclination, and compulsion of the individual members of the audience. Total functional apprehension of artistic meaning and experience will preclude the determination of artistic merit on the basis of specific individual analyses that deal primarily with parts of the work of art rather than with its total effect. For example, linguistic excellence will create a partial effect, but to consider only that one quality in determination of the artistic merit of the whole work of art would be to do a disservice to all the other qualities that make up the total presentation and to render invalid the appraisal in terms of the total effect of the work. But by the same token, no prescriptive device, such as predetermined focus, used by the artist to create the effectiveness of his work can be disregarded in establishing a total appraisal of merit. This is not to say that certain qualities of structure should not be isolated and their merits critically scrutinized, but rather that before final judgment is made, all qualities should be seen in relationship to all other qualities of the work and that the final determination of merit should be made on the total impression of the work, not on isolated parts of it.

V

THE CRITICAL IMPULSE

CRITICAL PRINCIPLE IS AS OLD AS MAN'S EXPERIENCE WITH the impulse to re-create, interpret, or communicate; for man, compelled by the peculiar and singular functions that designate him as something apart from other animated forms and impelled by a natural inclination to preserve and transmit the conditions of his experience, has sought to devise symbolic and representational devices—including language—to establish in substantial form the means to consolidate and reincarnate his sense of feeling for the effectual natures of the conditions of his experience. The moment man begins to establish a representation of experience by a grunt or a scratch in the sand the function of criticism becomes operative because the basic function of criticism is to examine the effectiveness of the representational experience; and man, the creature of compulsion to perpetuate his sense of experience, is also compelled to determine the effectiveness of his substantial form representation of that experience by observing its function in the responsive re-creation of the meaning of the experience by an audience. Ultimately, then, the artist and the critic should be primarily one and the same because both are concerned with the same consideration

110

—the effective functioning of the substantial form representation of experience-meaning; but there is, even though primal consideration of effectiveness is contemporaneous in both artist and critic, the difference in direction of that consideration. The artist looks at the form with foresight; the critic looks at it with hindsight. The artist tends to operate on speculative principles concerned with what *might* reincarnate his feeling and sense of experience, whereas the critic tends to operate on analytic principles concerned principally with the substantial form product of the artist's impulse to re-establish the experience-meaning of conditions. Ideally, the artist and the critic would remain one and the same; but, functionally, the contemporaneity of hindsight and foresight at the level of genius in one individual human being is unrealistic; Epimetheus and Prometheus are truer representations of human functions than is Janus, and Tiresias appears more often in re-created conditions than he does in original and natural conditions, conditions that have not undergone transformation in the artistic mediary between experience and substantial form representation of experience. It would therefore seem to be the role of the critic, as an entity separate from and with a different direction of view of the artistic process than that of the artist, to analyze the substantial form representation of experience-meaning to determine its effectiveness rather than to speculate on meanings and experiences extraneous to the immediate object of scrutiny. Flights of fancy, even though impulsed by particularities of a work of art, are invalid as critical criteria in the judging of that work of art; they may, in fact, be artistic representations in substantial form in their own right, but they hardly qualify as valid interpretations of the experience-meaning inherent in the work itself— the total of the accumulation and fusing of the conditions that make up the work and supply the three essential limitations on critical activity: that which the work itself permits, that which the work itself requires, and that which the work itself disallows.

A critical principle that operates on the assumption that any one or any two of the three limitations posed by the work are sufficient for critical interpretation is invalid. And a critical principle that is applied to the separate conditions composing the whole work, even though the three limitations are operable, without the qualification afforded by *all* the conditions and impulses inherent in the work, is invalid in terms of functional analysis and interpretation of the experience-meaning of the whole work. For example, a critical principle that allows an interpretation of Milton's Satan as an heroically righteous adversary of tyranny by selecting particular conditions from *Paradise Lost*, that by themselves and separate from other conditions in the work qualify that interpretation, does not give the experience-meaning permitted, required, or not disallowed by the totality of conditions that make up *Paradise Lost*. Valid criticism can come only from a critic who is capable of submitting totally to the totality of a work of art, who is compelled by the critical impulse to give everything the work permits and requires and to refrain from superimposing anything the total experience of the work disallows; who is endowed with a sense of critical integrity that voids any tendency to prejudice; and who is selfless enough to refrain from the impulse to find verification or justification for a pet theory, opportunity for self-aggrandizement, or occasion for a creative extension of the experience-meaning defined by the limits imposed by the substantial form of the conditions composing the work under critical appraisal. To use *Paradise Lost* again as an example, it would be invalid to interpret the work only in terms of a theoretical critical principle based on operative evidences of racial memory; too many qualities, too many conditions, of the work are demonstrably products of deductive intellectual exercise to give credence to an interpretation that depends on a few verifying conditions that tend to justify a particular critic's pet theory. The critic must serve art; art must not be made to serve criticism.

Once a critic makes the primary assumption that a particular work may or may not be judged as a work of art, he places himself under the obligation of determining the entirety of the experience-meaning inherent in the work itself, in that substantial form of the artist's attempt to express his impression of experience-meaning, insofar as his sensitivity, perceptivity, and receptivity will allow him to apprehend the experience-meaning contained therein. He obliges himself to submit to the experiencing of the work as *it* (not his preconception of what it should be or do) stirs the impulses of his responsive natures. And he should judge the effectiveness of the work, not by its adherence to his rules or theories, but by the intensity of the responses inhering in it; and he must respond to every impulse to respond that the work affords, every qualification, every condition. At the same time he must submit to all qualifications, all conditions, all impulses, without prejudice and without fear of finding a personal preference or theory unsubstantiated or inoperable. He must grant to the work everything that it requires; he must permit whatever the work permits; and he must disallow whatever the work disallows. These three things he must do, not only for and with the separate parts of the work, but also for and with the fused and merged parts of the work and conditions that constitute the qualified experience-meaning of the whole substantial form itself. The critic should be a reporter, an analyzer, a describer. He should not be a self-indulgent practitioner of esoteric cultism superimposing his theories on art; nor should he be a theorist foisting his ideas and prejudices upon art and audience; rather, he should be an honest scholar, judging with integrity and reporting the facts.

Every critic must recognize his own limitations—he must realize the practical improbability of such totally empathetic projection as would be required for infallibly accurate recreation of experience-meaning inherent in a work of art. The critic must admit that his degree of sensitivity, his perceptive

113

From Human Sentience to Drama

acuity, and his receptive capacity fall short of absolute perfection; and he must recognize that the conditions of his own nature —receptive, responsive, and critical—have impulses that are uniquely his own and quite apt to be at variance with the conditioned impulses to response inherent in a work of art, and that his judgment of the qualities of a work will of necessity be biased and prejudiced by impulses within the conditions of his own nature which determine the condition and manner of his will, inclination, or compulsion to re-create the whole experience-meaning of a work. Consequently, the critic should be not just an honest scholar; he should be an humble, cautious, and honest scholar. How many, O Lord, have been the critics since Aristotle, who possessed such qualities?

The inherent impulse principle in the analysis and interpretation of art is not a prescriptive formula designed to negate any other theory or formula. It is rather a descriptive synthesis of any and all approaches to the problems of critical analysis, allowing any critical theory its place and validity as it is justified by subjugation to the test posed by the whole context of the work of art under consideration and as that work of art requires, permits, or disallows in its totality or in its parts any or all of the particularities of critical orientation established by prescriptive points of view. The synthesis of critical criteria implicitly requires that the critical apparatus be tested by the work of art rather than that the work of art be judged in terms of the critical apparatus. It disallows the negative judgment of a piece of art merely because a part or the whole of the piece of art is inconsistent with, contrary to, or lacking in qualities complimentary to a particular critical theory unless it may be established by the work itself that it is deliberately structured on the pattern prescribed by a particular critical system. So too it disallows the positive judgment of a piece of art merely because it conforms in whole or in part to the requirements of a particular prescriptive formula. Consequently, the synthesis precludes arbitrary judgment of a work of art in terms of anything less or more than its total effect, and it would rule as invalid any interpretation based on excerpts, abridgements, selection of parts, or alteration of structural forms or ordering of materials within the work. It would invalidate prescriptive requirements that qualify evaluation of a work in terms of qualities external to the work itself or to the impulses created by the relation of conditions within the work which cause a knowing or experiencing of the work of art as a re-created or potential condition of life. As an example, the prescriptive requirement of a "flaw in character" as the cause of a tragic circumstance would be invalid unless the artist himself define "flaw in character" as the base of his creative interpretation of the cause of tragic condition within his work, or unless the work itself demand that a "flaw in character" be a noncontradictable, irrefutable, impulse toward tragedy generated by the conditions within the substantial structured form of the work and justified and verified by the total effect of the work (permitted, required, or disallowed by all the parts of the work in their synthesized wholeness) experienced in terms of the magnitude created by the structured relationships of all the parts. It would be fruitless to look for a "flaw in character" or to emphasize the concept of "flaw in character" unless the total effect in the experiencing of the meaning of the work demand "flaw in character" as the impulse-creating action within the work. Far too much critical work has corrupted the art it intended to serve because the prescriptive requirement of "flaw in character" had to be found and made to play a part in a context that neither allowed nor required such a concept as an integral experience-meaning function within the total structure of the work.

Art is an experience; it is a happening, a being in contact with conditions and an exposure to the impulses those conditions contain to stir imagination, create awareness, prompt analysis, and promote curiosity. The substantial form that art presents in its recognizable character is man's attempt to solidify, to capture in transmissible form his impressions of conditions whose impulses have stirred the responsive states and natures of his own existent qualities. It is the critic's obligation to appraise the effectiveness of the presentation, of the devices employed in the structuring of conditions to provide impulses to stir an audience to a re-experiencing of the nature of the experience the work itself presents. In this sense, art is the solid, substantial form of an impression or expression of experience. Nothing can be added to it or taken from it without transforming it into something it is not or was not, and the critic who is not aware of this fact, the critic who imposes on a work of art his own qualities and qualifications extraneous to the work itself, or who through ignorance, prejudice, or ineptitude does not give to the work all that it evidences, mutilates and castrates art, commits an atrocious act of disfiguration on the face of art, debilitates both art and Nature, and profanes very Nature; for art, that substantial and self-perpetuating expression and form, is man's impression of his experience in and with Nature made incarnate. And to art itself, this mutilation, this castration, this disfigurement, this profanation, is the destruction of the very spirit of art; for the spirit, the self-perpetuating impulse of art, cannot exist isolated from its own substance, or in a substance contaminated, distorted, or transformed by critical malfunction. All too often critical deficiency, or a critic's deficiency in analysis and appraisal, has left to posterity not the beauty of a genuine work of art but a deformed mutant, an ugly aberration, a travesty of Nature and her self-perpetuating likeness, Art. And man the artist, the being a part of Nature giving expression to that of which he is a part, creating a substantial form expressive of his impressions of the nature of his experience of the conditions and impulses of Nature, becomes the means through which Nature herself creates art out of her own being. And he, who through design or accident, adds to or detracts from the pristine quality of a work of art, commits an intolerable rape upon the body of the infant of Nature, the likeness of Nature, the nature of Nature.

Artist, critic, and audience, all are part of Nature for they form part of that which may evoke response; they are all part of the conditions that may be experienced; they all create awarenesses of their existence in Nature; and they all function as impulses giving meaning to impressions of their experiences. All, too, have obligations, obligations to that of which they are a part, to that which they are, conditions of Nature. For anyone or anything that has no control over that which causes its becoming or coming into being is a natural condition or quality of that from which it derives and that into which it arrives. Man is a natural condition of the creative functioning of Nature and a natural experiencer of the meaning he has as an impulse generating new qualities and conditions, new meanings and experiences, new impulses moving and motivating and evolving arrangements, fusions, and mergings of conditions to establish new meanings and new experiences. He is the supreme organ in the functional complex of evolutionary qualities and conditions and impulses that compose Nature, supreme because of all the organs that animate, that create and receive impressions, that order and disorder conditions, that differentiate between and among qualities, he is the most specialized in the totality of responsive natures—physical, mental, emotional, spiritual, and behavioral—of all the organs of Nature. His responsive states evidence greater variety, greater differentiation, and greater ranges of potential perfectibility than do the similar but limited responsive states of the other organs of Nature. That is not to say that he is superior in any one responsive state, but that the totality of his responsive potential in all the responsive states places him at the pinnacle in the hierarchy of conditions that define and delineate Nature. In such a position he has the supreme obligation—to master and control and order and seek perfection in and for all those conditions below himself in order and species. But he must strive with the wisdom of experience. He must master with justice. He must control with firmness and with self-discipline. He must order with knowledge of consequences. And he must seek with senses unimpaired.

Artist, critic, and audience, each has an obligation to bring to art—in his particular relationship to art—the totality of what his position demands. If he fails to function within the scheme of Nature as his position demands that he function, he becomes something less than man, something less than his primary condition and position as a part of Nature in Nature demands of man. In his failure he forfeits his position and becomes unqualified to create, to criticize, to participate in the experience of art. The integrity of the position man enjoys obliges him to observe the obligations of the position. His abdication of the position, with all its demands of justice, of fairness, of honesty, of wisdom, demeans man until he is no longer fit to concern himself with art; and if he continues to associate himself with art, he can only do violence to the meaning of art; he can only debase art to the level of his own degeneracy. And man who debases art provides the evidence himself in Nature's court where his sentence should be eternal silence. But unhappily the conditions of Nature are often too tolerant and Nature is condemned rather than the criminal against Nature; the criminal becomes a preacher, a politician, a professor, a purveyor of pseudo-artistic faddism, or a critic, and art and Nature suffer the consequences. The consequences are poor art, faulty criticism, prejudiced preaching, ineffectual teaching, and corrupt politics—the foregoing are merely selected from the great variety of man's endeavors wherein malpractice occurs, but similar conditions abound in any other of man's activities, and they reflect the disorder that man brings to Nature and to art, to himself and his posterity. They reflect also man's failure through history to play his role in the conditions of Nature with authority and integrity—with but few exceptions, the exceptions of genius.

But the genius among critics is as rare as the genius among members of any other genus of human activity, and the ismological species of the critical genus spawn most plenteously when parental genius mates with topical condition and produces a strain that inherits neither the insight of genius nor the range of experience. And, unhappily, the eloquence of an intellectual half-breed, the popularity of a faddistic mutant, or the excitement of an ismatic aberrant may all too often put the genuine critical genius in the lonely obscurity of an ivory tower or the limbo of intellectual suspicion, particularly among the legions of pretenders to scholarship and critical acumen that proliferate in the pseudo-intellectual ponds of Academe. Chance matings have produced such species as the psycho-artistic, the politico-literary, the religio-analytical, the socio-critical; and rarely have the parents of the species been the geniuses of their kind. Usually they have been the half-learned, the insecure, the pretenders, the undisciplined, the artistic failures, and the puerile purveyors of the inconsequential; but the impulse of publish or perish, the pursuit of the ephemeral, the pseudo-sophisticated faddism of esoteric popularization, the certitude of personal spiritual revelation, and the excitement of partially understood techniques of psychoanalysis have produced libraries of trivia that perpetuate and preserve more volumes of intellectual froth and critical nonsense about art than there are volumes of art to be criticized. Too often ignorance and inexperience with a loud voice become the authority, pretense and masquerade with the exciting demeanor become the rule, and popular fads become the vehicle of critical utterance. And the mild voice of intense scholarship and detailed descriptive analysis is drowned by the rush and roar of hyphenated, formula-fed, prescriptive, popular market-seeking purveyors of critical opinion. This is not to say that the genuine critic, the critic with integrity, will not or must not

119

make use of every available means to come to an understanding of the experience-meaning presented to him by the work of art. Nor does it mean that the critic should not use every legitimate device at his disposal to interpret and analyze a work of art. It does not mean that the critic should not speculate about meanings that are ambiguous or obscure. It does mean, however, that any speculation should be clearly labeled as such, that it is made obvious to any reader or hearer that the speculation is only that, and that it does not merit consideration as a definitive pronouncement. Too many speculations have become the bases of critical principles without valid evidence to support them, and too many works of art have undergone mutilating treatment when subjected to critical appraisal based on speculative principles with little or no validity. All too often a secondhand speculation takes on the character of valid truth and is presented in a prescriptive formula its innovator never intended; resultant interpretative analyses and appraisals may create exciting new qualities of counterfeit criticism, but they rarely add to functional understanding of, or participation in, genuinely creative experiencing of the nature and meaning of a work of art, though they may establish, and do establish, a certain sort of falsely intellectualized, dilettantish parlor game for the pseudosophisticated and a sort of celebrity for their pronouncers.

The critic should be a sort of superman who can take into himself an overwhelming amount of experience, knowledge, and information and keep it at call for whatever application it might legitimately have when it is necessitated by an impulse to respond generated by a condition structured into a work of art. The genuine critic should know and be able to apply any or all theories of critical interpretation whenever the conditions of a work demand; he cannot depend on any one theory or biased point of view to explain or appraise all the qualities or conditions inherent in any work of art. The human experience that generates the artistic impulse and that forms the bases for the impressions that take substantial structural form in artistic expression is too varied and complex to be explainable in any one manner or by any one approach; any critic whose stock in trade is a formulaic prescription based in one or a few critical principles or theories is a charlatan; he simply is not equipped to function as an interpreter of anything other than the artificial, imitative exercise that follows the same prescriptive formula. Unhappily for such limited, embryonic critics, great artists seldom have the particular kind of foresight, or the inclination required to fashion their arts into formulaic patterns that would fall within the limited range of prescriptive critical function. Indeed, the artist and the art and the critic with the qualities of predictability of critical functionality, of perfection in the re-creative expression of experience, and of infallibility in critical interpretation would form a Trinity whose qualities, separate and triune, would surpass those of any divinity yet dreamed of. Though many critics speak as though they were the mouthpiece of the Holy Spirit, seldom do new stars appear in the East as a result of their activities, and seldom do their pronouncements long retain the authority of Holy Writ.

Art, in its ultimate functional perfection, re-creates with its fused and merged conditions and impulses, as rich, varied, complex, and unique experiences as are found in Nature; and the critic not equipped to make a positive response to each and every one of the conditions, separate and together, that make up the structural unity, the wholeness of the artistic expression, the substance of the substantial form, and the experience of the meaning the work has as a re-creation out of Nature of the experience-meaning of man, can only fail to do justice to artist, art, and his own function as critic. The real critics, the geniuses of critics, those who really merit being listened to, are as rare in their field as are the Einsteins in his; indeed, the truly great critic may be as rare as Tyrannosaurus—and in the same condition. But it is not Tyrannosaurus who creates the current critical chaos; it is the psychological parasite, the spiritual saprophyte, the physical fungus, the intellectual tumor, and the emotional tapeworm, each with its limited range of function and adaptability, that have fragmented criticism and preyed upon art and Nature. Criticism has had bred upon her many new *isms*: Freudianism, Jungianism, existentialism, utilitarianism, and others, and each bastard offspring has produced a proliferation of even narrower, more limited and deformed, only partially functional, critical *isms*. And the closer the critic adheres to any one critical *ism* the more he neglects the totality of the artistic experience and the greater is his disservice to art—and greater is the danger to art that the *ism* will contaminate art, or strangle it, or drain the vitality from it, or destroy essential parts of it, or maim its potential of self-perpetuation. But happily, art is resilient; though an *ism* may drive it into quarantine for centuries, or debilitate it for an era, somehow it manages to survive the *ism* that would destroy it and reappears with new vigor and beauty following each ismatic invasion of its domain. Each critic must know all the *isms*; how can he appraise the subject of its condition if he doesn't know what the symptoms indicate? "The Roan Stallion" is more than an exercise in expression of a theory of racial memory; how can the critic who knows only the racial memory theory adequately analyze the other conditions inherent in the structural fusion of conditions and impulses that makes Robinson Jeffers' poem more than a reportorial account of Jungian speculation? Does the critic whose experience is limited to Skinner's albino rats know enough to grasp the entire functional coherence of the conditions in *The Divine Comedy*? Ridiculous, as ridiculous as a gnat trying to impregnate an orangutan—he may irritate her a bit, but he isn't equipped to get the job done.

Among the *ism* critics are found the proponents of most of the economic, political, scientific, psychological, philosophical, religious, and social institutions of man. What they say about their own institutional theories and practices and the art that is limited to a projection of the specific institutional view usually is valid in terms of the institutional concept; but usually there is also a promotional quality about such criticism, a bias favorable to the institutional image and unfavorable to anything that does not promote the institutional image. This bias tends to distort to an extent both the art based in the institutional perspective and that which has no affinitive base in the particularities of the institutional complex. Because of this rather natural tendency of man to promote whatever is familiar or native to him, to elevate those qualities that are a part of his own immediate knowledge and experience, to protect that which he represents in tradition, environment, and learning, and to perpetuate those beliefs and facts that seem to be truth to him, biases develop, both consciously and unconsciously, which are meritorious in terms of institutional loyalties, but which are certainly not conducive to legitimate, unbiased, objective, fairminded, critical interpretation of art. By the same token, this same natural tendency causes man to fear that which is unfamiliar or alien to him, to depress those qualities that are not a part of his own immediate knowledge and experience, to be antagonistic to that which is in substantial opposition to his tradition, environment, and learning, and to minimize the importance of beliefs and facts that are not immediately allied to his own version of truth or beauty. The conditions and impulses that constitute potential experience; the sensitive, perceptive, and receptive qualities that allow degrees of experiential apprehension; the natural and conditioned responsive states that differentiate the qualities of experience; and the will, inclination, or compulsion to retain impressions of specific experience, all combine to establish a complex variability of qualities and proclivities toward personally individualized and biased interpretive responses to art and experience.

It matters little whether art be under the subjugation of political, economic, religious, or patronage domination, or if it be under the subjugation of topical critical criteria or conventions. In either case, whether it be by direct doctrinal consideration or by indirect prescriptive formulation of rules and regulations tending to control the creative impulse and direct the will, inclination, or compulsion in the exercise of that impulse, art, artistry, and artist inevitably stagnate in the backwaters of political, economic, religious, and critical ideologies. Only when art, artistry, and artist are left free to test their own qualities under the timeless criteria of universality may there be a genuine evolution of qualities of artistic beauty and excellence that allow recognition of magnificence regardless of time or place and at the same time insure that a topical excellence become not a quality or standard for the arbitrary appraisal of extra-topical artistry. Critical doctrine that is non- or extra-artistic in its own formulation is no more valid in the appraisal of non-doctrinal art than is political or any other doctrinal ideology. Each will tend to appraise and interpret in terms of its own ideology rather than in terms of creative or re-creative artistry. Certainly reason would indicate that the criteria used for the judging of a jumper in the horse show should not be the same as those used to judge the hen in the egg-laying contest, though both be in the same county fair. By the same token, criteria applicable in one realm or era of artistry should not be sacrosanct in judging qualities in another realm or era even though both be re-created experiences in the county fair of human display.

Intensive experience with one or a few points of view or institutional truths combined with limited experience or minimal experience with all other points of view or versions of institutional truth can only create an imbalance in the responsive conditions of man's nature. When this imbalanced focus and perspective is allowed to function critically, the object of critical scrutiny is most apt to suffer, particularly if the object of critical scrutiny does not derive from the same focal and perspective conditions; and certainly the imbalanced focus and perspective can not allow for unbiased discrimination among the conditions and impulses either of life and Nature or of art. Bias, personal or institutional, religious or irreligious, practical or speculative, has no place in criticism; bias distorts, and it mutilates, and it camouflages; it warps the responsive impression, and it injudiciously selects parts of a whole and makes the parts represent the whole. Critically, bias and imbalance manifest themselves in one-sided argumentation, in overemphasis or underemphasis, in prejudice, in intoleration, in condescension, in inaccuracy, in misrepresentation, in error, in effeteness, and in outright untruth. Critical biases and imbalances, when applied to a work of art, may so misinform that they destroy the total experience of the work. For example, Faulkner's "The Bear" may become an example of Negro racism, of white racism, or of anti-Indian racism. It may be an example of racial memory, of social decadence, or of local color. It may be an example of irreligion, of primitivism, or of Christian fundamentalism. It may uphold the dignity of man, or it may express contempt for particular man. It will represent to the biased, imbalanced critic whatever the responsive impulses in the conditions of his nature permit, require, and disallow; for where bias and imbalance spring out, submission subsides; and when the conditions of the critic's nature permit, require, and disallow in contravention of that which the conditions of the work permit, require, and disallow, critical analysis and interpretation become invalid. When bias disallows submission to the conditions structured into the substantial form of art, valid criticism ceases to exist; when bias requires that its own nature be justified, valid criticism ceases to exist; when bias minimizes what the work requires, valid criticism ceases to exist; when bias permits more or less than the work permits, valid criticism ceases to exist; and when the nature of the critic takes precedence over the nature of the work being criticized, art becomes subservient to criticism. Art no longer has importance as the substantial form of man's impression of the experience that is his in the nature of the conditions and impulses that evoke his responsive awareness. Criticism becomes the object of man's study and the reflection of his sense of experience-meaning, and art becomes merely a springboard to catapult the imagination away from itself into a new element, the ethereal element of vaguely associational derivations, airy speculations, and diluted analytical substance. Such criticism may occasionally touch lightly on a work of art, lift a self-justifying fragment out of context to nourish its parasitic nature, and flit on to another work to perform its excremental functions as it sustains itself on those parts best suited to satisfy its specialized appetite.

Genuine criticism is not a thing of separate isolated parts, just as art is not a thing of separate, isolated parts. The parts form the whole, and each part functions in cohesive unity with all other parts to provide the structural magnitude of the entire experience-meaning fused into the combination of parts comprising the whole and qualifying each other to establish the impulse, in substantial form, for a uniquely re-creative experience. Criticism, to be functionally whole and valid, cannot depend on any one point of view, definition, approach, perspective, focus, theory, or institutional "truth." To be functionally valid and effective, it must command all knowledge relative to the requirements posed by the work under critical scrutiny. Psychoanalysis of Antigone is not critical appraisal of *Antigone*, though many self-styled critics would present it as such. But psychoanalysis of Antigone might aid the critic in coming to an understanding of the experience-meaning of *Antigone* if the psychoanalytical tool were used in combination with the other tools which would have as much applicability to *Antigone* as psychoanalysis. An understanding of the social environment of the setting, a knowledge of the familial customs and conventions of the time, an insight into the political atmosphere of the age, a feeling for the religious inclinations of the era, a firm grasp of the artistic requirements and tenets of the time and the proprieties of expression demanded of the artist by his contemporaries might well be as important, along with many other qualifications, to an understanding of *Antigone* as a psychologist's study of Antigone. Antigone on the psychiatrist's couch is not *Antigone*, nor is psychoanalysis artistic criticism. It is one tool, among many, that the critic may use; to use it exclusively may, perhaps, be good exercise in psychoanalysis; but it hardly qualifies as criticism in and by itself. No one specialized study or skill qualifies by itself as valid criticism. Psychoanalysis is not criticism; Protestantism is not criticism; Catholicism is not criticism; existential philosophy is not criticism; biographical study is not criticism; literary or social or political history is not criticism; nor is any other one specialized orientation criticism even though it be given such labels as speculative or aesthetic or practical criticism; and the substance may designate a particular emphasis in criticism; but until approach and substance combine to provide a completely balanced, cohesive, analytical, descriptive evaluation of the total experience-meaning inhering in the substantial form of art, criticism is nothing more than an academic parlor game using Nature and art as experimental toys to gratify the whims of the players and allowing such inanities as "Man, that cat really digs fornication" to become the last and authoritative word in critical appraisal of *Don Juan*.

The specialist in a field outside art who presumes to become a spokesman for art criticism is a distinct threat to genuine criticism; but he is no more so than is the specialist in art who dabbles in specialization outside art and arrogantly superimposes his inadequacies of peripheral skill and knowledge on art. Both are bound to sin against the whole of what art is. But equally as dangerous to art as these is the art specialist who is so overly specialized that he can see only particular qualities of art as determinants of the total artistic function: the prosodist

127

who creates an imbalance in critical structure by undue emphasis on prosody; the stylistics expert who can experience little more than complexities and variations in style; the tonalist whose appraisals de-emphasize by neglect everything but tone; the semasiologist who cannot range outside his passion for words or symbols; these and all other specialists who subordinate other qualities of art to their own specializations misinterpret art and deform criticism. Then there is the nonspecialist in critical function, and in understanding of the function of art itself, for that matter, who through ignorance develops and promulgates idiosyncratic artistic and critical attitudes: the thematicist-messagist, who looks only for themes, messages, plots, or story; the moralist, whose whole intent in relation to art is "to find the moral"; the ambiguist, who looks for or creates ambiguities for their, or his, sake; or the enigmaticist, whose sole artistic passion, critically and analytically, is to "find the hidden meanings." Also among those whose overemphasis of a particular specialization may perform critical mayhem on art, though their particular skills and knowledge may aid criticism and understanding, could be listed those scholars who trace down allusions and provide historical facts to establish allusive meaning; those who have the peculiar gift of sensing the echo and detecting its source; those who can spot *contaminatio* and establish its derivation; those whose particular skill enables them to detect shifts in symbolic function of words and to clarify meanings in relation to the time and place of usage; these and all other legitimate skills aid in the development of the knowledge and understanding the good criticism requires. But when one of these skills is employed solely for its own sake, it is not legitimate criticism of the art that evidences the applicability of the skill if either overemphasis of that skill or underemphasis of any other requisite skill creates an imbalance in the over-all, total appraisal of a work of art. Every skill that man develops is meritorious when it is employed legitimately; but any one

128

skill which purports to function as the sole legitimate object in criticism arrogates unto itself an infallibility that nothing in Nature possesses except Nature.

Arrogance or presumption of infallibility is all too often a quality, a condition, inherent in the nature of man; it comes into operation because of man's recognition of himself as a superior being in the order of Nature's hierarchy and is expressed out of an ego-centered impulse to gratify man's sense of esteem and accomplishment. Usually it derives from an overestimation of personal merits and abilities and an underestimation of extra-personal qualities and conditions, but it is the quality or condition that makes it possible for any man, with the limits of experience and knowledge that are his, to presume to judge that with which he has little familiarity; to define as superior that which most nearly coincides with the range of his own limited experience and knowledge; and to minimize the importance, deny the merits, or resist the experience-meaning of that which is unfamiliar or alien to his self-styled superiority. It is this quality which makes possible critical judgment, as well as art, based on bits and pieces of knowledge and experience. It is this presumptive quality that causes ignorance and inexperience to assume the role of interpreter, analyst, and judge, to bring down to its own level of quality and to its own limit of comprehension that which is superior to it. Good critics recognize the inherent, prejudicial to art impulses in either natural or assumed arrogance and carefully refrain from arbitrary judgment, categorization, or appraisal. Good critics recognize the limits of their own receptive and responsive natures, their capacities and their abilities, and qualify their criticisms to avoid the chances of error or the pronouncement of untruth. Great critics have such a range of knowledge and experience that they need guard against only the possibilities of misinterpretation or misunderstanding of minute bits of conditions comprising the work they are criticizing. The monumental critic, the rare genius among critics, gives to art everything that it deserves and takes from art nothing that it possesses, and in the process he enlightens lesser men and lessons them in the experience-meaning of art. But there is a fourth category of critic, the bad critic, and he is probably in the majority. It is he who, through ignorance or design, misinterprets art, misinforms his audience, and misdirects his own limited abilities, knowledge, and experience toward objects to which they do not apply or have limited application. Usually the bad critic is unaware of his dearth of critical tools and of the violence he is doing to art; he is an ignorant fool and guilty only of involuntary mayhem on art. But sometimes the bad critic is aware of his lack of proper personal equipment and proceeds anyway; he is a criminal against art and deserves no better than to be required to do nothing but read his own drivel to himself, to hear nothing but his own blather, and to see nothing but his own corruption for eternity.

Among the presumptive, the arrogant, the bad critics are many who succeed in disguising their ineptitude or their inadequacies of knowledge and experience with persuasive rhetoric and distracting showmanship. They may go undetected for ages, corrupting art and contaminating audiences with their profane nonsense. They, and their brothers, the pseudo-humility school, are most often members of the great *ism* fraternity, that single specialization faculty professing formulaic approaches and writing prescriptive dicta based on uni-specialization. Foremost in the pseudo-humility school are the fetishists, they who hold in adoration single-minded theories of criticism and accept as an act of faith the absolute truth, for them, of the theory. They are usually fanatic in their belief in the divine nature of inspiration, and of their insights into critical function; they tend to present their criticism as though it were divine revelation unto them and them alone. What they can't explain they can dismiss as being unrevealed, and what they don't know they can say is unknowable except to God alone. Their wildest speculations take on

130

religious garb and are uttered in the most acceptable pulpit manner. The fundamental religiosity of their manners and sentiments precludes debate, the fervor of their faith attracts and excites, and the sincerity of their utterances convinces. Who dares quarrel with what may be attributed only to God without offending God? We will be damned. And so will most of the great art of the ages.

Divine revelation may come to the prophets, and the prophets may speak with theological authority on matters divine, but once past the prophets even divine revelation becomes hearsay and the pulpiteers become pronouncers of secondhand gospel —though in the divine tradition, the tradition attributing directly to God the truth. But art is of earthly origin, and man is the creator. Whatever his origin, man creates only in the sense of transforming into substantial form his impressions, conscious and unconscious, of the reality of the substance of the conditions of his experience. Whether he be a divine creation or a happenstance transubstantiation of inertia into vitality is immaterial; each man is a neoteric entity, not a facsimile in any reproductive detail of any identity that preceded him, particularly not in the creative impulses given form and substance in his works of art. The attribution of divine conditions, of godly impulses, to either artist or critic renders them incomprehensible save in terms of divine revelation and denies the nature of humanity in man himself. This denial would, of course, facilitate the critical functioning of man incapable of apprehending experience-meaning beyond his personally unique capacities by transferring to a superhuman intuition the essence of that which man finds incomprehensible. Man thereby frees himself of the obligation to go beyond the immediately topical conditions to apprehend the meaning of experience by attributing to divine nature all that he does not, cannot, or will not comprehend. The Prophet-critic passes the buck to God, or gods, whenever his ignorance denies him authority to speak, whenever his comprehensive faculties fail him, and whenever his apprehension of man's artistry is too little to afford adequacy of experience-meaning. God becomes the scapegoat for man's inadequacy and the source of his superiority. That is an easy way out for man presuming to explain what his abilities do not equip him to explain, and it is characteristic of certain schools of criticism. But art is a man function; its impulses are in man nature; its conditions are in man experience; and its meaning is man meaning. Theology relates God to His universe; Art relates man to his universe; criticism relates the expression of man to his impression of the experience-meaning of his universe. Theology is not criticism, and when the critic falls back on theological premises to escape his obligatory functions as a critic, he testifies to his own failure as a critic. Escape into any associational realm is crucial malfunction attesting to the critic's receptive and responsive inadequacies in relation to the man-derived impulses and conditions that provide the essential nature, the essence, of art.

Genuine criticism is not divine revelation, and critics are not prophets serving as intermediaries between God and man. Even the prophetic image that certain critics assume arises from an impulse in man nature, an ego-superioritive symptom of man's sensing of his personal inadequacy. And even the most ecstatic of man's mystical experiences are still experiences of man's responsive nature; the impressions of those experiences are man's impressions; and the substantial form re-creation of the impressions is a man-made substitution for the fundamental impulses in the originating conditions. Man-oriented in impulse, in condition, in impression, in expression, in response, in interpretation, in meaning, and in experience, art should be criticized in terms of man's nature in Nature. To use the suppositions of religious faith, even the primary certitude of dogmatic theology, as bases of critical interpretation and analysis, requires the substitution of the suppositional for the evidential. It is not good critical sense to disregard the evidence of the substantial form in favor of the speculative theory that is not substantiated in the substantial form. The essence of art is inherent in the work of art itself; it is not an emanation from an ethereal, mystical force outside itself and associated with it only by a link of verbal religiosity. The essence of art is art itself, and its impulse is based in the responsive nature of man, created by the conditions that comprise the nature of man's experience in the Nature of which he is a functional part, the interpretative, responsive, re-creative part, responding in accordance with the variably complex laws of that Nature. Theologically that Nature may be God created; scientifically it may be an evolutionary process; imaginatively it may be the nightmare of a mutant bedbug; but artistically it is the substantial form of man's impressions of experience-meaning.

So often mere man is mystified by the seeming remoteness of the impulse that impels another man's artistic response, so awed by the process of establishing the substantial form that another man's impressions demand, that he creates a myth-superstition, an aura of mystery, about art. Both artist and critic have, to an extent, fostered the great art-myth—not the greats of either art or criticism, but the second-raters, the non-geniuses; and the mythopoeic mania of those who try to glorify their own mediocrity by deliberately vaunting obscurantism and ineptness as mysteries of art lessoned a vast audience of misinformed people in one of the greatest anomalies of all time: that which should be closest to man, the nature of his involvement with the conditions of his world, has become the most remote of his logically responsive natures, and he has become awestruck by the artist who dares to examine the mystery and overawed by the critic who, he has been taught, can divine the meaning to be found in the occult world of art. Too many critics are infected with mythomania; they create a critical ritual which excludes all but a few subservient initiates. Art becomes an altar about which the artist-priest and the critic-witch doctor lead the dance of blindly following non-initiates. The pages of Nature's open book blow too wildly for careful scrutiny: her lines are blurred by the motions of the priest; and her meaning is lost in the incantations of the witch doctor. Her experience becomes a *mélange* of fantasy and reality, with the reality of common sense rarely gleaming through the smoke and flame of the altar fire. The expression of man's sense of experience-meaning becomes as a dream; and the humbuggery of the initiates becomes the impulse to create a conditioned response by the audience, a response that has little relation to the experience-meaning inherent in the conditions of the work of art, but one which is based almost entirely upon the secondhand frenzy and weird substance manipulations and mutilations of the critic-witch doctor.

There is something awesome about art, real art. The degree of sensitivity, the colossal range of perceptivity, the tremendous depths of insight evidenced by great artists should strike with awe and respect upon the conscious responsive natures of less gifted persons. The prodigious skill the great artist uses to structure the conditions of life into a substantial form to re-create the substance of experience-meaning that is his for the subsequent re-experiencing by an audience of that experience-meaning in substantial, essential reincarnation of the artist's impression of experience-meaning merits the utmost admiration. The mastery by the artist of the tools of the particular art form, the devices of representational experience, the sound and color and tone impulses used to establish meaning and create responsive awarenesses, these all command attention and require diligent effort to comprehend. But mysterious? Otherworldly remote? Incomprehensible without a medium? Mystically elevated beyond the range of common sense? Too deep to plumb? Too exotic for common experience? Hogwash. Anyone with common sense; with the normal sensitivity, perceptivity,

and receptivity required for living; with unimpaired responsive
faculties; with the will, inclination, or compulsion to submit to
the experience-meaning of living: anyone can understand and
appreciate the great arts without the mumbo-jumbo humbuggery that constitutes so much of the critical canon. Great art is
life; it is Nature; it is truth; it is beauty; it is the substance of
life made meaningful and put into a substantial form so that it
may be re-experienced without the clutter of nonessentials that
usually obscure the experience-meaning of the conditions in the
non-artistic "real" life of everyday existence. The essence of art
is life, and its essential conditions are the experiences of life that
have meaning. Anyone capable of experiencing, of responding
to life, can make a meaningful response-experience to art without a critic's telling him how. The authentic critic, the genuine
critic, the genius among critics, may aid the layman-experiencer,
however. He may be able to draw attention to technical details
that would escape the awareness of the inexperienced. Out of
his greater experience he may be able to ascertain the qualifying
relationships of associational conditions with greater accuracy
than that of the inexperienced. His greater familiarity with
method and manner of expression might enable him to give
pointers to one less familiar with techniques and devices of artistic expression. His greater knowledge should enable the good
critic to go deeper into the meaning of the artistic experience
than the nonspecialist could go, and he should be able to transmit to the less qualified the necessary information.

Response to life is the experiencing of life; the meaning of
life is the awareness of the import of experience as experience
and of experience as an impulse stimulating knowledge and understanding of the conditions out of which experience arises.
Wisdom comes as a result of fusion of experienced conditions
stirred to meaning and understanding by an impulse of will, inclination, or compulsion that leads to profound comprehension
of the relation of experience to the qualities of the conditions

and impulses that constitute experience, that constitute life, that constitute Nature and man's place in Nature. The great critic is he who can bridge the chasm between the actuality of firsthand involvement in the experiences of Nature and the representational impression of Nature that is art, and, as a result of his wisdom, transmit to another the relational profoundness of his wisdom, judgment, and understanding to such a degree that another may share in the re-experiencing of the conditions and impulses of Nature, through art, as though they were the natural, actual experiences of firsthand response. The "representational impression," as it is used here, has nothing to do with a photographic or phonographic reproduction of experience. It is used rather in the sense of fidelity to the qualities of Nature and experience that command responsive impulses, and integrity in the structuring of conditions into substantial form in such a manner that the substances of Nature and experience are not deformed in the process to a semblance of something that does violence either to prior or potential experience or meaning. Indeed, the "representational impression" may not have a facsimile in natural actuality. It may be strictly the impression of fused and merged conditions in the artist's subconscious that have taken such substantial form as to seem to be exact reproduction of external actuality, whereas in substance the like may never be found in native experience. But the semblance of actuality may be so intrinsically faithful to the response-provoking impulsive qualities of actuality that the representation of impression takes on the appearance, the meaning, and the nature of feasibly actual conditions. In essence, art would not exist if it had no relational affinity in its substantial form to the impulses and conditions in Nature that provide the source of experience-meaning. Art does not exist in a void; it is a product of experience; and it has significance only in relation to experience-meaning. Art does not exist outside the responsive states of man derived from Nature, based in Nature, and

136

expressive of man's substance as part of Nature. Man's responses are essential qualities given their essence as impulses
in the conditions of Nature. Void of experience, man is void of
responsive impulses; void of responsive impulses, there is no
meaning significant to man; void of meaning, there is no art in
the experience of man. Without art, criticism ceases; art is the
impulse of criticism. It behooves criticism, or critics, to practice
integrity in relation to art, to use fidelity in the interpretation
and analysis of art. If they do not do so they destroy the very
essence of their craft; for that which mutilates art or destroys art
mutilates and destroys that which functions as a result of art,
criticism. Art may exist without formally delineated criticism,
but criticism cannot function without its impulse, art. Art is to
criticism as an eye is to sight. If the first proposition is not, the
second is nothing; nor can all the theories and principles and
hypotheses in the condition of man make it something. If anything in the conditions of Nature and man's associative responses to Nature is sacred and inviolable, it is art. Anything
that distorts or disturbs or destroys or misinterprets the impulses to meaning inherent in Nature or art is profane, for it
corrupts the essential substance of Nature and the elemental
bases in art for man's apprehension of experience-meaning, for
his growth in knowledge, and for his attainment of wisdom.

Art is a renewal of experience and an awakener to experience. It, in itself, is experience, a condition of life and Nature
that stirs the responsive impulses of man and creates for him
a source of meaning and an experience that he might not be
able to find anywhere else in the conditions of his environmental
existence. Art supplies an insight into the nature of impulses,
into the essential qualities of conditions, and into the essence
of the substance of life and Nature itself for him who has the
qualifications of a sensitive, perceptive, receptive nature and a
responsive state of being. Art is second only to Nature as a
lessoner of man, and indeed many of the lessons of Nature are

unavailable to man except through art. Great art provides the only path to knowledge and wisdom through experience for many; for many have only art as a source of the experience from which comes knowledge and wisdom and meaning. Art may provide what the happenstance of environmental conditions may exclude, and in the provision create impulses and conditions so purified of the extraneous that the essence of the experience is more totally apprehensible than it would be if encountered in any other manner. Art is experience and the conditions of experience and the impulses requiring response to conditions put into substantial form. It is the substance of experience compressed into a form so that it may be re-experienced again and again, and it is the essence of wisdom and beauty preserved and protected from the drift of time and the ebb of memory. It is not transitory and of the moment as are experiences out of art, for it may be returned to for the refreshing of spirit and the renewal of experience that most other forms of experience deny. It is self-perpetuating and self-glorifying; it is the permanence of experience in an impermanent world; and it is the eternal source of wisdom that outlives its builder and defies the death and forgetfulness that is the fate of the nonartistic, mortal things. But art has one great enemy, ignorance. Ignorance may place in obscurity what time cannot touch. Ignorance may corrupt where the greatest of corrupters, death, can find no place to light. Ignorance may distort where the drift of time leaves no trace. Ignorance may destroy the wisdom, the meaning, the experience of the ages though the ages themselves may be powerless to alter a single condition in a great work of art.

Though Nature herself cannot re-create in substance the absolute identity of a moment, and the essence of the moment alters materially in the inexorable evolution that is the movement of time across the face of Nature and through the conditions of Nature, the impulse of the moment is caught fast by art. Art freezes the lapse between now and then and stops the movement of time and experience in a substantial form to perpetuate the identity of the moment of experience and the meaning of the moment. Only in art may the moment be re-experienced, for only by art may the moment be stabilized, be halted for scrutiny and re-examination without the fickle faultiness of that most unstable quality of natural Nature, memory. Art is the real memory of man, the stable, immutable memory upon which man builds his wisdom and fastens the roots of his progress. Art preserves the past experiences of conditions and impulses, conditions the present by providing the comparative bases for judgment and circumspect evaluation of values, and prepares the future by circumscribing and delineating the sources of man's inspiration and aspiration. Without memory man may become nonhuman, a walking vegetable with no creative function other than self-reproduction, a machine incapable of altering the conditions of its environment or oiling its parts for more efficient functioning. Memory is the motive-impulse of man's evolutionary process as a sentient being, and even his unconscious memory or his physical memory will be preserved in his art—but nowhere else other than in art will it find expression in substantial form and become an available experience for a community of men. Man may subsist as a machine, a vegetable, an animal, an object, without art—art not just as an aid to memory, but the substance and substantial form of memory itself, the essence in solidity of man's comprehension, and the essential substance of his apprehension of the basal impulses of his progress as man.

Because art is memory and experience, art teaches; it teaches as memory and experience teach, not as the preacher or professor teaches, not with the externality of superimposed moralizing and theorizing and expostulation, but with the organic functionality of experiential participation in the conditions that create awareness, that supply impulses to stimulate knowledge and impress meaning, that determine the qualities that demand response, and that provide a primal source for the attainment of wisdom. Wisdom is not derived from hearsay; it is a product of experience. Nature and art supplement each other and complement each other as sources of experiential wisdom, real wisdom, not the secondhand, hearsay, errorful accumulation of disassociational facts that too often passes as wisdom, and not the speculative theorizing that the unwise would foist onto the unaware as wisdom. Art is a functional, dynamic teacher because art is experience; art is a lesson in participatory experience because art is the retained memory of the meaning of experience; and he who is susceptible to the nature of the impulses and conditions that constitute the qualities of experience in Nature and in art and the meaning that is implicit in those qualities of experience has no need of any other teacher, particularly not of the critical theorist or the inexperienced pedant. Too often these intrude between the experience and the learner, distort the experience and obscure the meaning of experience until all that remains is the image of the critic and the pedant rather than the meaning of the potential experience with art or Nature. The experience remains potential until it is had functionally. It can never be had functionally as long as the critic remains between the experience and the experiencer, and the meaning can never be the experiencer's meaning until his has been the experience. He may experience the critic, he may learn the meaning of the criticism; but he cannot experience art or Nature, nor can he apprehend their meaning, functionally, while the critic remains the source of his knowledge. Consequently, the critic must step aside, or be pushed aside, once he has imparted the information he has which might make the experience more meaningful to the experiencer; and the criticism must be relegated to the trash heap once its function of describing the structure of conditions comprising the experience is accomplished or once the experience itself establishes doubt as to the validity of the criticism. Art is its own reason for being and its own evidence of quality and the nature of its experience-meaning. Criticism is an adjunct to art and to Nature, not they to it, and it must not be allowed to become the object of experience-meaning at the expense of that upon which it depends. When the critic becomes so vain that he would substitute, to teach others, his criticism for the experiencing of art, he is forcing them to eat the regurgitation of his own corruptness, instead of the purity of the original vitalizing sustenance of untampered experience-meaning of art grown in the conditions of Nature and fruited by the impulses of Nature.

Critics may till the field of art, and the critical plough may turn up treasures of meaning and experience; but if the critic plants weed seeds of ignorance and error, weeds of ignorance and error will grow. They will choke the beauties of art and deprive them of the nutriments in Nature's soil that would cause them to flourish. And if the hailstorm of criticism goes unabated, it will pound into pieces what it does not smother or beat into the mud of the field. What should grow under the sunlight of knowledge and the gentle rain of wisdom will be destroyed by the darkness of ignorance and error.

The craft of criticism is culpable of great crimes against both art and Nature. It should not be guilty and it need not be guilty, but guilt is apparent: criticism has too many faces, too many "points of view," too many prescriptions that only partially deal with art or define only parts of an art. There are too many "fields" of criticism, each with a separate specialized approach to art, and each contradicting all other approaches to art. The inconsistencies among the various approaches to art, and inconsistencies within particular approaches to art, create frustrations for students of art, for anyone who goes to art for firsthand experience-meaning of art. The vagaries of the various schools of criticism, the personal caprices of critics, have evolved into a formless monster of critical criteria that is unexplainable as an affinitive adjunct to a particular work of art or as a generalized relative to art as a whole. They have created a series of gigantic sieves through which art is passed, allowing only those qualities of the art to survive the sieving process which fit the prescribed refining techniques of the particular school of criticism. That which will not flow of its own accord through the critical sieve is cast on the artistic slag pile, the dross heap of rejected art. When a work of art has gone through the refining process of a number of sieves of various critical schools, little remains to be identified with the work in its native form. The refined-out bits become the capsulated "artistic truth" of the particular brand of criticism, labeled, and peddled in the halls of Academe by salesman of pedantry, hawkers of patent medicines to cure the ills of ignorance. But too little of art remains in the capsules, the solution is too thinned out with dilutants of opinion, prejudice, ignorance, and dissemblance to be efficacious. All too often the ingredients added to the mixture are incompatible with the primary substance and create worse than that which they are supposed to cure. Certainly the diluted substance cannot command the same intensity of response that the unadulterated work would impress; the critical capsule may serve as an emetic, but it rarely succeeds in purging ignorance. There are too many witch doctor, patent medicine, quack critics around, and they have too many remedies to hawk. The labels on their medicines are misleading, and the potions themselves are contaminated. They create more ills than they cure, but their merits are bruited by the ignorant and they so disguise their nature that a popular taste is stimulated.

The multiplicity of schools of criticism puts too many points of view in the market place for criticism, too many critics looking for a unique, different, approach to the problems of criticism in an age that demands difference or newness as a quality of excellence. The result is that often expedience replaces experience as the basic criterion of the critic, and celebrity is sought rather than the sounder but slower and more difficult to attain reputation founded in solid, scholarly, honest effort and excellence. A guest shot on a television panel show is more rewarding financially than a lecture in a classroom, but the panel-critic needs the celebrity-image to qualify him for the show, and the celebrity-image requires a showmanship appeal to a mass audience, not the limited recognition generally accorded the serious scholar. Even Academe has succumbed to the celebrity-image, and the person with popular appeal who is known by the number of books he has published or the number of appearances he has had on television will often command a higher salary and position than will a person of greater intellectual and scholarly ability. The ivory tower and the ivy tower are forced to compete with the television tube and the paperback, and under the ground rules of "publish or perish," the latter is the odds-on favorite in the great game of critical commentary. Mass popularity should be no gauge in judging anything other than mass popularity, the appeal to the greatest number, the acclaim of the average, the satisfaction of mediocrity. But mediocrity with a flair, with a touch of the unique, with the celebrity of difference pays off, and mediocre celebrity wins public acclaim hands down over retiring excellence; department stores peddle second-class art acclaimed by second-class critics to buyers with second-class judgment and taste, and they hail each other as the greatest thing ever to hit the scene—the apathetic, complacent, superiority of mediocrity. But why should the average, the mediocre, the popular, be the standard for judging art? Most of those who would have it so would not use the criterion for judging auto mechanics or brain surgery. They would demand the best; they would hardly allow the great television comedian to perform brain surgery on them no matter how great his celebrity, yet they allow that same television comedian to tamper with and mutilate their communal memory, their permanent mind in an impermanent world, their art. Faddist popularity is allowed to take precedence over universal excellence; topical whims are allowed to submerge timeless truths; great art languishes while billboard advertising strikes the level of popular taste, and more viewers know by sight the young lady who sells deodorant than know the Mona Lisa, except when *she* sells the deodorant. Great art becomes a commodity in the market place, an object of speculative enterprise; and critics become stockbrokers, financial pimps, selling their prostituted product to a public whose only basis for judging excellence is the price the last bidder put on the object. Art cannot flourish where money and mass appeal are the primary bases for judgment. Honest criticism cannot be popular where such criteria prostitute art, and where the critical review becomes advertising copy for second-class art.

Genuine critics as well as genuine artists suffer in an age of status image-making; all men exposed to a cultural atmosphere that gives precedence to image over reality, that vaunts celebrity rather than sound contribution, that practices spectatorship rather than participation, that establishes possession rather than accomplishment as the mark of success, are products of a degenerate, decadent world. Such a world is marked by the image maker, the status seeker, the celebrity figure, the restless preciosity of its elite, the pretentious imitation of its lower classes, by the insatiability of its appetites, the voraciousness, the degenerate fickleness of its taste, the distortion of its traditions, the disrespectful contempt for its heritage, the notoriety of its leaders, the alteration of its morals, and the pseudoappreciation of the objects it establishes as status symbols. Art, in such a world, becomes a status sign, a mark of distinction, a possession to create a visual image of cultural achievement. What is decadent here is the assumption that cultural achievement may be bought, that it is marketable, and that possession rather than understanding and appreciation is the sign of culture. There is an ignorant degeneration inherent in such an attitude, and it is

144

a manifestation of all decadent times that the possession of art establishes the class superiority of the self-styled elite. Understanding? Appreciation? What have they to do in a world that bases its values on the prestige of possession and the image of material achievement? How can they advance or flourish when the arbiters of art are the unlearned in art, the manipulators of finance, the professors of mediocrity, the image makers in a pseudosophisticated, degenerate, status symbol society? What qualities of artistic merit can a stockbroker's ticker tape ascertain? What values attach to art in an age that says "My new mink stole must be seen at the opera tonight" or "I'll be the talk of the country club; no one else has a Matisse in his bathroom or Michelangelo prints on his toilet tissue"? What is art to a society whose acquaintance with literature is limited to the dust jacket blurb and the popular critic's column and whose appreciation of Van Gogh is summed up with "I bought it because it matches my drapes"? What is literature in an age when the excellence of a work is judged by the number of copies it sells and the publisher creates the best seller by buying back the books he has placed in the bookstore? These are questions the good critic must answer and attitudes he must counter. But how can he answer them honestly or counter them effectively when he is a part of the order that creates the need for the questions and the obligation to counter the attitudes? Artist and critic are caught going two directions at the same time; they find a contradiction in impulses quickening their attitudes toward their arts and their crafts. The conditions of decadent, degenerate times stir impulses mutually irreconcilable: a fine sense of integrity in relation to art and the social sense of material accomplishment in an atmosphere that correlates success with celebrity and financial gain. The result must inevitably be a withdrawal into the "ivory tower" or a scaling-down of the integrity impulse. The former may maintain for posterity a respect for art, an appreciation for its universal qualities, and a gratitude for its existence. The latter, of necessity, requires a defense of mediocrity and the establishing of popular taste as the criterion for judgment; this compromise, practical from the societal materialistic point of view and perhaps even desirable if the artist or critic can succeed in refraining from going all the way and can maintain some qualities of integrity in the face of mass taste and demand to keep alive those qualities beyond the period of decadence, is still a degenerating influence on art and criticism; and the apologist for art must apologize for his craft or tout a bastard craft as though it were legitimate to gratify the preferences of a public that doesn't know the difference between quality and gilt-plated mediocrity. If man can serve two masters, the bastard craft critic is the exemplar of duplicity; he pays lip service to art and soul service to anti-art, to corruption of art and the Nature for which art speaks.

The great critic must be selfless; he must be able to set aside all personal prejudices, all institutional loyalties, all social fealties, all inclinations to judge on the basis of familiarity and association, when he approaches art. He must be capable of going outside the impulses and conditions of his own experience. He must not judge the artistic merits of the *Kama Sutra* in terms of Christian morality or of primitivism in terms of sophisticated superimpositions: he must not derogate the quality, the experience, the meaning of capitalistic art because it does not satisfy a familiar regard for the communistic point of view; he must not appraise contemporary European painting with only a knowledge of Classical Oriental miniatures as his comparative standard of judgment. He must not allow the social, religious, economic, academic, scientific, artistic conditions of one time or place to influence his attitude or condition his responsive impulses toward the art of another time or place. If he does these things, he cannot criticize; he can only quibble, apologize, distort, or misrepresent. Great art is of Nature before it is of topical institution, and the great critic must recognize that fact and turn his loyalties to art and Nature or he becomes a mere propagandist for a limited environmental or hereditary point of view.

Neither art nor Nature nor human experience can afford the luxury of supporting anything that tends to limit, qualify, distort, or mutilate the substantial form expression of man's condition in the Nature from which he is the artistic voice, the impressionable recorder, the sensitive interpreter of his own evolutionary processes. The *Oresteia* is not great because it is pagan, classical, Greek, dramatic, tragic; it is great because it perpetuates the meaning and the substance of human experience through conditions that are conditions of human experience with impulses that stir human responsiveness in the timeless nature of human commitment to participation in the processes of human responses to life. Man's essential commitment is to life regardless of the topical impositions of fads, loyalties, and pressures; art is the reflection of that commitment; criticism should be the appraisal with fidelity and integrity of that reflection, but it cannot be with fidelity and integrity if the critic is committed to any peripheral association, institution, prejudice, fad, or loyalty. Art must soar above the smog of technology, beyond the restraints of science, over the limitations of philosophical or religious systems, outside the corruptive and corrosive influences of chauvinistic fealties or it becomes apologetically limited; but it must not minimize the influences of any condition that affects impulses of man in his world, because man in his world is the substance and the source of man's total condition in his evolutionary experiencing of his own meaning. But the artist must see man in his great perspective-relation to his nature, not just in his topically limited focus of time and space and environmentally curtailed experience. The critic must see the work of art in that same perspective, in the totality of man's affinitive nature with the conditions of his universal nature, and only secondarily with the focal conditions of his topical time and space impulses.

The critic must be capable of, and he must practice, submission to experiences and meanings completely alien to his own cultural, intellectual, social, political, economic, religious, philosophical milieu without losing his own identity as a participant in his native milieu of conditions, impulses, experiences, and meanings. What he must do is to specify value qualities from his own milieu and attach their significance in their own relational context to an expression of milieu experience that does not relate to the same value qualities. This value appraisal requires a level of knowledge and a depth of functional submissiveness that is beyond the receptive capacities and the abnegational propensities of any but the rarest critical genius. In addition, the powers of sequential thought in the great critic must be so disciplined that he will not only be able to ascertain the relational sequence of conditions and impulses in the work under consideration, but also he will be able to apprehend the meaning and total effectiveness of the work as a re-experience of the conditions and impulses that constitute the whole nature of experience given substantial form in the work.

VI

THE ETHIC-AESTHETIC IMPULSE

WHATEVER DISTURBS THE INTEGRITY OF NATURE, HER wholeness, her completeness, her self-perpetuating identity, her self-completing and self-sustaining ethic-aesthetic, disturbs the tolerable mean, the harmony between allowable tolerances of excess and deficiency, the variable continuity inherent in adaptability of parts to the functional evolution of those parts relative to and consistent with the evolutionary processes of the whole as the infinity of parts coheres into the finite identity of the whole of self-defining Nature. Any disturbance of natural order, the phenomenal ethical prerogative of Nature, that exceeds the tolerances established by Nature or that is deficient in the qualities essential to the evolutionary processes of Nature, upsets the mean formulated by Nature as the basis of her harmony, her order, her making of reaction of parts proportionately relative to the object of reaction—subservient to the integral functional integrity of Nature—and creates mutants intolerable to Nature. These mutants, the tragic offspring of Nature, Nature destroys or adapts to her identity at the expense of their identity. If that identity of the mutant is sentient, its destruction or adaptation is a tragedy to it even

149

though its sentient identity is erroneously self-conceived or self-defined. But self-deception, whether conscious or unconscious, may be a primary quality of sentience and in itself may promote a disharmony that has the tragic consequence of suffering the pain occasioned by the inability to adapt painlessly to the exigencies of conditions necessary to survival in the self-identifiable form of the mutant faced with the insurmountable obstacle of shaping the whole of Nature to the requirements of any of her minor parts. Thus Hamlet must be destroyed in his attempt to alter the nature of Denmark just as the Denmark of Claudius must have its identity destroyed to restore the harmony and balance essential to the well-being of the state as that state-part conforms to the integral order of the natural, as well as the topical, ethic. Destruction is tragic to the sentient being caught by the forces of the natural ethic, or of the topical ethic, whether he is an instigator of disharmony or a subject of disharmony attempting to re-establish an order beyond the abilities of a mere sentient being to cope with conditions and impulses external or internal to his own being, or of a nature alien to his own bent, topically temporal and environmental or ubiquitously ranging outside the facilities and faculties of his command.

Balance is the first law of Nature, of survival; and adaptability is the second law, dependent on the first and inextricably involved in its function. Balance and the adaptability to achieve balance are the functional processes in Nature's evolution; and natural integrity is the maintenance of that balance, through adaptability, between the extremes of excess and deficiency. Excess or deficiency in function is due to failure to adapt and results in discontinuance of form, substance, impression, condition, impulse, or style, both in Nature and in art. Excess and deficiency are relative to the function of an object in congruence with the conditions of its environment and the impulses of its heredity. If hereditary requirements for survival are not satisfied by environmental conditions, if there be either excess or deficiency in those conditions relative to the survival requirements or the survival disallowances, and adaptation does not ensue to create new requirements in harmony with environmental conditions, extinction is Nature's way of creating a survival conducive balance. If deficiency of food of the right sort is present to maintain hereditary dietary requirements, excess population of food consumers results, and the surplus consumers either starve or adapt to different foods in Nature's maintenance of balance. Balance is essential to the functional whole, sound, complete perfection of Nature; and any part of Nature must adapt to the whole order of Nature to play its role in the entirety of natural function. Each part is relative to the whole and dependent on its functional relationships with the rest for its survival in its adapted form or substance. Balance is functional harmony, the truth of what is in the natural processes of Nature's evolutionary adaptation of her parts to achieve the interdependent order of her conditions and to maintain the soundness of her substance, the wholeness of her identity, and the perfection of her forms. Without balance, with imbalance in her relative conditions, discord and disharmony would prevail; there would be no wholeness, no soundness, no perfection in forms, substances, or identities.

In Nature whatever is, is; and it is, it exists, as an indisputable fact as evidenced by its existence in the awareness of it by its responsive parts and the functioning of those parts to make it what it is in perceptible forms and substances. The parts, the conditions of Nature, in their fusing and merging and Nature sustaining processes, are the structural components of the whole of Nature. Each part performs in conjunction with other parts or conditions, and if the balance of performance is upset the order of Nature is upset and a new order is established, always in conformity with the evolutionary processes of Nature's own reshaping identity. Nature is ruthless in her re-forming, sustaining, evolutionary processes. She destroys one form to nourish another; she starves one part to provide a balance between sustenance supply and sustenance demand. She tolerates no excess and no deficiency in the conditions that make her soundly whole because the principle, the natural principle, of her being is the incorruptible soundness of her complete, unbroken condition, and whatever must be destroyed to maintain her perfect condition is destroyed; and whatever must be adapted to meet the requirements of her complete, functional perpetuation is adapted; and whatever must be supplied to maintain her soundness is supplied out of the complexity of her diversified evolutionary processes. This is the integrity of Nature: the incorruptible soundness that creates rightness out of what is required to maintain the identity of Nature; the perfection of condition that makes right whatever is permitted by herself to remain unimpaired in her wholeness; the complete, unbroken experience that creates and destroys to establish the perfect evolutionary balance that preserves the primal integrity, the natural truth, of Nature's functional self-perpetuating, self-justifying, self-creating, self-glorifying, and self-evolving standards of conduct. The conduct of Nature is the integrity of Nature. The function of Nature is the natural ethics of Nature's standard of conduct, and the morality of Nature is what is made right for Nature by Nature's functional processes in maintaining her evolutionary identity. Whatever is of Nature's doing in the preservation of her integrity is her moral right. The excesses and deficiencies, the imbalances that must be put into balance, the disorders that must be structured into the order of the whole, are Nature's ways to bring about change, to evolve; and the destroying-creating processes she works in the practice of her evolutionary integrity are the evidences of her ethical conduct in conformity with her elaborately complex code of ideal perfection in constant flux to achieve her self-defined perfection.

The integrity of Nature is the morality of Nature, and the ethics of Nature is the standard Nature creates to maintain her character of integrity. The parts are diffused in the whole, and the whole is the focus of the ethical integrity of all the correlated parts; each part depends on the whole, and the whole is entire and unimpaired and in perfect condition only when each and every part performs its function as an integral, ethical, sustainer of the whole. So it is with Nature; and so must it be with art, the substantial form of impressions of experience implemented in the functional processes of Nature and translated into expression through sentiently representational media. For Nature cannot become reincarnate in art if art has not the same ethical conformity to the functional processes of her model, Nature, that Nature herself evidences. What does not re-create the ethical function of Nature cannot reincarnate the relative conditions that are the experiences of Nature; and what does not fix the experience of Nature in substantial form with all the ethical integrity of Nature fused into its conditions and that ethical integrity acting as the impulse of its being is not art; it is artistic pretense, and it deserves the fate of those parts of Nature that are destroyed to preserve the integrity of Nature, for it disturbs the balance of art as excess or deficiency disturbs the balance of Nature.

Excess and deficiency are the sins of Nature against Nature, and so they must be considered the sins of art. These sins must be destroyed or adapted as Nature destroys or adapts; otherwise there will be no art, only grotesque mutant distortions of natural impressions with no relevant truth, no integrity, no meaning in experience except the negative, alienating meaning of the lie. The ethical conduct of Nature and the self-imposed standards of her integrity, the natural consequences of Nature's natural self, must be the standards and conduct of artistry, if artistry is to perpetuate in substantial form the experiences of Nature. Art is the expressive representative of Nature, and art must conform to the natural code of ethics to re-create or reincarnate the experience-meaning of Nature in the form of art. Artistic

153

integrity and ethics derive their impulses and their meanings from the functions of natural experience as man the artist replies to Nature through his sensitive, perceptive, receptive responsive natures and forms impressions of natural processes which become the bases of his artistic code.

The ethical code and the integrity of Nature are based on and derived from what it is; what is is the truth of Nature, the absolute, the irrefutable evidence inherent in the conditions of Nature and emanating from Nature as impulses demanding response to the manifest qualities of Nature. Nature is truth, ethical truth, the truth of integrity; and whether god created, God created, or happenstance created, what is is; and Nature is the only source, directly apprehensible by the responsive natures of man, for the perceptible substance of man's impressions and the object of his responsive faculties. Man's expression of his impressions of natural substance, his substantial form devices for reincarnating his experience-meaning of impressions and impulses transmitted by Nature, involves the natural compulsions man has to find means to represent his experience-meaning impressions in substantial form with symbols and representational devices that have a significant communal communicability. If there is no significant communal comprehension of the meaning of the symbols and devices employed by art to transmit the artist's impression to the responsive condition of an audience, there is no functional affinity established in the transmission sequence—natural experience, reception of impression by the artist, retention and transformation of the experience into experience-meaning, expression of experience-meaning, reception of experience-meaning impression by an audience, retention and reincarnation of experience in an audience responsiveness. Because art is a functional process in the nature of man as a part of natural Nature, because man depends on communal understanding and comprehension of transmission devices, and because these devices are conditions of man's compulsive nature to receive, retain, respond, and express, it is only reasonable that man should employ the same codes of ethics and integrity in his reincarnation of experience-meaning that he finds in the sources of conditions and impulses that give him the initial substance of his experiences and meaning of his impressions. Anything less than total artistic adherence to the natural principles of ethics and integrity is a travesty of Nature and of the receptive nature of man; it is an immoral prostitution of man's artistic impulses and an immoral rape of man's potential as the predominant expression of Nature herself. The ethics of Nature are not the artificial conventions and mores of topically institutionalized human societies; natural ethics is the evolving principle of functional Nature perpetuating herself despite the topical digressions of incoherent conventionality and transmitting throughout time the contemporaneity of universal truth and beauty. To the genuine artist conventional loyalties to topical conditions are subversions of natural law whenever those topical loyalties lead to contravention of Nature's ethics. An artist who places convention above natural ethics is the anti-Christ of Nature, and in his fall he will exchange his seat in an artistic paradise for a hell of his own contriving.

Balance—attraction-repulsion, love-hate, equal and opposite actions-reactions—maintains the integrity of Nature and creates the ethics of Nature; and balance—equilibrium between excess and deficiency—in relation to natural conditions and impulses must maintain the integrity of art as an impressive expression of Nature and create the ethics of artistry as a function of the truth of natural impulses to impression. Without balance, both natural and artistic, neither Nature nor art can remain complete, sound, unimpaired, in an unbroken condition. Natural integrity, the incorruptible soundness of natural Nature, is the model for the integrity of art just as the experiencing of Nature is the source and the model for the substance and conditions of art. Because integrity is the essence of natural

155

ethics, it must also be the essential quality of artistic ethics if art is to function as art, as an expression of impression of natural phenomena, including all responsive impulses: physical, mental, emotional, spiritual, and behavioral.

Integrity, as well as being an essential of ethics, is also a contributive essential to the second quality of Nature and art, the aesthetic. If ethics, the moral judgment of standards of conduct, is a functional derivative of Nature, then aesthetics, the philosophy of beauty, is an essential result of ethical function; and consideration of the one without consideration of the other is a fragmenting of the essence of the whole Nature-art complex of interrelated conditions, impulses, expressions, impressions, and responses. Ethics is the soul of Nature and art; aesthetics describes the perceptible form and substance of that soul as it generates impulses requiring responsive impressions. If there is no fidelity in the reincarnation of experience, there is no beauty and no truth in the resultant impression, and the substantial form expression of conditions and impulses will be void of taste other than that topically conventionalized, of naturally substantive moral judgment, of standards of normal and natural behavioral function, and of impulses generating soundly founded responses for worthwhile experience-meaning.

Excess and deficiency are matters of prime significance in the consideration of the ethics of Nature and of art, but they are not exclusively negative qualities or conditions of ethics alone, nor are they exclusively negative qualities of that integrity which is the basic functional determinant of natural ethics. Excess and deficiency are also significant considerations in the analysis of the substantial form expression of ethical function as that substantial form's affinitive impulses—between Nature and art—create the impressions that may be designated as the substance of a work of art once they have been structured by man into a form that fixes a particular experience-meaning in the multi-complex fusion of conditions that is the work of art. Excess and deficiency are likewise negative qualities of fidelity, the accurate, faithful, loyal presentation of what is in the ethical function of Nature, the natural beauty of Nature in both the panoramic perspective and the specific focus of natural conditions and impulses. Fidelity to natural impulses—the accurate, faithful presentation of those impulses as generators of responses that come without corruption from a naturally sensitive, perceptive, and receptive responsive nature—is the essential quality of aesthetic reincarnation of natural experience-meaning, of non-aberrant experience-meaning, of ethical experience-meaning. Aesthetics can no more tolerate excess and deficiency than can ethics; for either excess or deficiency is a breaking of the balance, the creating of an imbalance, that is as detrimental to aesthetic result as it is to ethical function.

There is in Nature, in the balance of Nature, a clearly evident cause-effect relativity in the conditions and impulses that comprise natural experience-meaning and that create impulsive response-impressions; there is inherent in this experience-meaning of Nature, the reality of cause-effect relativity, a causal-effectual derivative: ethical-aesthetic relativity as congruently consubstantial corollaries in natural and artistic function. Just as there can be no effect without a cause, there can be no aesthetics without ethics: ethical function, both in Nature and the translation from Nature into art, is the essential cause of aesthetic result, and integrity is the essence of fidelity. Artistic aesthetics can no more be alienated from artistic ethics than can natural aesthetics be alienated from natural ethics without creating a monster-mutant-aberrant imbalance that negates both truth and beauty; for truth and beauty depend on the essentials of ethics and aesthetics, integrity and fidelity, in both Nature and art, for the mutually dependent cause-effect relativity that establishes the functional experience-meaning that emanates from both natural and genuinely artistic processes. It is not to be inferred here that either the panoramic perspective or the definitive focus of the ethic-aesthetic complex is to be construed in the artistic expression of impression as being a photo-phono representation of Nature; rather, the implication is that the representation in artistry of natural phenomena must conform with the principles of natural ethics and aesthetics, and that the expression in substantial form must obey the same natural laws that initiating experience in Nature evidences, within the limits established by Nature on the natural receptive, retentive, responsive faculties of man, the highest order in Nature's functional forms.

The ethics-aesthetics relativity in Nature and in art is not necessarily an in-sequence relationship; indeed, the relationship is one of concordant and concurrent interdependence in a cause-effect fusion of simultaneous functions, and to separate the one from the other for consideration would be to lift the one out of the qualifying and modifying context determined by the other. This is true both of the Nature-art affinity and the ethics-aesthetics affinity; and it is true, also, of the co-relativity of the natural ethic-aesthetic and the artistic ethic-aesthetic interdependent identity of each and both at the same time. There is contemporaneity of ethic-aesthetic process in the Nature-art relational function, and the cause-effect relationship is necessarily sequential only in the sense of the practical problems involved in describing the functional processes of ethics and aesthetics simultaneously. Perhaps the beautiful truth of Nature, and of art, may best be described as the ethical aesthetics of Nature reflected in art, the substantial form expression of the experience-meaning of Nature. In most instances the ethical and aesthetic function, the cause-effect process, will be so completely assimilated into the conditions and impulses of either the natural or the artistic event that the distinguishing identities of neither can be extrapolated from the fused and merged qualities of both as they together make up the total ethic-aesthetic impression of experience-meaning; and the integrated whole of the genuine, Nature-based and Nature-generated, experience-meaning will not be separable into differentiated ethical or aesthetic parts without the destruction of experience-meaning as the essence of truth and beauty in Nature and in art.

Both ethics and aesthetics are intrinsic qualities or conditions in Nature, independent of external conditions for their impulses; neither, in its basic state, is independent of the other; and neither, in its pristine condition, takes precedence over the other. Nature is and Nature does. What Nature does is right and beautiful in terms of Nature's functional determination of her own conditions of rightness and beauty; and what Nature is, is what Nature determines in her organic, functional processes of evolution. Man, as an objectively differentiated form in Nature, may alter surface features of Nature: he may level mountains and pollute streams, but he cannot create the sensitivity, perceptivity, or receptivity with which he is endowed by Nature to enable him to respond to Nature, including his own nature, as Nature supplies him with the faculties to discern, form impressions, apprehend experience-meaning, and comprehend his place as a condition in the structural whole of Nature. Man is of Nature, and being of Nature he is subject to the laws of Nature and is an object of natural function. His attempts at altering the ethical and aesthetic conditions of Nature are as contrary to natural function as his defacing of the surface features of Nature and his pollution of her waters. When man arrogates unto himself the prerogative of altering Nature, he creates imbalances that the rest of Nature must put to rights, even at the expense of destroying her most elevated form, man. The ethical and aesthetic functions of Nature preclude drastic alteration of the non-Nature oriented whimsy of any of her parts; as a whole she determines her own destiny, and it is therefore incumbent on any of her parts, and especially on man, to be aware of the rectitude of her function and to adapt to her order, both in his direct contact with her and in his re-creation and reincarnation of her experience-meaning. The artificial conventions of man's invention are meaningless unless they conform to the qualifying standards imposed by Nature on each of her parts separately and on the merged totality of all her parts collectively as they are structured into a complex whole meaning of Nature. If man persists in cluttering Nature with nonessential or excessive conditions, or if he is deficient in adhering to his obligations as a functional object in Nature, he may well find himself swept into the trash heap of Nature's discards when she re-establishes the balance and order essential to her perpetuation of her own ethics and aesthetics.

Man's arts, as conditions of man's functional process in Nature, must also adhere to the principles of Nature within the limits of excess and deficiency imposed by Nature's ethics and aesthetics, or those arts may well suffer the same fate as any other useless, meaningless, superfluous, or deficient condition in Nature. Man must operate within the limits of what Nature requires of him, permits him to do, or disallows his doing; and his arts must be submitted to the same natural impulses that he is submitted to by Nature, or there will be no ethical or aesthetic quality to his expressive impression in substantial form of the experience-meaning of his condition in Nature. It cannot be overemphasized that art is simply man's, Nature's man's impression of himself as a functional part of Nature amid conditions of Nature responding to impulses emanating from Nature and expressing his impression in a substantial form that preserves the moment of expressed impression for future reference. Art centers about, focuses upon, man's relationships with whatever touches him, with whatever evokes the responses that he makes out of the nature that is his in the Nature that is his. His physical, mental, emotional, spiritual, and behavioral responsive natures are just that—natures, states of Nature—and they are both subject to and object of all conditions and impulses in Nature—physical, mental, emotional, spiritual, and behavioral

—that evidence themselves by commanding response and creating impressions. Man's arts, his memory of experience-meaning in Nature, his impression of his place in the scheme of Nature, his preserved responsive impulse, derive from a condition of Nature inherent in his being as a part of Nature: the will, the inclination, the compulsion to maintain his identity as a part of Nature by his expression of the experience-meaning Nature has for him. Unhappily, man cannot freeze time; he cannot congeal movement; he cannot solidify thought; he cannot jell emotion; he cannot forge spiritual experience; he cannot fix behavior. He may only freeze, congeal, solidify, jell, forge, and fix his impression of experience; and he can do it only with the materials of art to put into substantial form that which has no physical substance in its own nature but which may through art re-create a semblance of the initial experience-meaning event in Nature. The pain felt in a thumb hit by a hammer cannot be bottled, preserved, and released so that another thumb may have that same experience-meaning of pain; it is not possible to preserve the actuality of an experience sempiternally in the form of its non-substantial condition or nature; it is possible, however, to put into substantial form a selected set of conditions that will give impulses to and suggest a semblable impression of the actual experience to an audience quite without supplying the audience with hammers to hit thumbs to create similar experience. It is the province of art to reincarnate the pain without repeating the actual primary experience, to put the impression of pain into a substantial form that will have communal significance to an audience, by structuring into the form the conditions that will create impulses demanding responses that will form impressions semblable to those elicited by a primary or initiating experience. Because experience, the meaning of experience, experience-meaning, is in itself without substance, without discernible form that may be retained in the substance of its innate qualities of conditions and impulses that excite responsive impressions, because ideas, emotions, feelings, senses are not physically substantial, art must find the means to transfer the meaning of experience into forms that will give its audience the impulses to re-create from the art expression, the substantial form suggesting the initial experience-meaning, a reincarnation of the nonsubstantial initial experience through the responsive natures of the audience as they are stirred by the conditions and impulses of the work of art to re-create in impressions of experience. A mystical experience that has no material or physical substance must be suggested with and by materials of physical or material substance to convey and establish and excite impulses that will cause an audience to re-create the mystical experience in the apprehensive natures of audience responsiveness. The transference of experience into material substance—words, paint, forms, or other ways—to be transferred again into reincarnate experience must be accomplished with fidelity and integrity or the meaning of the experience will be lost in the process of transfer; there will be no semblable relativity of the initial experience with the reincarnate experience, for unless the experience-meaning of the initiating experience fructifies in the reincarnate experience and provides the impulses for semblable meaning, there is no art in the intermediary form; and unless the ethical integrity and aesthetic fidelity of the initiating experience is reproduced and preserved by the substantial form and in the audience's responsive reincarnation, the art is a travesty on Nature and a hoax on audience susceptibility.

The incidence of natural ethics and aesthetics in the substantial form of experience-meaning, and that same incidence in the reincarnate experience, is the essence of both the artistic re-creation of experience-meaning and the audience reincarnation of that experience-meaning. The degree of artistic excellence may then be determined by the degree of success of the artist in transferring the incidence of natural ethic-aesthetics to

162

the nonnatural but substantial form of the experience-meaning and by the suitability of the materials and the conditions of the substantial form to create the impulses evocative of the reincarnate experience. Because it is not possible for an audience to make a direct comparison of its experience-meaning as that experience-meaning derives from impressions of a work of art with the experience-meaning of the set of conditions that were the experience of the artist, and thereby determine on the basis of comparative standards the extent of representational fidelity, and because photo-phono representation is a sort of forgery of Nature, it is the incidence of the principles of Nature on the work of art and in the responsive natures of the audience that will determine the quality of the artistic ethic-aesthetic or the audience ethic-aesthetical response. The extent and intensity of incidence of natural principles will determine and delimit the perspective range and the focal depth of the work of art; and, depending on the quality of the receptor faculties of the audience, they will define the apprehensibility of the audience in relation to the transference of experience-meaning from the substantial form to the artistic susceptibility of the audience, as well as detailing the influential nature of the impulses structured into the conditions of the substantial form by the artist to incite responsive impressions.

It is the materials of artistry—the words, the paint, the sounds, and the solids—with physical substance, that must suggest and create impressions, that must prompt impulses, and that must represent conditions to re-create in substantial form qualities that in themselves have no substance, but, in a sense, give form to formlessness, give body to the incorporeal, give substance to the unsubstantial, give permanence to the impermanent. Art is the artificial, imitative form of reality in its inception, but it becomes a natural reality to the audience to whom it conveys its conditions and impulses. Just as surely as it receives its meaning from experience, it becomes an experi-

163

ence and emits meaning to those capable of responding to the experience it manifests. But its experience-meaning is not only the impressions received of the impulses in the representational conditions of its structured form; its experience-meaning is also inherent in the materials of artistry used to make the substantial form representation of experiences. Art is a dream made real to the nondreamer; it is feeling given substance so that it may be felt communally; it is sense put into physical form; it is experience made available to the inexperienced; and it is meaning put in a manner that may be re-examined at leisure. The materials used to give form and substance to the unsubstantial must be of such nature and used in such manner as to re-create the identity of that which they represent and transfer the experience-meaning of that which they represent to an audience so that the experience-meaning may be reincarnated in the impression-forming responses of the audience.

The materials of art are not the sense, the feeling, the meaning of experience, but they are made by art to convey impressions of sense and feeling and meaning, and they are made so by the suitability and manner of their use, their function in the structure of conditions that make up the substantial form (they themselves are among the conditions that are part of the whole of the work of art), in forming the impulses that reincarnate experience-meaning in the apprehensive natures of receptors. The materials themselves are matter, and matter has no innate mind, emotion, or spirit. Those qualities are infused into the conditions of art in the structuring of conditions evocative of mental, emotional, or other responses. They are the attributes of response to matter rather than essences of matter, and though they are directed toward matter, matter provides the impulses for their activation. Consequently, the matter of artistic expression cannot be separated from conditions composing the substance of the substantial form; and the manner of expression, the means of conveying impressions or conditions and impulses evoking impressions, is an essential to art as is the experience that provides the conditions of the substance of art. The devices used by the artist to give permanence to his impressions serve as representational substitutes, or suggestive means, for the artist to reconstitute his experience-meaning in a form that is not the material form of the initial experience for him; and if he is successful in finding the proper substitutes and structuring them into a substantial form that will reconstitute the essential experience-meaning of his experience in such a way as to cause an audience to apprehend a semblable experience-meaning through the medium of his work, art has been made and the principles of Nature's ethic-aesthetic have been served, insofar as imitation or translation can serve as a substitute for actuality of experience.

Intellect, feelings, senses, emotions, insights, spirit: these are nonmaterial conditions, but they provide experience, and experience is the substance of meaning. Nonmaterial substance, however, is as real a condition of Nature as material substance, and it depends upon material association for the means of its expression in substantial form. But because the materials of expression are by the nature of their substance different from the nonmaterial, or even physically material, objects or concepts they are made to represent, and because the materials of expression have no naturally innate identity with the substances they describe, a communal comprehension of associationally attributive meaning must develop if art is to have other than a uniquely personal and individual experience-meaning, and that only for the expresser of the experience. A word is not the object or thought or feeling it describes, and it has meaning and prompts meaningful experience or impression only when its function is comprehended in the same way by both its user and its receptor. Consequently, because the means of expression are merely sophisticated representations in forms different from the objects they represent, there is a correlative sophistication in the principles of the ethic-aesthetic that provides the essential functions in the transference of experience-meaning from one form to another, but the principles themselves must remain grounded in the integrity and fidelity of Nature or they will be destroyed in the transference process and with them will be destroyed the potential for experience-meaning in art. Art can have no ethical or aesthetic quality if the principles of the ethic-aesthetic are destroyed in the transference process between natural Nature and represented Nature; indeed, ethical and aesthetic control must be maintained with the utmost care in the transfer to an art process because the probability of excess or deficiency in expression of impression is much greater in the representational form of experience than it is in initial direct contact experiencing of conditions and impulses in Nature. This is due to the difficulties of total transference from one form to another and to the fallibility of communal comprehension of the devices of transference as well as to the variability in recognition of relational meanings by audiences and to the complexity of response-apprehension and variety of receptor faculty capabilities and capacities.

Man may come to know only by experience, experience real or vicarious, and in art man may find two basic experiences: the experience of the work of art as substance for intellectual analysis and the experience of the work of art as a source of conditions for total responsive submission. Intelligentially analytical experience will be concerned principally with the devices and means of the artistic presentation of substance—with matters of diction, style, rhyme, colors, forms, structure of conditions, and meter; whereas submissive experience will be concerned with the reincarnation of the experience-meaning, the impulses to impression, of the total structural identity of the substantial form of experience and the conditions and impulses that provide its materials and substance. In the first instance, the experience will be primarily an intellectual recapitulation of the artistic

166

conventions employed by the artist to create the possibility of the second instance. The second instance will involve all the responsive states appealed to by the impulses inherent in the fused and merged conditions of the whole synthesized substantial structure, and it will be real experience in the sense that responsive involvement with the impulses of the work of art will create a direct experiential affinity of the work to the receptor as well as an indirect, or vicarious, re-experiencing of what has already been experienced by the artist and put by him into the form that is being experienced by the audience. Herein lies the sophistication of Nature—of man nature concerned with the perpetuation of his experiences through the application of man's superior natural function of intellect finding the means to reincarnate his experience in substantial form.

It is through intellect that man devises the means of expression, the words, the sounds of his intellect functioning to transmit his impressions of experience-meaning and to voice his memory of experience. Words, and all other devices of expression transmission, are learned representations of experience-meanings; they are form substitutes for whatever they are made to represent, whether what they represent has form or not; and in use they must be made subservient to the same principles of ethics and aesthetics as are the objects of their representational function if they are to become legitimate devices of art because they are the means by which art impresses its impulses and its conditions on the submissively receptive nature of man and presents the reincarnate experience-meaning potential that art has re-created from man's experience in his ethic-aesthetic world of conditions and impulses derived from Nature.

Just as ethics and aesthetics fuse and merge in Nature to become one entity, the experience-meaning of Nature, so do ethics and aesthetics fuse and merge in art to become the experience-meaning of Nature in art. But the experiencing of art also has two fused and merged identities that are made one in the func-

167

tional processes of artistry: the real experience and the artificial experience, and both must be apprehended and comprehended if art is to have experience-meaning for its audience, its receptor; the function of each separately and in affinitive relation to the other establishes the total effective potential of the work of art as an affirmation of man's evolutionary heritage as an elevated creature in Nature. If man regards only one of the attributes of experience in art, he can have no apprehension of what art really is as an experience-meaning. If he regards only the artificial experience, the devices used by the artist, he may become conversant only with tools of artistry, not with the product made with those tools. The tools make the art, but they are not the art; they only put conditions and impulses into expressible forms capable of being used by the artist to create art. The tools of art, the devices used by the artist to shape conditions and impulses of Nature and experience into expressible forms, are the hammer and saw of artistic carpentry, sawing and nailing to build a permanent structure, the work of art. They are neither the work of art nor the substance of the work of art; and to judge them as such would be to judge a mansion by the hammer and saw used to build it; but the judge the mansion without consideration of the use or misuse of the tools and materials, conditions and impulses, used to build it would be to neglect the manner and means by which it comes into being as a recognizable form, a structural identity of interrelated and interdependent parts standing as a whole and inseparable from its parts, and they from it. Its wholeness, its soundness, its perfection, depends on the integrity of its structural functionality, its ethics and the ethics of its builder. Its aesthetic quality, the resultant beauty of its structure, is inseparable from the functional relationships that create its form, its substantial representation of the design that was its initial impulse, out of the sand and cement and lumber and paint and nails that are the conditions of its structure, selected and ordered, shaped and put into place relative to all other parts, to create a thing of use and beauty. Art has a dynamic functionality, but to use it only as an object for consideration of devices would be to belie its functionality and to make of it a static record of topical artistic conventions. For example, linguistic analysis of a work of art would not reveal art; it would only reveal a tool of art, and that, isolated from all the rest of what the work is, would be a static quality divorced from its functional, relational affinity with the entire structure that is the re-created experience-meaning of the work, the dynamic experience-meaning potential that the work has to reincarnate perpetually the experiential nature of man in the world of Nature that is his, past and present, evolving into the Nature of posterity.

Insofar as experience is a natural function, a function of response to impulse in Nature by an attribute of Nature, man, and may be interpreted only by man in relation to conditions that touch him, actually or vicariously, in the processes of his being, the quality and the range of his wisdom is determined by the depth and the extent of his responsive comprehension and apprehension of his condition insituate in Nature. The impulses of Nature are infused into the nature of man, and from them he derives the instinctual, physical, mental, emotional, spiritual, and behavioral natures that project his identity in relation to Nature and that instill into his expression the meaning he abstracts from his experience and institutes in his arts. Even his most abstract processes of sequential thought, even his most psychic or spiritual extension outside physical relationships, are bounded by and put into expression through devices conjured from and congruent with impressions of experience-meaning. Experience has meaning only in relation to man and man's ability to comprehend and apprehend experience-meaning; meaning is man-centered because only man has developed the sophisticated devices to express, record, and preserve experience outside the limits of genetic memory and to develop the

169

arts that may transmit experience-meaning from one being to another or from one age or place to another without the limitations of biological inheritance or environmental determination. Though we do not deny the possibility of biological inheritance of abstract wisdom, we do maintain that through his arts, a non-biological function, man may pass his wisdom beyond biological barriers and share it with anyone capable of responding apprehensively and comprehensively to his expression. Not only may the physical form of art be transmitted, but also the abstract wisdom inherent in the structured conditions and impulses of the work of art may be transmitted, and the memory of man may transcend, through his arts, all the physical and material properties of man that must decay in the evolutionary processes of Nature establishing her perpetual and perpetuating balance. It is his arts that enable man to accumulate knowledge and to preserve it from one time to another, to share his wisdom and to perpetuate his identity. For art to function so, there must be a communal understanding, a communal meaning, a communal experience; otherwise there will be no perpetuation, no sharing, no preserving, no accumulating of experience-meaning, and consequently there will be no evolutionary progress, only a static chaos of "different meanings for different people" or an intellectual litter of only partly formed ideas being foisted off as authoritative interpretive truth to disguise the ignorance that substitutes "my meaning" for "its experience-meaning" in relation to art. The ethic-aesthetic of Nature's elementary functional processes must be the model for artistic processes if art is to serve other than a merely topical utilitarian purpose, for art is founded in the functions of Nature in being and essence and if the conditions of Nature are violated there is no permanence or perpetuation.

Artistic fidelity and integrity and responsive fidelity and integrity, the being and essence of the natural ethic-aesthetic, require a compatability, a congruent conformity between the experience-meaning inherent in the work of art and the meaning attributed to the work by the audience receptor. The work cannot function as a record, as a preserver of wisdom, as an accumulator of experience-meaning if it has different meanings for different receptors and if its experiential substance is responded to in either an excessive or a deficient manner. Here, as in Nature, excess and deficiency function as crimes against ethics and aesthetics, against truth and beauty, against what is as opposed to what might be, against the evidence of the work as compared to the opinion of the audience receptor; and the substance of wisdom, of experience-meaning, is prostituted by ignoramuses who excuse their ineptitude and ignorance by averring that a work has "different meanings for different people." A genuine work of art has its own unique experience-meaning; what should be said is the responders have different degrees of ignorance, of ability, to apprehend the real meaning of a work of art. A genuine work of art does not have "different meanings for different people"; it has in its audience different degrees of ignorance and stupidity as well as different degrees of responsive ethic-aesthetic sensitivity, perceptivity, and receptivity; and art must not be allowed to be a scapegoat by persons who would use it and the "mystery" attributed to it as a means of celebrating their own ineffectuality. The natural demands of Nature's ethic-aesthetic must transfer from Nature to art to audience receptor, and it must be a prime consideration in receptor reincarnation of experience-meaning.

Ethic-aesthetics, derived from Nature and sustaining the integrity and fidelity of art and maintaining the inherent quality of Nature in responsive reincarnation of experience as a sophisticated natural function in man's relationships with gods, man, nature, or abstract ideas, must be the base upon which is built the whole descriptive structure of analysis, interpretation, understanding, appreciation, learning, and entertainment if there is to be positive value attributed to art as a functional representation of man's place amid the conditions and impulses of the world that is his. God, man, nature, idea: these are all functions of Nature or of man's impressions of Nature, sophisticated by the devices of transmission and retention and made complex by the differentiating processes of man's ingenuity and the variability of responsive natures. But they are qualities of Nature, however abstract and immaterial they are made to seem through the operation of man's responsive natures and man's ability to extend meaning beyond the limits of material or physical properties or sensory perceptions. Man's responsive natures transcend material objectivity, they transmute sensory impression into immaterial concepts, and they too often attempt to regulate natural and infinite function with topically transient conventions and prescriptions derived from immaterial concepts rather than from determination of the validity of the immaterial concept by testing it against the ethic-aesthetic principles of its source, Nature. Behavioral principles in the unique world of man, and in man's arts, must be a translation of natural principles into the artificial order of man's conventions rather than an infusion of the artificial orders into man's impressions of natural principles.

Meaning derives from ethic-aesthetic experiences which are the bases for the order and form essential to the structure of conditions that provide the impulses of re-experience to be translated into the impressions that constitute experience-meaning, and they are the internal and eternal properties of Nature. Man, too, is both an internal and an eternal property of Nature so long as Nature tolerates his particular processes as an integral function of Nature. Man's arts are man-nature creations to express his functional relationships just as man is a Nature-nature creation to express her sentiently functional relationships and processes; but man-nature is merely a sophisticated definition of a particular Nature-nature identity, a superlative in the comparative responsive natures of mineral-nature, animal-nature, god-nature, idea-nature, man-nature, because it is man-nature that has the qualities of sentience allowing representational definition of itself and the other identities of Nature. Man-nature should differentiate among material, nonmaterial, submaterial, and supramaterial substances, but too often man's fallibility causes him to confuse qualities or conditions or impulses and to attribute the qualities of one to another. In so doing he disguises the real, natural identities of each and creates a reversal of natural cause and effect relationships in responsive impressions of conditions and impulses. Thus man is often led to impose artificial conventions on natural processes and to judge natural processes in terms of that which is derivative rather than in terms of that which is contributive. This reversal of identities confuses and misleads; it creates obscurity and "mystery." It substitutes man's fancy and his error for evidential experience, and it presents erroneous impression as experience-meaning.

The fallibility of man's intellectually responsive nature creates topically limited instruments for measuring the infinite relative conditions of man's associational impulses in the tangible and intangible relationships he has with Nature, the world that is his as a responsive physical, mental, emotional, spiritual, and behavioral experience-meaning. The internal and integral function of man as an essential of Nature precludes the validity of externalization of his processes either in direct associational responses to the conditions of Nature or in the expression of his impressions of experience in Nature—physical, mental, emotional, spiritual, or behavioral—from which he draws the inferences that become the meaning of his experience, even when he provides tangible, material representational devices to record immaterial relative decisions or impressions. When man forgets that he is an internal, integral functional quality of Nature and attempts to impose his will on the integrity of Nature, as an externally impositional substance of man's concoction that is nonessential to natural functionality, he creates a discordant imbalance in natural processes that can lead only to excess or deficiency disruptive of the affinity of man with his source and conductive of distorted and corrupted ethic-aesthetic expression of experience-meaning.

Causal identification in Nature is essential to the determining of effectual excellence in the substantial form of expression termed *art*, and causal identification in art is essential to determining of effectual validity in audience apprehension of the experience-meaning transmitted by art to the responsive and retentive faculties of its receptors. There is no effect without its cause; causal-effectual relativity is the first principle of human-nature perception; it is the principle that establishes the natural balance between act and nonact, thought and nonthought, sense and non-sense, meaning and nonmeaning; in function it creates the primary conditions that are termed experience and from which all meaning is derived as products of experience. The complexities of cause and effect in the conditions and impulses of Nature are the sources of all conflict, all motive, all inspiration, all aspiration—all apathy, all complacency, all hopelessness, all inaction. But these complexities are of natural origin and of natural order, and as such they are subject to the natural principles of ethic-aesthetics. It is therefore incumbent upon man—artist, critic, and audience—to determine and identify not only the causal-effectual relationships of the impulses that activate all his responsive impressions, but also to identify the principles that effect the determining influences in his expression or reception of impression so that he may evaluate the validity and effectiveness of the natural or substantial form experience that subjects him to experience-meaning and evokes his responses. In the natural order, the ethic-aesthetic order of cause and effect, the first consideration is for experience-meaning; the second consideration is for the means and manners of transmission of the experience-meaning. What is transmitted is more important than the vehicle used to transmit it, but the vehicle is essential to transmission. In art the one cannot function without the other; there is no meaning to experience if experience-meaning is not transmitted, but there is no worth in the vehicle of transmission if it transmits nothing. In the best of art the vehicle not only transmits the experience-meaning, it also enhances it, presents it in its most effective manner to intensify the impressions emanating from it; but it must carry a causal substance of experiential conditions and impulses before it can effect a meaningful impression of natural validity, no matter how beautiful the external appearance of the vehicle. Beauty, natural beauty or artistic beauty, is inherent in the internal substance of Nature and representation of Nature; it is not an externally superimposed ornamentation or a superficial surface gilding of natural substance, nor is it an artificial coloring of a natural object. It is a functional complement of the substance of Nature or of art that derives its quality in either instance from an essential fusion of causal-effectual harmony in the relationships of conditions and impulses that make up the experience-meaning of an event, natural or artistic. True beauty, the ethic-aesthetic beauty of Nature and of genuine art, scorns both excess and deficiency in the presentation of the qualities of experience; what is is, and its beauty is intrinsic, native, and natural. In the natural ethic-aesthetic of Nature, the ethic quality is the essential determiner of causal function and the aesthetic quality is the essential determiner of effectual function; in their fusion as ethic-aesthetic, mutually interdependent functional qualities, they form not only the essence of cause-effect harmony, but also the essence of the truth-beauty complex.

Art is a translation; it translates experience into expression, into substantial form; and, if the principles of the ethic-aesthetic integrity and fidelity are not adhered to in the translation, the translation will not be a re-creation, either in substance or in form, of the original experience from which it derives or extends. The art of translating experience into expression requires minute attention in the selection of equivalences that have the suggestive characteristics to convey the semblance of the substance of experience and to mold it into a new or different material substance without mutilating the experience-meaning of its evocative impression. Man becomes an artist only when he is capable of evoking, with his substantial form representation, expression of impressions that have a natural affinity with the conditions and impulses of natural experience and that have evolved out of the principles evidenced by Nature as the focus and perspective of natural order and that have taken on the expressive reality of re-created experience as a faithful translation of natural derivation from the fusion of impressions of experience in the conscious and subconscious nature of the artist. In addition, man becomes an artist only when he is capable of mastering the forms of expression required by the substance of the conditions and impulses being structured into the substantial expressive form to re-create the experience-meanings that are not unrelated to natural principles of the ethic-aesthetic integrity to which he must submit. The artist is required by Nature to adhere to her principles and to master the materials with which he re-creates conditions suggestively native to Nature; otherwise he is no artist.

Likewise, audience reincarnation of experience-meaning is a translation. An audience, if it is to have genuine appreciation and apprehension of the experience-meaning of art, must translate the total substance, structure of conditions and qualifications of form, of the substantial form into impressions that reincarnate the meaning-experience inherent in the work of art. Such translation requires that the audience bring to the work of art the same principles that gave creative impulse to the artist and that permeated the conditions out of which he structured his art. For valid audience reincarnation of experience-meaning and for interpretive analysis and evaluation of consequences, the same terms and principles that were operative in the substantial form creation must, *ipso facto*, be the terms and principles operative in audience exponent response. Natural ethics denies the right to judge under laws that were inoperative in the commission of that which is to be judged, and natural aesthetics demands that the intrinsic qualities of the object be the source of the impulses of the beautiful rather than that the receptor of impression originate the conditions of beauty, external to the object of scrutiny. Natural order, the order of sense, requires that no variation be made in the sequence of Nature to artist to art to audience transmission of impressions of conditions and impulses and the ethic-aesthetic principles that govern their validity. Any rearrangement in the sequence and any imposition of externalized or topicalized principles, other than those governing modes and manners of expression, distort the principles of the ethic-aesthetic and extort from Nature and from art their primary merits, the integrity and fidelity that make of them substances of potential perpetual experience-meaning, of experiential pleasure and comprehensible response.

Experience-meaning is an intrinsic quality of the impulses put in motion by the fusion of conditions making up the structure of the substantial form of art, and the principles of ethics and aesthetics native to the source of those conditions in Nature are the determinants of the order and of the subsequent validity of the impulses as they activate submissive responses in the receptive natures of an audience. But the receptive natures, the responsive states, of man are no less appealed to by the extrinsic qualities of the substantial form of art, the devices of transmission, of translation, of experience into impression evoking forms; and there is a degree of topicality, of time and place convention, insinuated into the devices of transmission by the processes of social and institutional evolution of manners, styles, modes, and forms. The most fitting expression of an experience-meaning will, because of the nature of the devices used to translate experience-meaning into expressive form, incorporate extracorporeal substance into the nature of the initiating and natively impermanent experience-meaning (considering the primary experience as the corpus of the substantial form) and thereby, through the external imposition of substitutional devices of expression for the primary experience, create an interrelationship of substance and form, with form a contributing but subservient instrument of presentation, of expression, and a matter of secondary and peripheral consideration in evaluative response. Out of the fusion of substance and form, the merging of the qualities of the primary substance and the secondary device of transmission, the intrinsic and extrinsic qualities of substance and expression, will emerge such tertiary qualities as tone, atmosphere, style, or color, which by complementary association intensify, enhance, emphasize, and expand experiential impressions and provide means of qualifying or modifying focus and perspective. Although the devices of transmission develop artificially, independently, and peripherally as intellectual equivalences of that which they represent, and although they evolve into sophisticated and often precious affectations of expression, they are still the means by which man preserves his experience, transmits his impressions, and perpetuates his understanding of experience-meaning. Therefore, evaluative response, in the best of ethical practices and aesthetic apprehension, must take into account the time and place context they represent. Otherwise the expression of one time or place will be judged by the topical conventions of another; and because there is no absolute conformity to natural progressive order in the evolution of artificial devices and because of the whimsicalities of topical intervention of faddist or cultist modes and manners, the attribution of the particularities of one context to another will most certainly lead to misapprehension of the experience-meaning of the work of another time or place. Submission to experience-meaning must include comprehension of the contextual use of the devices of transmission in the terms of their own topical functionality, not in terms of audience-oriented topicality of meaning, aesthetic comprehension, or environmental experience.

Artistic beauty is, then, that quality manifest in the total impression of the experience-meaning re-created in substantial form by man the artist and subjected to scrutiny by an informed audience unbiased by extra-artistic peculiarities and considerations and unprejudiced by topical criteria. Artistic truth is that quality manifest in the presentation of conditions structured into the total substantial form of the experience-meaning presentation and evocative of the impulse to respond to the conditions of the presentation in their merged and fused nature obeying the principles of Nature's ethic-aesthetic, limited only by the finiteness of man the artist's experience, meaning, imagination, and grasp of the complexities of artistic adherence to principles of both topical and universal significance in the structuring of a new experience-meaning. Artistic integrity is the fusion of artistic beauty and artistic truth within the limits of the media of expression in substantial form and the mean-tolerance balance of Nature's ethic-aesthetic principle, with the best possible use being made of the materials of the particular medium to re-create the most intense response-demanding impulse that the substance and the substantial form will permit or require.

Beauty, then, will not be merely a matter of current or topical definition; it will also be that quality evocative of response outside the bounds of topical time and place. Truth will not be merely the expression of complimentary similitude bounded by time and place; it will also be the complementary expression of experience-meaning that is the communal meaning and experience of universal sentience. Integrity will not only be the adherence to topical or biased interpretation; it will also be the infinite variety and complexity of man's natures merged and fused and selected by the artistic genius of their re-creator in substantial form, making best use of the limited tools and materials available for his essay at putting into transmissible form the substance of his apprehension of artistic excellence. Beauty, truth, and integrity merge and fuse, assimilate and synthesize, in art, man's re-creative expression of experience-meaning.

Artistic beauty derives from the artist's concern—his will, inclination, or compulsion—to perpetuate experience-meaning in the most suitable manner, using the devices of transmission in the most effective way, and creating the means of most efficient reincarnation of the experience-meaning in the receptor-responsive faculties of an audience. Derived naturally from Nature, which is the source-impulse and the inspiration for the conditions that go into the structure of substance of art, artistic creation of beauty is consonant with the beauty found in Nature, and both natural beauty and artistic beauty depend upon responsive apprehension of the qualities that may be said to please the responsive natures of a receptor of impression. To be beautiful an object must adhere to the natural ethical principles of incorruptible soundness, of unimpaired and perfect condition, of wholeness and completeness, principles which establish the integrity of the object, the perfection of its substance. In addition, artistic beauty must evidence fidelity in its representational function, harmony of the representational devices with the substance of conditions fused into the composite whole of the substantial form to evoke impulses to impression that elicit responses proportioned among the responsive states of man's receptor faculties in consonance with man's cognizance of his function in the nature of the world that is his. Art, to be beautiful, must also show an excellence of form dependent on the genius of the artist to adapt the devices of representational form to the structure of substance in his re-creation of experience-meaning. These three qualities—the ethical quality of integrity, the aesthetic quality of fidelity, and the artistic quality of structural genius—are, in art, inseparable and indispensable; for an object to have beauty these qualities must be fused into the whole of the object, must be incorporated and integrated into the entirety of the structure of the substantial form, and must be capable of assimilation by the response-receptor faculties of an audience to such an extent that the audience may reincarnate the experience-meaning of the art presence in substantially the same manner and form as it was for the artist as he structured conditions into the substantial form of re-created experience-meaning.

Artistic genius—the genius of adaptation of device and the genius of translation of experience into form, the power to transform the transitory into the permanent and the abstract into the concrete, the intellect to transfigure experience into meaning, the knowledge to select conditions from Nature to create the impressions and the impulses from which experience-meaning may be reincarnated, the wisdom to retain without mutilation the ethic-aesthetic principles of Nature that provide the essential bases of all worthy and valid re-creation of experience—artistic genius is not just skill or intellectual imposition of external qualities. Artistic genius is also a matter of internals, of compatibility with the conditions of Nature and the impulses of those conditions, ethical and aesthetic, that signify the perpetuity of Nature in evolutionary process and give to art the permanence potential of man's impressions of his place in the infinity of natural affinities. It is a matter of submission, of submitting the whole of man's responsive natures to the qualities of conditions and impulses in Nature, that provides the substance of man's experience-meaning; and, by the nature of their function in the ethic-aesthetic order of Nature, these conditions and impulses determine the most effective manner and form of expression—translation, transformation, transfiguration—as re-creation of experience-meaning capable of reincarnation as substance-condition and substance-impulse of significant re-experience. The artist must not only be capable of adapting forms and devices to give expression to experience-meaning, he must also be capable of submissive adaptation of himself to experience as a means of apprehending the meaning of experience and comprehending the demands that the substance of experience makes on the modes of representational expression. Without the capability of adaptation and the capacity for submission there is no artistic genius; only skill and craft are possible, and skill and craft alone are insufficient for genuine artistry. Intense responsive natures, exceptional sensitivity and perceptivity, singularly capable receptive states, and superb will, inclination, or compulsion to re-create the impressions formed by submissive apprehension of experience-meaning are essential to genuine artistry—and to the most effectual of reincarnate experiences.

For art to persist, to persevere, artist and audience must exercise diligence in their adherence to the ethic-aesthetic principles that give impulse to the substance of art experience and that provide the essential means of separating the universally valid from the topically curious work of art expression and impression. A low level of art, strictly topical art, may subsist as an object of curiosity; but great art exists as an ultimate monument to man's genius for re-creating the meaning of experience with integrity and fidelity. The beautiful, the usable, and the pleasurable are inseparably fused in great art; they remain separately identifiable or of lesser quality in lesser art, and each exists only for its own sake in craft.

Man is a sounding board for Nature, an instrument upon whom and through whom Nature plays the symphonies and songs that are her experience-meaning, the impulses to all the experiences and meanings and feelings and responses capable of being elicited, consciously or subconsciously, from Nature's most superior instrument, man. But for man to be an artist, the perpetuator of Nature's music, he must be most perfectly in tune with Nature and with Nature's ethic-aesthetic principles of integrity and fidelity, of mean-tolerance, excess-deficiency laws of balance and order. Not all men have the capacity, the capability, the will, the inclination, or the compulsion to harmonize with, to be attuned to, the supreme creative source, Nature. Man out of harmony with his source and the impulses and principles of that source cannot be an artist; he can only be a negator of artistry in either the re-creative or the reincarnative function of expression in substantial form or in reincarnating response to the experience-meaning of the substantial form re-creation of experience-meaning. If man, artist or audience, is not in harmony with the functional processes of Nature, his art and his response to art will be discordant, aberrant, perverted; and though he may topically establish a fad for discordance, aberrance, or perversion, the integrity of Nature, the ethical and aesthetic balance in Nature and man's ultimately pliant submission to the demands of natural evolution and the natural principles of adaptation or extinction, will eliminate the imbalances of excess and deficiency and retain only that which has maintained the universality of natural principle. One era, one age, one topical faddism may strike a sour note in the infinite symphony of Nature; but Nature has means to correct her errors as well as the errors imposed upon her by the dissonant and aberrant and perverse behavior of her subject parts. Nature, in keeping with the natural principles of balance, ethic-aesthetic, will not long tolerate imbalance in the representational records of her evolution, the expression of man's concern for and identity with the processes by which Nature organically moves through the events and conditions and impulses by which she brings herself to the apprehensive responsiveness of man, the one creature capable of recording her experiences and translating them into substantial form other than the forms Nature herself supplies. Aberration and dissonance and perversity may flourish sporadically in man's arts, his transformations of experience into meaning, because man's ingenuity and his capacity for error and his curious search for the new and different may at times lead him to establish concepts and forms and meanings out of affinitive context with the processes of natural principle, and often his comprehension of the relation he bears to natural processes will be inadequate and his expression of impression of that relationship will be deficient in the substantial form into which he infuses his experience-meaning. Nature, in such instances, inexorable in her purgation of the excessive or the deficient, through time sweeps the dross of excess and deficiency from her records and from the conscious apprehension of man. But man, if he will, may, by diligent adherence to the natural principles of Nature's ethic-aesthetic, lessen the duration of unnatural divergence from natural order in his arts.

Man, artist and audience, must realize that in violating the sanctity of Nature he denies his own nature the order and the truth and beauty which is his inheritance; and that he enslaves himself to error, anarchistic processes, regression, and artlessness by his failure to submit to the principles of natural order. Man must substitute submissiveness to natural principles for the permissiveness that he allows himself in his relationship with Nature or he will become extinct, as have other qualities of Nature whose overly specialized functions have led to excessive or deficient practices in the evolutionary order of natural processes. Man may attribute his superiority and his principles to deity, to his own creativeness, or to chance; but at the level of perceptive awareness, evidenced in the responsive accumulation of his impressions in substantial form, man must function within the limits imposed by natural environment of substance and principle, experience and meaning, to which he is exposed actually or vicariously; and his experience-meaning is environmentally limited in transmissibility by the qualities he possesses as a creature of Nature, sensitive and perceptive and receptive and expressive. Only figuratively may man go outside natural principle for experience-meaning; and even then the forms taken in expression of figurative impression are dependent on natural

responder, receptor, retainer, and expressor qualities for transmission, and man still cannot escape his essential nature as a
creature deriving both his impressions of experience and his
expression of meaning from association with natural experiences of which he is a functional part and from which he
receives the impulses that move him to attempt to re-create
his sense or feeling of associational relativity with the processes of natural evolution of experience-meaning, natural or
imaginative.

The imaginative quality of man's genius, while at times it
seems unrelated to actual experience, is grounded in the fused
and assimilated and synthesized accumulation of experiences
and conditions that give impulse to impressions that often have
no seeming relationship to reality. The qualification and modification that experience-impressions undergo through fusion
and merging within the receptor-retainer faculties may create
images and senses and impressions and meanings quite out of
the context of reality even though the essential qualities of those
images and senses and impressions and meanings are scattered
among the multitude of conditions that provide experience. But
once the impressionable faculties of man consciously or unconsciously bring together an accumulation of divergent and
disassociated impressions and out of them fashions a new combination of conditions, man creates out of the diverse raw materials of experience a new experience potential with a new
experience-meaning inherent in the impulses contained within
it. In substantial form the new experiences may then evoke
responses that change the experience potential to experience
actuality and provide the source conditions and impulses for a
reincarnation of experience-meaning that is the reality of experience for an audience even though the initial impulse to
create the substantial form of the impression is seemingly only
a product of the artist's imagination. Imagination, as all other
responsive qualities of man, is a product of Nature and is given

185

impulse only by experience; but it is this imagination that experiments with combinations of conditions and out of them and associations of combinations finds the impulses that lead man to new ideas, new wisdom, new arts, and progress—and to error, ignorance, and regression if he fails to pay heed to the ethic-aesthetic demands of Nature inherent in the conditions he employs to create his imaginative improvisation of impression. The ethic-aesthetic qualities of Nature do not inhibit imaginative and creative art; they give order and direction and provide the natural means for control of its potentially unnatural effect. Without the restraint of the natural ethic-aesthetic, art would be chaotic, without order, without form; the principles of art would be anarchistic, untransmissible; and experience-meaning of art would remain with the artist, not re-created in the work of art, and incapable of being reincarnated by the audience. Imagination is conducive to excess and deficiency because of the fallibility of man's faculties; but Nature, the ethic-aesthetic of Nature and of man's dependence on Nature to establish his place in Nature, will find the balance that makes creative imagination the impulse of evolution and invention and provides the good and the bad in topical environments of man.

Imagination is impulsed by Nature—in the sense that all experience, all conditions, and all impulses eliciting response from man and capable of man's apprehension are found in or derive from man's hereditary and environmental situation in the world that is his—and functions as an adjunct of the responsive qualities man evidences in formulating and forming devices for translation of the substance of his nonmaterial experience into substantial form. Imagination is an experiential extension of the impulses of conditions stimulating the responsive states of man to go beyond the obviously perceptible attributes of an experience into the tangential impressions of substance relative to that experience and out of the fusion of tangential impressions deriving a new experience-meaning and a new substance for impression-forming impulses. But no matter how remotely-seeming is the product of imagination from the substance of environmental reality, it will be found that not only is the substance of the imagined condition derived from the experience of man in the nature of his world, but also the means of translating the substance of that condition into images that may transmit its experience-meaning to a receptor derive from a naturally developed impulse in man to find a communal expression for his most esoterically developed extension of experiential imagination and tangential impression. Man may attribute to gods the seeming mystery of his imagination, but imagination is an experience, and the experiences of man relate him directly to the world that is his in his own nature and in the Nature of his surroundings; and his responses are governed by the qualities of the natural responsive creature that he is and are subject to the ethic-aesthetic laws that permeate the evolutionary functions of natural processes in the conditions that touch him.

It has been said that only the good and the beautiful should be the province of art. This is true, but true only when the good and the beautiful are defined in terms of the integrity and fidelity of natural ethics and aesthetics. It is not true when the good and the beautiful are defined in terms of topically faddistic values limited by time and place environments to the promotion of unnatural or imbalanced conditions relative to the standards imposed by Nature in the perpetual propagation of her evolutionary identity. All experience, all meaning, is the proper province of art when the ethic-aesthetic standards of the excellence of Nature are the impulses providing the will, inclination, or compulsion to re-create experience-meaning and when the substantial form of art transmits that experience-meaning to the receptive faculties of an audience. The "good" and the "beautiful" are terms too often used to describe qualities arrogated to themselves by topically determined environments to laud the artificial codes and concepts that are the unique consequence of individual environmental conditions. When so used, the "good" and the "beautiful" take on as many meanings as there are environments that attempt to glorify their own unique qualities, and there is no communal comprehension of the meaning of "good" or of "beautiful" outside topically faddist or cultist conventions. It is only when "good" and "beautiful" are ascriptions to the functions and forms of nontopical conditions as evidenced in the processes of the natural ethic-aesthetic that they can have a universally valid comprehensibility. So comprehended, "good" and "beautiful" are descriptive terms of the ethic-aesthetic of natural order and balance and have specific meaning as a communal experience of natural integrity and fidelity emanating from and established by the rightness of natural processes as they are apprehended by the impressionable nature of man. Consequently, "good" and "beautiful" are only coincidentally valid descriptive terms when the topical concepts of "good" and "beautiful" accord with the natural processes which are the "good" and the "beautiful." When those natural processes are at variance with topical definitions of "good" and "beautiful," the function of Nature must take precedence over the artificial sophistications of topical environments; otherwise the part becomes superior to the whole, fragments are better than entire and sound objects, and impairment is more to be desired than perfection. Man is only a part of Nature, albeit an important part, and as such he is inferior to the whole of the Nature which includes him only as a part. Out of his imagination man may find the means to adapt certain qualities of Nature to his unique specifications, but that only when Nature accords him the privilege of altering her parts within the tolerance limits of excess or deficiency. What man impairs in the alteration, Nature destroys. That is, the "good" and the "beautiful" in Nature function even when they go against the will or the artificial codes of man's topicality. Nature allows man degrees of variance between excess and deficiency to provide range for his imagination and his adaptive inventiveness, but she will not tolerate a degree of either excess or deficiency that would destroy her evolutionary processes or circumvent her ethic-aesthetic practices or prerogatives.

"Good" and "beautiful" are descriptive terms of natural validity only when the experience-meanings of conditions and impulses being described are consonant with the functions, processes, and principles of Nature in her continuous striking of balance between excess and deficiency, in righting the imbalances that constantly appear as the products of the perpetual change that marks the evolution of Nature's forms and substances. They, "good" and "beautiful," are prescriptive terms when their experience-meaning derives from the conventions of topical environments, from institutionalized versions of man's associational conventions relative to the artificial or nonnatural concepts he invents to explain or protect the identity of his topically limited "truths." Descriptive "good" and "beautiful" are in and emanate from whatever Nature is and does. Prescriptive "good" and "beautiful" are external labels designating a topically limited value judgment that is subject to the fallibility of man's immediate environmental experience-meaning resources. In other terms, the descriptive "truth" is what is; the prescriptive "truth" is what it seems to be and what is hoped for, and it is subject to error-impulses by its limited time-place-convention environment. "Good" and "beautiful" are generally separate terms in prescriptive analysis; but in the descriptive sense of natural origin they are inseparable and synonymous, each qualifying and enhancing the other as they fuse into the function of the ethic-aesthetic of natural process. The "good" in Nature is what Nature is; the "good" in topical environments is what man deems proper to protect the identity of his conceptions whether or not those conceptions violate the integrity of natural ethical order and progression. The "beautiful" in

Nature is also what Nature is; the "beautiful" in topical environments is what man deems proper in his institutionally conditioned definitions of beauty whether or not those definitions violate the fidelity of natural aesthetic harmony. Prescriptive definition goes before the fact of re-creation in substantial form in interpretive analysis, and it is an artificial topical imposition upon the re-creative impulse as well as a matter of prejudgment of the art process and a conditioner of audience response. Descriptive definition is an after the fact comparative device that is determined not by the whims of topical convention but by its inherent quality of condition in Nature, and it is a source of the re-creative impulse rather than an imposition upon it. Description judges on the achievement in presenting the innate ethic-aesthetic qualities evidenced in the substantial form as they accord with natural principles, rather than on the artificial conceits of topical arrogance and imposition as does prescription. Identification with Nature and the principles that guide Nature, the source of experience-meaning for man, is the only common ground for all men upon which they may construct the monumental substantial form of art that will have meaning beyond the quagmires of topical environments. The "good" and the "beautiful," the "truths" of universal proportion, the "art" of man's natural evolution, all must have a common identity, an apprehensible commonality of source, a synonymity of comprehensibility despite the topical analogies used in modes of expression and manners of reception, if art is to function as a medium of memory and pleasure. And that sole common ground, that singular identifiable universal experience of man, that common denominator of man's comprehensive and apprehensive natures, that communal source of responsive faculties, is Nature—the Nature of man's sources, existent and subsistent, and the infinite environment of his evolutionary experience-meaning—good and beautiful, the truth of what is, the impulse of all that may validly be termed art.

Ethics, the "good," and aesthetics, the "beautiful," are not external impositions on either Nature or art. They are the internal qualities infused throughout Nature and art and inherently fused in Nature and art by the relativity of conditions and impulses that provide the experience-meaning of an apprehended experience in Nature or an apprehended experience reincarnated from the substantial form of experience re-created in the work of art. Neither Nature nor art requires the externality of divine nascence as a consideration in the apprehension of the natural or the art experience; nor do they require it in the comprehension of natural or artistic meaning. Each is its own substance and its own experience-meaning despite external curiosity concerning its ultimate origins and the nature of the impulses that antedate the experience itself. This is not to say that antecedent experience, experience of conditions and impulses predating the substance of the conditions and impulses of the immediate experience, may not be revealed in the immediate experience of either Nature or art. It is to say, however, that speculation concerning antecedent experience is not essential to the apprehension or the appreciation of the immediate experience unless that antecedent experience is, by the nature of its inclusion within the substance of the immediate experience, made to be an essential condition of the immediate experience and of the subsequent experience-meaning of that immediate experience. Generally, then, antecedent experience and identification of antecedent experience are peripheral matters of scholarly sleuthing rather than matters of immediate responsive apprehension and appreciation of either experience in Nature or re-created experience in art or reincarnate experience in response to the substantial form that is art. The valid re-creation of experience in substantial form and the reincarnation of that experience in responsive reception of impression are functions of the will, inclination, or compulsion of the artist and of the audience, resulting from the immediacy of experience, not from

191

speculation about antecedents; and the natural commitment of man is to the nature of his experience-meaning, not to artificial externalities of nonsubstantial theories. This is not to say that antecedent experience, the generally peripheral matters of relative conditions that so often excite the curiosity of scholars, must be excluded from consideration or analysis of a work of art; whenever that antecedent experience may contribute to the comprehension of the conditions that fuse to form the total impression and experience of the work of art, the peripheral scholarship is an essential to the establishment of the knowledge necessary to give meaning to particular topical conditions that may otherwise remain outside the total apprehensive natures in audience response, and without the peripheral knowledge erroneous impression or reaction might be formed and might lead to inadequacy of comprehension and distortion of experience-meaning.

Obviously, because art uses the devices and the limited comprehensible topical modes of transmission that will convey experience-meaning to its contemporary audience, the artist may unconsciously take for granted that the audience will be aware of or familiar with the significance of certain topical allusions or conventions he may employ in the creation of the substantial form; and in so doing, but without intent, he may make scholarly recapitulation of antecedent or peripheral experience to be an essential of subsequent audience apprehension of the no longer topical conditions that give impulse to the focal experience-meaning of the work or to the perspective range of impressions inherent in the work and emanating from it only to the informed apprehensive nature of its audience. For example, comprehension of the topical implications of royal election as an antecedent experience focusing impulses in Hamlet to respond to conditions in the particular way that is his, is essential to the total apprehension of the experience-meaning of *Hamlet*. So also, comprehension of the implications of details of canon law in the Gertrude-Claudius relationship is an antecedent experience that must be taken into account in reincarnating the conditions that determine the socio-religio-political rottenness with which Hamlet must contend in the setting of conditions and impulses that compel him to respond in the way that he does. This is to say that topical reference, antecedent experience, and peripheral conditions must be taken into account whenever total apprehension of experience-meaning depends on the comprehension of their import in a particular work of art; but whenever their definitive interpolation is not essential to apprehension of the total experience-meaning potential of the work, their inclusion in interpretive analysis goes beyond the requirements of the work and becomes an excess in audience response, violating the natural principles of ethic-aesthetics. By the same token, failure to include comprehension of the import of topical reference, antecedent experience, and peripheral conditions essential to the total apprehension of the experience-meaning potential of a work would be a deficiency, violating the natural principles of ethic-aesthetics. But topical reference, antecedent experience, and peripheral conditions must be comprehended in the context of the understanding or comprehension of them that was the artist's understanding or comprehension, not that of any other person at any other time. The significance of canon law in the Gertrude-Claudius relationship interpretation must be apprehended in the same total sense that Shakespeare understood and used it, not in the sense of a canon law scholar's definitive interpretation of theological implications. The scholarly interpretation, although it might be completely accurate as far as theological implications are concerned, might be totally inaccurate so far as Shakespeare's experience-meaning use of canon law is concerned, and in such a case the imposition of scholarly interpretive implications as a condition in the apprehension of experience-meaning recreated in *Hamlet* or reincarnated in audience receptor natures

193

would be an excess and a violation of the natural ethic-aesthetic principle.

Adherence to the natural principles of ethic-aesthetics as an essential of art does not, however, preclude use of substance that is not in conformity with those principles in the conditions that make up the structure of the substantial form. Indeed, conflict is an essential of action, of dramatic interplay, and conflict requires variance in opposing impulses. Balance may be achieved only when equilibrium is established between contrary impulses; and there can be no action, no movement, no conflict, except when there is disharmony in the variance between excess and deficiency in the meeting of impulses and in the proportional relativity of conditions and impulses as they come together to form new conditions and impulses. Balance, the ethical focus and the aesthetic perspective, is not an exact distance or weight relationship between two object impulses; rather it is an ebb and flow relativity of complexly associated, or disassociated, impulses as they vary in intensity in the impressions they evoke within the receptor natures of man in Nature as he relates them to the merits of their object. Natural evolution depends upon that relative variability; without it there would be no change, no progress, no regression; there would be only a static, impulseless similitude of experiences that would excite no response, create no impressions, and demand no re-creation or reincarnation. Just as it takes two parts of hydrogen combined with one part oxygen to create the equilibrium, the balance in Nature of two conditions that may be identified as a third condition, water, so it may take varying degrees of other conditions and their impulses to strike a balance that is identifiable as a disposition of natural, or artistic, ethic-aesthetics. Balance, then, is a matter of relative proportion of conditions and impulses effecting a change that is still a product of natural process and a function of the ethic-aesthetic principles of Nature.

The conditions in art combine to create in the substantial form the conditions and the impulses that are not just hydrogen and oxygen in their separately identifiable natural substance forms but are also water as a new substance of experience-meaning. Water, though a condition derivative from the conditions oxygen and hydrogen, performs quite another function than do the separate elements from which it derives. So too in art, condition C, which is a derivative of the combination or fusion of conditions A and B, performs quite another function than do the separate conditions of A and B and is identifiable as a new condition with new impulses emanating from it. Condition A may be quite out of harmony with condition B in matters of any measurable ethical or aesthetic principle; but to form the proportionate relationship with condition B that will through fusion create condition C as a balance or focus, which is the ethical state of what is in Nature, imbalances are necessary between A and B as separately identifiable conditions or impulses (at least in proportion) to cause the change in the resultant conditions and impulses that is the functional evolution of Nature or of impression of the experience-meaning inherent as potential in conditions of Nature. Balance, as an operable function, requires varying degrees of imbalance to provide the impulse that makes it operative or evolutionary. A child is an evolutionary, ethical, balance between the conditions of the sperm and the egg, but without both the sperm and the egg, imbalances separately, and without the coming together of the particularities of both, there would be no child, no substantial form identifiable as a product of the conditions that make its being possible. The impressions derived from a work of art are the children of the conditions in the work and are dependent solely for their being on the fusion of parental conditions and the qualities those parental conditions, together with their associated impulses, allow, require, or disallow.

The integrity of Nature, the natural functional processes of

195

evolutionary ethic-aesthetic order re-created in substantial form displaying the fidelity of natural balance and proportion of ethic-aesthetic principles identifiable in the work of Nature, of necessity not only permits, but also requires or disallows, divergence in the separate parts of Nature from the balance Nature maintains in the harmonized fusion and interrelationships of those parts together. But Nature disallows the continuance of any condition of excess or deficiency that cannot be made to come into harmony or balance with the conditions that become associated with it. The "good" and the "beautiful" in Nature are the functional balances established by Nature from among conditions that in themselves, separately, may not be "good" or "beautiful"; but in the juxtaposition of their qualities and the fusion of their impulses they become "good" or "beautiful" because they are what is right for Nature in her self-perpetuating processes. So too in art the "good" and the "beautiful," if they result from principles founded in the "rightness" of Nature from which all re-creative impulses emanate, may derive from a fusion of conditions that in themselves and taken separately may signify qualities of the "bad" and the "ugly," not only in the prescriptive terms of topical identification, but also in the descriptive terms of natural principles of ethic-aesthetics universally identifiable by their conformity with the apprehensible qualities of natural processes and functions varying from the tolerable mean to the intolerable range of excess and deficiency. The imbalances in Nature, as in art, may well derive from topical disorientation toward the ethic-aesthetic of natural order and result in a momentary disharmony in functionally organic representational expression of impression, or in natural adaptation of natural topography to the exigencies of excess or deficiency and mean seeking imposed upon either the substantial form of Nature herself or on the substantial form of man's impressions of natural experience. In one sense, the excesses and deficiencies then become functions of natural process in the corrective order of natural principle even though they may derive from the disorientation of natural determination through the topical fallibility of human ingenuity; and the "bad" and "ugly," the excesses and deficiencies in terms of prescriptive identification, may well function as conditions and impulses in both Nature and art contrary to the principles of ethic-aesthetics, the descriptive identification from Nature of the "good" and the "beautiful," that seek to establish the evolutionary balance between excess and deficiency. But the "bad" and the "ugly," as descriptive of excess or deficiency in relation to natural principle, may also be the "good" or the "beautiful" in topical prescription, and as such will be the topical determinants of functional experience creating the conditions and impulses of responsive reception and retentive impression at variance with the exigencies of natural order and determining the correlative conditions and impulses essential to the creation of proportion and balance in the natural cause and effect relativity of natural principles to the object conditions and impulses of experience-meaning. Descriptively or prescriptively, the "good" and the "beautiful" and the "bad" and the "ugly" function as conditions and impulses in both Nature and art, providing the substance essential to the striking of balance and the establishing of proportion and order. Without the negative conditions and impulses to balance the positive, there would be no equilibrium, no balance, in the evolutionary processes of Nature; and impulseless, inanimate conditions would prevail without the constant interplay of divergent conditions and impulses creating the new forms and impressions that represent the movement of natural order obeying the principles of natural ethic-aesthetics inherent in the perpetual balancing act of Nature. Instead of the harmonious fusion and merging of conditions to establish experience-meaning beyond the bounds of

197

singularly separate and unrelated conditions, there would be a dreary monotone of impressionless, responseless, meaningless, and static sameness to experience.

The implication here is that the "bad" and the "ugly" as conditions of Nature, and consequently of art, are as essential to the functional processes of natural evolution as are their contraries, the "good" and the "beautiful," though the "good" and the "beautiful," in the natural process, are the end result, the rightness, of the natural ethic-aesthetic. This seeming dichotomy is not really a contradiction in descriptive terms if the "bad" and the "ugly" are understood as the two extremes, excess and deficiency, which must be balanced in relation to what is permitted, required, or disallowed by the object toward which their qualities are disposed and if the balance achieved between these two divergent extremes is recognized as the ethical and aesthetic rightness of natural order, the "good" and the "beautiful" in Nature. Only prescriptively, in topically selective formulaic terms, will there be contradictions, and then only when topical self-justification causes disregard for the naturally inherent affinities of man to the Nature which is the accumulation of the conditions and the impulses of his experience-meaning in the experience that is his world, subjectively and objectively, finitely and infinitely, consciously and unconsciously. The "good" and the "beautiful" depend for their ultimately valid experience-meaning on balance between their excessive and deficient contraries, and so, by comparison and contrast, as well as by identification of natural order, values may be ascribed to the qualities emanating from the functions and processes of natural evolution and translated into the substantial form of impression of experience-meaning as man's artistic expression of "truth." For what is, is truth—the "good" and the "bad," the "beautiful" and the "ugly" functioning under the ethic-aesthetic of natural law. And that law is one law, truth, the fusion of two processes, the ethical and the aesthetic, the

198

rightness of natural process under the aegis of the only arbiter and ultimate determiner of her own conditions and impulses, Nature, in the inexorable integrity of Nature and her fidelity to the principles of functional evolution that are her prerogative and her practice.

Ethics and aesthetics are the dynamics of Nature: the natural impulses to movement, to change, to experience, to meanings; the natural processes by which Nature identifies herself and perpetuates herself; the natural order of form and substance; the natural source of the conditions that are the materials attracting man's responses; the natural lessons in harmonious fusion of qualities, the achievement of balance, establishment of integrity, creation of impression, and development of proportion. Without these qualities of Nature, to be identified and stirred into the conscious and unconscious receptor-retainer faculties of man together with the impressions of experience-meaning he apprehends, there would be no form, no order, no balance, no proportion, no integrity in the behavior of man. And without their essential presence in the works of man there would be no art, no progress, no morality, no meaning to experience and the functional processes of life. There would be only disharmony, imbalance, disorder, distortion, formlessness, separateness, falsity: anarchistic chaos. Art, the nonstatic, non-genetic, nonmortal but substantial form of the memory of man's experience-meaning, must obey the fundamental laws of Nature and adapt to Nature's evolutionary principles of balanced, orderly ethic-aesthetic fusion or suffer the fate of all aberrantly unadaptable conditions in the natural process, extinction of identity, the ultimate manifestation of tragedy, the loss of identity through operation of conditions failing to find the ethic-aesthetic balance in disproportionate fusion of their impulsive qualities.

Ethical and aesthetic art, a derivative of the ethic-aesthetic function of Nature, is the process by which a sentient being puts

199

into substantial form the impulses to real experience-meaning that emerge from the fusion of experience-impressions that has formed within the receptor-retainer faculties of the sentient being in compliance with the laws of natural functionality, taking shape as prescient sources of new experience to be translated from the nonmaterial substances of artistic compulsion into the material substance of artistic expression in substantial form, to become, in turn, the medium of experience-meaning transmission between artist and audience. Artistic prescience is, however, not necessarily a consciously intellectual foreknowledge of the total impression potential of the substantial form as an experience source for its audience; that is, the artist himself may be unaware of the impulsive implications inherent in the totality of the conditions structured into his work and fusing, merging, and synthesizing to form other conditions of different impulsive nature and function; though, even without his conscious intent, these conditions may be conducive to experience-meaning impressions or impulses validly attributable to the work itself as an object source of conditions and impulses demanding response from an audience receptor of impressions. This implies, in the Nature-artist-art-audience hierarchy, a Nature-artist, Nature-art, Nature-audience, artist-art, artist-audience, art-audience complexity of relative associations that qualify and modify, each in its own particular focal perspective, the responsive potential; the sensitivity, perceptivity, receptivity faculties; the will, inclination, and compulsion proclivities; and the submissive abilities and capacities of each sentient or naturally determined entity in the total hierarchy. But art, because it is the product of man's ingenuity in translating experience-meaning into substantial form, relies on the sentient qualities of man to apprehend that experience-meaning—without sentience in the artist there is no functional or valid re-creation of experience in artistic form, and without sentience in an audience there is no reception of experience-meaning by a responsive being. Natural

200

sentience, a quality that man has not invented but one which derives essentially from man's condition as a part of Nature, is the essential prerequisite for both artist and audience to enable them to perform the function, through art, of transmitting human experience-meaning via the medium of the substantial form from the artist to the audience. Both artist and audience are subjects of Nature and of the qualities of sentience Nature gives to each individually, though the sentient prowess of each individual is not identical to that of any other individual, nor is the sentient capacity of any one being identifiable with the sentient capacity of any other being. Consequently, the receptor acumen and responsive acuity of each being will vary in accordance with the natural capacities and abilities of each being and in relation to the natural or the conditioned will, inclination, or compulsion of each to apprehend the experience-meaning potential inherent in any experience, either natural or artistic. The meaning of an experience is there as a potential in any experience, but sentience is required for that potential to emerge as an experience-meaning, and sentience is inoperable whenever will, inclination, or compulsion denies submission to the experience or whenever conditions in the sentient faculties disallow response, reception, or retention to, or of, impulses evocative of responsive impression. It is an obvious fact that sensation does not exist for the insensate or insentient being incapable of receiving the impulses creating sensation; just as obviously experience-meaning cannot exist for a being not capable of apprehending the impulses of experience-meaning that depend on sentience for both their transmission and their reception. Sentience is the capacity, both conscious and unconscious, of being susceptible to and aware of the experientiable impulses emanating from the conditions that make up the Nature of each individual being's world—involving ubiquity, ubiety, and contemporaneity—and creating the necessity of sensory perception. That sentience is determined by the nature of the

201

genetic memory and the experiential conditioning to which each being is uniquely both subject and object in Nature's ethic-aesthetic balancing functionality.

Natural sentience does not imply that man will always respond in a manner compliant with the ethic-aesthetic principles of Nature, nor that his responses, though compelled by his nature as a functional part of Nature, will be in accord with an arbitrarily compulsive pattern in natural evolutionary function. It is the unique prerogative of man's ingenuity, his topical identity, to overstep the bounds of an unyielding natural determinism in his naturally curious experimentation to experience for himself the limits to which he may exercise a role in adapting Nature to his desires or himself to her demands without upsetting the integral balance of natural order to the extent that destruction of man and his works will be the inevitable result of his experimentation. Man, as a part of Nature and as the sentient quality in the functional processes of Nature, is the prime mover in the sophisticated utilization of Nature's resources, including man himself, to create an adaptable evolutionary atmosphere in which he can enjoy the benefits his ingenuity would deem possible or probable in topical definition of utility or of desirability, with the result that oftentimes man is the creator, out of the impulses of his natural inclinations, of the very excesses and deficiencies that cause him discomfort in his striving against the conditions that oppose, in the sense of the natural ethic-aesthetic, the achievement of the balance conducive to his sense of well-being in relation to the conditions of Nature juxtaposed with the conditions of his invention. Consequently, man, as a condition of Nature, may find that his condition is one that must be balanced with a condition contrary to what his topical definition would determine as right or desirable. His enjoyment of and involvement in topical excesses and deficiencies can be only momentary, for ultimately balance must be achieved or the impulse of natural integrity will destroy the excessive or deficient condition despite the exercise of man's ingenuity in de-vising extranatural extensions or sophisticated deployment and substitution of natural conditions to effect a topical contain-ment of natural condition exploitation.

Man's sentient qualities enable him to convert conditions of Nature into forms and substances amenable to his topical taste and sense of utility and to divert natural impulses into forces gratifying to his self-oriented state in Nature, if he does not violate the essential principles of natural order and commit an aberrant act to create conditions beyond the limits of Nature's tolerance, either as excess or as deficiency. Because of his adap-tive ingenuity, the exercise of his sentient qualities and his in-ventive potential, man may hold temporarily in abeyance the integral achievement of natural order by topical substitution of temporary conditions for the universal conditions of natural evolution and, in so doing, create a transitorily impermanent, but a seemingly substantial, condition of natural environment; but unless the conditions of man's inventive ingenuity coalesce with the conditions of natural order, there can be no perma-nence, no universality, no integrity in the artifices emanating from man's sentient inclinations nor from the compulsive quali-ties of his ego-gratifying nature. Man at the same time epito-mizes Nature's achievement and tests her tolerance, and it is in the conditions of his invention that her most devious devices of ethic-aesthetic practices are tried in the determination of bal-ance between excess and deficiency. Nature may endure for a time the excesses and the deficiencies derived from man's fallible and selfish nature, and she may delay for a time the reckoning to be exacted, but her qualities of endurance and her toleration of delay are superior to all the qualities of any of her parts, and it is the ultimate tragedy of temporal impulses and topical aber-rance that the endurance and the tolerance of the parts cannot match the inexorable stamina of the whole of Nature's ethic-aesthetic functionality, though it is in the functional processes of natural order that the toleration and the endurance of the parts are tested and determined in either an apprehensible or a comprehensible state, a state that depends for its meaning on the physical, mental, emotional, spiritual, and behavioral experience responses of sentient creatures.

It would be all too easy simply to insist that Nature is the absolute determiner, arbitrarily, of all the conditions that make up the world of man's sentient response and the impulses that stir him to experience. This, however, would deny the obvious, the state of man as an evolutionary creature in an evolutionary atmosphere of complexly varied and mutually influential conditions and impulses constantly refocusing and re-establishing perspectives in a perpetual excess-deficiency balance and counterbalance in relation to the particularities of contingent conditions and impulses as they create new experience-meanings. This would deny the variability of experience as it impresses the uniquely individualized responder-receptor-retainer faculties of man; and it would deny the natural prerogative of man to experiment and invent and question as the sentient quality of natural resourcefulness. It is just that quality, the sentient quality of man, that supplies a natural impulse-moving man to excess or deficiency in all his responsive attitudes and aptitudes and that creates the imbalances that require him to compromise with Nature and find resolution of the evils created by his excesses and deficiencies under the aegis of ethic-aesthetic principles that are generated by natural processes. Nature, in this sense, is then a guide to right principle rather than a determiner of acts. But if the act violates principle, then principle must prevail or the act will lead only to destruction or to the establishing of a balancing or countering act in accord with the principle of natural integrity. Nature, then, is not a haven for escape, but rather it is the generating source of the impulse to escape. It is the cause as well the effect of its own variability, versatility, and complexity, and escape into Nature in its most precise sense would be commitment to the principles of Nature and submission to the experience-meaning implicit in the function of Nature. In this same sense, Nature allows latitude of movement to her parts, and, in so doing, she provides for the continuation of her evolutionary processes. Nature permits, requires, and disallows; she permits error, but she requires rectification and restitution; she requires excess and deficiency to shape her evolution, but she disallows the degree of excess or deficiency that would compromise her self-perpetuating processes. She determines the integrity of her own evolution by the functional balancing of the contraries in her character and establishes the ethic-aesthetics of her identity by the processes of her evolution.

In terms of the ethic-aesthetic as a natural emanation of the germinal functioning, self-perpetuating process inseparable from the being of Nature in her primally generative harmony of variable balance functions, tragedy emerges as a profound, sentiently perceptible disharmony, an awareness of loss of equilibrium, of mutation, within the delicate tolerances allowed by a Nature jealous of her identity as the arbiter of truth and beauty. It follows that sentience, the uniquely human quality of Nature's elements, is the one constant in the perceptive-receptive-retentive-responsive function in experience-meaning relationships derived from the only source of generative impulse, Nature herself. Since sentience is a Nature-human quality generated by Nature and giving impulse to the recognitive process possessed by human nature alone, it follows that sentience is the essence of all experience-meaning that is not merely an automatic mechanical function of the natural entity separated from its sentient parts. Experience-meaning requires sentience; and tragedy, or at least the recognition of tragedy, requires experience-meaning, human nature awareness, as do all recognitive response functions requiring sentience as the faculty of awareness. Man is the sole quality of Nature to possess awareness as either a cognitive or recognitive memory responsiveness, and man is therefore the sole receptor-responder of and to tragedy in any sentient sense. Tragedy is Nature's curse on man, her means of balancing man's sentient inquisitiveness and curiosity against his sentient potential to recognize the disharmony his sentience may create or apprehend. Whenever a mutant order is created, either by happenstance of Nature or out of man's sentience, the ethic-aesthetic re-establishment of harmony or balance or equilibrium will of necessity focus on the mutant, and tragedy will result, for the mutant, both in Nature and in the nature of topical adjustment of temporal conditions and conventions relative to the mutant. Mutation and aberrancy are the direct results, both in Nature and in art, of violation of the ethic-aesthetic principles of natural order. They are the deviations, both in action and in condition, from the desirable mean to such a degree that their identity as functional entities in the excess-mean-deficiency tolerance scheme of Nature is compromised and they no longer fit into the harmonious whole of the integrated integrity-fidelity, ethic-aesthetic, order. Such deviations are not tolerable to Nature, and they should not then be tolerated in art; for whatever is in violation of the principles of Nature's law is in the nature of its condition an abomination, and as an abomination must be scourged from the presence of the dynamically functional conditions and impulses that adhere to the principles that provide functional harmony in Nature and in that derivative of Nature called *art*.

The major complication here would be the dichotomy of sentient creatures subjected to two sets of complex laws: the law of Nature and the law of topical expediency. Aberrance or mutation could easily occur as a result of violation of the *status quo* of either law; and, though an act, condition, or impulse might be contrary to one set of laws, it might well be in concert with the other and establish a set of tragic conditions and impulses to suffering, the consequences of which are tragedy in terms of the one law but nontragedy in terms of the other. But man, sentient creature that he is, caught in the inconsistency between the topical and the universal law, must suffer if he is an aberration or mutation of either law, and his topical tragedy is no less tragic in terms of individual sentience than his universal tragedy, for his feeling responses are no less involved if his suffering is from topical or from universal causes, and the effect is the same, for him, in either case. The mutant or the aberrant must be destroyed, even if, under topical law, the mutant or aberrant adheres to universal law in violation of topical law; or if, under universal law, the mutant or aberrant violates universal law to uphold topical law; for mutation or aberrance cannot be tolerated by either topical law or universal law if either wishes to defend its integrity and identity, even though, particularly under topical law, that integrity and identity are not sanctioned under the contracts man has with the other law.

VII

THE EXPERIENCE-MEANING IMPULSE

THE SUBSTANCE OF ART, AS OF LIFE, IS EXPERIENCE, EXPERI-
ence—real, vicarious, or imagined—that has stirred the receptive and responsive impulses in the natures of man and that
has stimulated the retentive impulse that makes man a storehouse of experiences as a source upon which the re-creative
impulse acts to impel a reincarnated version or impression that
takes structural shape in the substantial and material forms
of artistic expression: stone, sound, words, paint, or others.
Genuine art is the tangible expression in substantial form of
those experiences as they become structured into a response-
demanding form by the re-creative genius of man the maker,
the poet who structures the conditions of his experience into
expressions that become the experience of an audience.

As a child experiences sounds and attaches significance to
them and retains them within his individual being until conditions demanding a response from him provide an impulse for
him to utter those sounds as a symbol of his needs, his ideas, his
responsive nature, so do all men of experiential receptivity
attach significance to and retain within their beings the impressions they have of experience until conditions demand a

response and provide an impulse either for overt expression of responsiveness or for covert submerging of the responsive impulse. It would, however, be presumptuous to maintain that any individual human being is always intellectually aware of having retained a particular experience or even of having had a particular experience. Indeed, just as the child may never be intellectually aware of having learned the meaning or significance of a particular sound or combination of sounds, just as he may never be able to attach significance to the time or occasion of having experienced the sound but uses it as a natural and seemingly unlearned expression of his impulse to respond, so may man become a storehouse of other experiences and meanings of which he is unaware until conditions demand their utterance either overtly or as an experience retained within the consciousness of a sentient being. The impulse to respond may then evoke conditions and structures and forms and impressions of experiences that are not a part of the conscious awareness of a particular sentient being, and he may put into substantial form experiences of which he was unaware and express meanings that he did not know he knew. His expression or structuring of those meanings or experiences as conditions of his world need not then to be always and invariably expressions or structurings involving intellectual awareness or even intellectual activity. They may be the putting into substantial form of experiences derived from sensory impression and retained in the subconscious spirit or created by the chance juxtaposition of conditions of experience within the unconscious nature of man, taking shape as conditions or experiences containing impulses demanding awareness only when they have been given structural relationships through expression in forms demanded by the conditions themselves in whatever medium is employed to give them substantial representation. A John Milton may so thoroughly apprehend and experience the mode, the spirit, the personality, the substance, and the form of classical artistic expression that

209

without intellectual consciousness of their presence in his personal world of responsively creative genius, he may, without exercise of conscious intellectual faculties, re-create the manners, the sentiments, the moods, the echoes of and allusions to the substance and forms of his classical experience. The result will then be the artistic expression in a natural English linguistic environment of a natural classical aesthetic presentation of a naturally apprehended condition of personal and topically learned substance. A *Paradise Lost* could then develop, naturally and without the conscious effort of pedantically intellectual exercise, as a classical epic in English on a personal thesis with a Judaic base and a Christian application. A contemporaneity of classical, Judaic, and Christian spirits would exist in the retentive capacities of the artist and emerge in a re-creative artistic expression that would defy identity of any one spirit as a dominant feature justifying critical interpretation in terms of that one spirit alone. The commingling of qualities and conditions and impulses within the spirit of the artist would so thoroughly merge their natures as to create a new quality of spirit unlike that of any of its sources but echoing a material substance of all of them, each qualified and modified by its relation with the others. Within the spirit of the artist, or of any sentient being, for that matter, there is established a contemporaneous presence of all the conditions and impulses and experiences that constitute the personal world of man. As an overly simplified illustration, the seventeenth-century classical scholar who has submitted himself to the classical materials and who has absorbed the nature of the classical spirit along with the nature of the immediate environmental spirit may become, if the proper impulses are put into motion, a genuine and natural assimilation and synthesis of two separate worlds brought together outside the limits of chronological time into a contemporaneity of spirit and quality that is unique and universal, personal and substantial, and topical and timeless, all in the same expression of artistic substance. The merged and commingled influences as they are structured into a work of art would then be so complexly modified and qualified as to defy analysis or interpretation through the media of any one prescriptive formula, but would require descriptive submission to their expression for valid appraisal. Contemporaneity, in this context, has no reference to time in a sequential or chronological sense. It is, rather, a bringing together out of time sequence or chronological order qualities, conditions, impulses, meanings, and experiences that find focus within a particular or unique structural relationship bounded only by the perspectives native to the receptive and retentive capacities and the expressive inclinations inherent in the nature of the being in whom concomitant relationships are merged. Contemporaneity in this sense may establish third century B.C. pastoral elegiac structural form as a native and topical seventeenth century A.D. vehicle for *Lycidas*. It may establish fifth century B.C. tragic mode as a topical seventeenth century means of expression in *Samson Agonistes*. And it may establish for twentieth-century artists a natural affinity for and expression of qualities and substances in topical art that are centuries out of context in calendar time measurement. The foregoing is not a denial of deliberate intellectual choice of forms, substances, or allusions, on the part of a particular artist; it is, however, a suggestion that not always is a particular echo or quality necessarily a matter of deliberate intent, imitation, borrowing, or adaptation.

Man—artist, critic, or audience—is at the same time a receptor, a retainer, and a responder; impressions of experience flow into his nature as a sort of current, joining him tangibly, intangibly, and tangentially to the conditions and impulses of his experience. The emanations of conditions, the impulsive currents of experience, are drawn to the receptor by the sensitive and perceptive qualities of man's states of responsive nature —of his physical, mental, emotional, spiritual, and behavioral

211

conditions—as impressions of the nature of experience or of the conditions establishing experience. The intensity of the impressions is modified and qualified by the degree of sensitivity and perceptivity of the receptor, by the nature of the impression itself as an impulse-requiring response, by the qualities of responsiveness in or by each of the five separate responsive states, by the condition and nature of each of the five responsive faculties, by the nature of the fusion and merging of the impression in and among the responsive states, by the modification of the impression to fit the receptive capacity of the receptor, and by the will, inclination, or compulsion of the receptor to receive the impression in a particular manner, form, or intensity. Man the receptor does not receive the experience itself or the condition generating the experience; the condition or the experience sends an impulse toward the receptor; and if the receptor responds to the impulse an impression of the condition or the experience is created. Man is the recipient of the impression and the impression only, but that impression is uniquely his because it is determined by the complex variability of all the qualities that establish the uniquely individual characteristics of each individual human. The impression to one receptor is universally similar to the impression of the same condition or experience as it is received by another receptor because the condition originating the impulse has its own identity as originator; but, at the same time, the impression is uniquely different for each receptor because the experiencing natures of the receptors are unique. Consequently, the same experience will create different meanings for the two receptors. Similarities in general perspective will occur, but the identity of focus and intensity will be as rare as identity of total molecular accumulation in two separate individuals.

Tangible impressions will be formed, either negatively or positively, when the experiencing of a condition establishes distinct relativity between the condition and the receptor through impulses generating responsive awareness of the impress of the experience of the condition on the nature of the receptor. The tangible impression may establish identification with, recognition of, feeling for, alienation from, or behavior toward the object condition; but whether the response is one of attraction or repulsion, the tangible impression will be such as to alter perceptibly some quality of the receptor, particularly as a conscious awareness of the nature of the condition, a distinct feeling or sensing of the qualities of the impulse that generates response to the condition, or overt response to the experience as a new condition adding to or subtracting from the accumulation of conditions that give evidence of the nature of the receptor as an identifiable form in Nature. Just as rain and wind conditions may erode and tangibly alter the face of a landscape, so may the conditions of experience create the impressions and the impulses that erode and alter identifiable features in the nature of man; and man, by the nature of his susceptibility to a greater variety and a greater complexity of experiential conditions because of a greater refinement of his receptive and responsive natures, is more inclined to undergo tangibly identifiable alteration and perceptible evolution than are other qualities of Nature. Man is capable of enlarging his perceptive awareness, his comprehension, his apprehension because he is capable of receiving and retaining a greater variety and complexity of lessoning impressions of conditions and experiences than is any other quality of Nature; and man is capable of remembering, through art, the substantial form of his impressions, the conditions and the impulses and the experiences of his heritage. Art, the evidence of man's nature as a former of impressions of experience, also evidences his nature as a receptor of impressions, for something cannot be created out of nothing in the experience of man, and only out of impression may the substantial form of impression arise.

The transformation of man is not, however, only a product of tangible impression; it is also a product of intangible impression and of tangential impression. Much of the experience of man, many of the conditions that touch upon the nature of man, make no perceptible impression on man the receptor, either as a matter of tangible alteration of his condition or as evidenced by perceivable response. In the conditions of such impressions the impulses denominating overt responsive awareness of impression of condition or experience remain latent as do the impulses that impress perceivable alteration in or on the nature of the receptor. Particular notice of condition or specific awareness of condition does not determine the particularities of impression so much as do the qualities of the receptive nature of man; so, too, obvious awareness or direct response is not the only source of latent impulses of impression. Those qualities of conditions and experiences that imperceptibly flow into the receptor are intangible impressions. They may become tangible only through the intermediary of impulses emanating from other received impressions creating an associational responsiveness that finds perceivable expression or awareness. This could establish for the artist, consciously or unconsciously, objective correlatives that seemingly have no source other than the native intuitive responsiveness or the racial memory of man. Under such conditions, however, when the impression is intangible to the receptor and becomes tangible only after the impression has flowed imperceptibly into the receptor, the nature of the impression becomes that of a felt or sensed recall of initiating experience rather than that of involvement within the conditions of the experience that supply the impulse for the impression. Indeed, the fusion and merging of the intangible impression with all the other associational impressions stored within the retentive nature of the receptor may so alter the qualities of the impression that identification with the initiating experience becomes impossible, and, under certain imbalances in the responsive states of man, might seem to be a psychically generated experience originating beyond or outside the physical world and appearing spontaneously without intermediary of Nature or responsive impulses as unique revelation from the supernatural. But whatever the personal explanation of the source of the intangible impression, its experience, once it becomes the object of experiential significance, may seem as real to the experiencer as any tangible impression; and its expression in substantial form may become an experiential reality to anyone who submits responsively to the conditions and impulses structured into its transmissible nature; it may become, through art, a tangible impression of experience even though its initiating impulses remain intangible to the creator of its substantial form. Often, too, what may be a tangible impression of experience to one may, because of the individuality of receptor qualities, be an intangible impression to another; degrees of sensitivity and perceptivity and intensity of the impressive impulses on the responsive natures of the receptor may well determine tangibility or intangibility. Within the receptor intangible impression may become the impulse to tangible personal experience, and, conversely, what is received as tangible impression of experience may be so modified by fusion with other retained impressions that it becomes intangible. Nature is so lavish with her conditions and experiences and impulses, separately and in combinations, and so variable in the complexity of her parts, including the receptor faculties of man, that no two impressions are ever identical, and the apprehensive range between tangibility and intangibility of impression is universally infinite, subject only to the variable receptive capabilities of each one of Nature's receptors of impressions. Experience, in this discussion, and the impression of experience, are not limited to personal environmental conditions; indeed vicarious experience probably accounts for more of man's impressions than do conditions of personal involvement; nor does this discussion rule out psychic experience or even hereditary experience as sources of impres-

215

sions both tangible and intangible. Fundamentally, man is probably a greater storehouse of intangible impressions than he is of tangible impressions because the range of his awareness is not broad enough and the acuteness of his responsive faculties is not differentiated enough to allow him to make tangible impressions of more than a minute quantity of all the conditions that have an effect on him.

Many of the mysteries of art, the substantial form of impressions of meaning and experience, particularly in relation to the so-called mystical or metaphysical arts, may originate in intangible impression; and because of man's limitations in the means of establishing tangible expression of intangible impression, reincarnate experience-meaning is difficult to achieve or apprehend for anyone not initiated into conditions from which the tangible impression derives, and the differentiated natures of the art experience may be obscure to the noninitiate. What is obvious to one is not necessarily obvious to another; one man's mysticism may be another man's reality, and the tangibility or intangibility of impression may well determine the experience-meaning for each in a different manner and depth of apprehension. Intangible impression is quite obviously functioning in a near tangible manner when there is a sensing of, or feeling for, a condition or impulse that has no discernible relativity to conscious or perceivable experience; and certain responses to particular conditions, especially emotive responses, that seemingly have no evocative impulses to prompt such a response, likely result from intangible impression moved to tangibility by unconscious associational reference, creating a seemingly incongruous responsive impression: laughter when the normal response would be sorrow, pain when the conditions would seem to produce pleasure or like reactions. Perhaps, too, premonitory impression that has no evidential source in external condition may arise from a merging of intangible impressions causing an impulse to be activated that gives rise to a tangible premonition.

The associational affinity of impression to experience is so infinitely complex and variable, so subject to transformation by the conditions of the receptor, so liable to mutation in the fusing and merging processes within the retentive nature of the receptor, and so certain of alteration by the expressive abilities of man, that a multiplicity of impressions, both tangible and intangible, may be evoked by one experience and take on a multiplicity of nonidentifiable characters in the expressive reality of the substantial form, and this in relation to all the functional responsive natures of man: physical, mental, emotional, spiritual, and behavioral. It is quite probable that most tangible impressions may have no experiential significance, that they will remain latent, until an impulse is generated to command overt response; it is also quite possible that the initial overt response will be an internal impression within the experiencer of the response and that subsequent expression of the impression will be discernible externally. It is not necessary, however, for the impression to have an external expression to cause it to be a real experience of the experiencer or to have meaning for him. Nor is it necessary for the experiencer of an intangible impression ever to be consciously aware that he may have given expressive reality to the impression. In art the artist may structure into the conditions of the substantial form what for him may never be more than an intangible impression; whereas that same impression may establish for an audience a fusion of conditions, an impulse, a meaning, a tangible impression of experience, that is as real to the audience as any other experience-meaning could be; and the artist may remain eternally unaware both of the intangible impression that he has had and of the tangible impression that he has created. A conclusion here is that the work of art is the proper object of examination, not the nature of the artist, for the experience-meaning that is art. Art, once it comes into being as a substantial form, is self-sufficient. The artist is merely an intermediary

217

who has brought it out of Nature into a form that may be perceived by an audience. Once this intermediary function is performed, the artist ceases to be essential; the only legitimate source of the experience-meaning of the art is the art itself. This does not mean that knowledge about the artist may not be an aid to understanding if that knowledge be the essential substance of the work itself, but rather that knowledge about the artist is not the experience-meaning implicit in the work of art. The work is the art, and any knowledge extraneous to the implicit and explicit experience-meaning of the work is nonessential to the total context of what the work requires, permits, or disallows. However, if knowledge of the artist is a fundamental requirement for a reincarnative experience-meaning of the function of the work, then, most certainly, a valid audience-critic response must require that same knowledge.

Art functions as experience-meaning: its conditions and impulses produce an experiential impression of Nature for whoever responds to it, and its meaning is inherent in the structure of the conditions that comprise it. It is its own substance and only its own substance, and its function is the presentation of that substance to the experiential responses and apprehensions of its audience. Its function is not to provide identification for its structural organizer, its maker, unless he be of the substance of the work; nor is its function to provide creative impulses to an audience to create outside the inherently indigenous experience-meaning of the work of art itself other experiences and meanings, audience created, to be attributed to the substance of the initial substantial form. It may stimulate impulses in an audience to create or generate new impressions of experience-meaning for the audience, but to be an attribute of the work of art itself, that experience and meaning must be a functional part of the experience-meaning that is the work of art itself. If the impression of new experience-meaning, either tangible or intangible, is the creation of the audience, even though the impulse arises from the work of art, the new creation by the audience must not be regarded in the descriptive interpretation of the work of art. If a Cézanne painting arouses an impulse creating a recall of an actual scene from personal experience, the recalled scene must not be imposed on the critical interpretation of the experience-meaning of the Cézanne painting; the recall is a function of the audience, not of the painting; and the qualities of the recall are comparative, not attributory, to the qualities of the painting. Art functions as experience-meaning, but only as its own experience-meaning. It may contribute impulses stirring other experience-meanings, but they are not its experience-meaning, and they are not the experience-meaning of the artist, the functioning maker of forms between Nature experience and art impression of experience. Nor is the artist necessarily a functioning substance, a condition, of the work of art itself; the nature of the artist is not necessarily revealed by the art. Is Shakespeare Juliet, or is he Iago? Or is he both? Great art, unless consciously oriented to be so, is seldom autobiographical, and audience response and critical interpretation should not be biographical unless the work functions as autobiography. Is the Hamlet of Ernest Jones Shakespeare's Hamlet? Is the Hamlet of Shakespearean texts Shakespeare? If so, is the Hamlet of Ernest Jones's interpretation Shakespeare, Shakespeare's Hamlet, Ernest Jones's Hamlet, or Ernest Jones? Who reveals what about whom? Functionally, the Hamlet of art is the Hamlet of *Hamlet*. And the impressions, tangible and intangible, of the experience-meaning of Hamlet emanate from *Hamlet*. *Hamlet* is the substantial form of the experience-meaning of Hamlet, not Shakespeare, not Jones, not Pollard and Pollard. And *Hamlet* provides the only essential substance of conditions and impulses to know Hamlet as an artistic impression of experience and meaning. Peripheral knowledge and experience may aid in coming to apprehending, in coming to total experience-meaning; but peripheral knowledge and experience are not Hamlet, nor are they the experience-meaning of *Hamlet*. *Hamlet* is evidence of an accomplishment of Shakespeare and his editors; it is not evidence of the total character or nature of Shakespeare. *Hamlet* is the substantial form of impressions, tangible and intangible, structured by Shakespeare and those editors into the associational and qualifying fusion and merging of conditions and impulses that create the reincarnated experience-meaning of *Hamlet* in an audience-receptor of impressions of the textual *Hamlet*.

Tangible and intangible impressions as dealt with above have a direct involvement of experience-meaning with the conditions of Nature and art and with impulses for impression flowing directly from the essential or causal nature of the experiencing of the conditions in their pristine or most uncomplicated state. But the experience-meaning complex in conditions often emits impulses that are not generated by the particular conditions themselves in their most directly apprehensible natures. Most conditions have impulse-generating qualities that are not part of their own essential nature but merely attributory or affinitive natures associated with the essential or basal natures of the conditions. These attribute or affiliate natures have experience evocative impulses in their own right, both tangible and intangible, that may create their own impressions isolated from the experiencing of conditions with which they are associated; or they may perform as complements to the conditions with which they are associated and create a variable complexity of experience-impression impulses that qualify and modify the experience-meaning. The impressions that qualify and modify and complement the direct condition to receptor basic impression are tangential impressions, as are attribute or affiliate impressions. Tangential impression may originate both outside the receptor, as emanations from conditions, or inside the receptor, as associational qualities of the received impression of the experiencing of conditions. In both Nature and art the

220

tangential impressions add color, tone, atmosphere, nuances of meaning, modification, and qualification to the experience-impression of the receptor. Prior experience of sound adds tangential impression to the experiencing of the stillness of a remote desert environment. Change in tone may modify the experience-impression of the reading of *Euphues* drastically from that of a handbook on gentlemanly behavior to that of a satire on the stylized artificialities of a "euphuistic" gentleman. The hieroglyphical structure of "Easter Wings" may create a tangential impression complementary to and elevating the word-meaning experiential impression of the poem. Sensitivity is the prime positive requirement in tangential impression. Ignorance, insensitivity, prejudice, and inexperience are the major detriments to the experience-meaning impulses of the tangential impression.

Because art is the substantial form of impressions of experience-meaning with conditions structured by the artist into a substance from which will emanate impulses to activate responses in an audience to reincarnate the experience-meaning impressions of the work in an audience receptor, it is necessary for the artist to structure condition relationships and impression-creating impulses in such a manner as to evoke tangential impressions, either consciously or unconsciously on the part of both artist and audience, to create perspective breadth of the artistic experience and the focal depth of its meaning. Creation of impulses for tangential impression then becomes the major artistic function of the artist in establishing in substantial form the means of arousing re-creative responses in the receptor, and the sensitive submission of the receptor to the tangential impressions generated by the work becomes the major artistic function of the audience-receptor to reincarnate the experience-meaning of the work within the cumulative response-states of the receptor. Tangential impression is the grasp of the artist on the fine details of experience; it is the shades and nuances of tone and mood in the structural unity of experience-meaning created by the substantial form of the art; and it is the perspective-focus relationship of experience-meaning in the art-apprehensible capabilities and capacities of the audience-receptor. Tangential impression is that quality of experience response that may change a photo-report of conditions to an art expression of experience-meaning or journalese into fine art. In the work of art the tangential impression determines the quality; the potential for re-creative response; the implicit conditions that permit, require, and disallow particular interpretive responses; and the inherent experience-meaning structured into the associational relationships of the conditions composing the substance of the work. Tangential impression elevates art above the commonplace, turns unique experience into potential communal experience, and differentiates the communal response in terms of individual receptor qualities of comprehension, apprehension, and responsive will, inclination, or compulsion. Control and discipline in the structuring of tangential impressions may well establish the division between craft and art in the expression of experience-meaning, for tangential impression is that quality of experience which modifies, qualifies, complements, and creates the ultimate essence of experiential significance of the experience-meaning. The impulses to experience-meaning apprehension in art inhere in the tangential impressions of artist and audience merging in focus and perspective within the apprehensible substantial form of conditions unified by artistic structure into the communal experience of both artist and audience, the one functioning as intermediary between Nature and audience, the other functioning as receptor-responder to the expression of the intermediary, and within the limits of its re-creative proclivities making the reincarnate experience its experience and the reincarnate meaning its meaning. Tangential impression bears to commonplace impression a relationship similar to that a full-flowered plant bears to the seed from which it grows. Tangential impression is the wealth of experience-meaning rather than the condition from which it grew; it is the intrinsic beauty attributable to an object rather than the mere recognition of the object; it is the magnitude of love compared to indifference; it is wisdom contrasted to a few facts; and it is truth made manifest in the mutual integrity of Nature and art. Tangential impression is "divine" added to ecstasy to create divine ecstasy; it is the "im" that changes mortal to immortal; it is the pressure that makes a handshake take on meaning; it is the process that changes fruit juice to wine; it is the impulse that changes the intangible to the tangible; and it is the sensitivity that gives experience its meaning. Tangential impression is a light that seeps through darkness, and it is the glow that reveals happiness. Tangential impression gives color to the dull, makes the ordinary extraordinary, and flames feeling into passion. It is the breathtaking hope kindled by an unexpected pulse in a loved one, and the single sob that tears the mask of sorrow. It is the condition that changes pathos to tragedy, and the experience that turns happiness into bliss.

The establishing of the identity of the tangential impression does not carry any implications of license in artistic interpretation. The genuine tangential impression is firmly rooted in the conditions, the experiences, the impulses, and the meanings with which it has affinitive, complementary, qualifying, or modifying functions. The tangential impression, if genuine, if relative, if associationally sound, if evidencing responsive integrity and experiential fidelity, is the product of that in and with which it is found; it is not genuine when it is the invention of the audience observer, but only when it is the re-creation by the audience observer of that which is intrinsically and irrevocably delineated by the substance of the condition from which it emanates as a substantial evidence of the innate experience-meaning of that particular condition. The tangential impression begins as a functional quality of the condition itself; and it must retain its identity as a function of the condition to have any validity in interpretive response by the receptor who must not go beyond what is permitted, required, or disallowed by the condition for identification and significance of the impression relative to its source. The grasping of tangential impression significance is a matter of audience re-creation, not of audience creation; and that re-creation must substantially reincarnate the totality of the germinating conditions of experience-meaning to give valid, meaningful impulse to the substance of the tangential impression. For whole audience response to an art substance of creative impression, nothing must be added to or taken from the fused assimilation of conditions that compose the substantial form; if addition or subtraction of any substance, any condition, any impulse, occurs, the tangential impression will be invalid in terms of its relational significance to its source, the originating experience-meaning of the conditions inherent in the work of art. A flying saucer impression created by audience imagination out of a high-flying piece of toilet paper is not a re-creation of a flying saucer and has no relational significance to a flying saucer; and its description in flying saucer terms does not transform the toilet paper into a flying saucer, nor does it validate any substantial impression of a flying saucer. Relational identity must be preserved to validate any impression; and any unvalidated impression must not be regarded as having relational significance to the identity of its source in interpretive function. Malfunction in establishing relational affinity of tangential impression and source is conducive only to error and misinterpretation, distortion, ignorance, superstition, disorientation, and corruption of truth, beauty, and integrity.

Relational affinity of tangential impressions with the source of impression must be validated with care and with utmost regard for point of view, intent, identity, nature of receptor response function, and response significance. The presence of a horse in the flower garden may be an identical condition for a lady intent on winning first prize in the flower show and for a dung beetle; but the tangential impressions evoked by "horse in the flower garden" will be drastically dissimilar for the two; although the initiating condition remains, the responsive realities of the tangential impressions will vary according to the natures of the receptors of the impressions and will be significant to each in relation to functional association of relative conditions determining impulses prompting differentiated functional response as well as differentiated tangential impressions. Because the responsive natures of dung beetle, lady, and horse are dissimilar in degree and form of specialization and sophistication, and because the personal point of view or prejudice of each is different, the tangential impressions determined by the condition, which is the same for each, will inevitably be oriented by and toward their differentiated natures; and the significance of the condition will be relative to the functional impulses in the condition as they pertain to each individually. But "horse in the flower garden" will evoke substantially the same responsive tangential impressions for two dung beetles or two horses or two ladies, although there may be greater variation in impressions for members of each group as it is placed higher on the scale of group responsive sophistication. The differentiated impressions by horses will be substantially more sophisticated than the differentiated impressions by dung beetles, and the specialized responses to tangential impressions by ladies are apt to be more sophisticated than those of either dung beetles or horses. Horse and lady might both have a preference for petunias, but the evoked responses will be at extreme variance. Horse impression might be "Oh, boy! Petunia fodder." Lady impression might be "Damned horse, there goes my petunia prize at the fair." The basic condition evocative of responsive impression has remained the same "horse in the flower garden," but the responsive impressions have varied because of species differences in response function; there will always be great variance in responsive impression when two or more orders or species of response natures receive impulses from the same condition. When two or more response natures of the same order or species receive impulses evocative of tangential impression, the evoked impressions will be substantially the same, varying only in degree as determined by levels of sensitivity, perceptivity, and receptivity, by balances of responsive natures—physical, mental, emotional, spiritual, and behavioral—and by will, inclination, or compulsion to respond to the particularities of the condition. "Horse in the flower garden" will evoke variations in responses and in tangential impressions for two ladies, but there will be a similarity in total apprehension of the condition and the experience and the derived impressions from that experience. Variations will be personal and not of order or species nature. But the structuring of conditions in art, by the very nature of the substantial form that solidifies experience into a perceptual unification and modification of conditions and impulses, establishes a control of impressions not found in the disassociational conditions of natural Nature where extraneous and peripheral nonselective impressions disorient the focus and perspective of both the initiating experience and the receptor impression of the experience. Art, then, functions as a means of establishing order out of the experiences of Nature, and reluctantly it directs and limits the tangential impressions it evokes in focal and perspective response. "Horse in the flower garden" becomes a focus for responsive attentiveness; tangential impressions evoked by "horse in the flower garden" are directed by the structure of conditions relative to "horse in the flower garden" to define the perspective bounds of tangential impressions delineating the experience of conditions depicted by "horse in the flower garden" and determining the impulses evocative of response to "horse in the flower garden." The meaning, then, of "horse in the flower garden" is only what is permitted, required, and disallowed by the substantial form of focal and perspective impressions structured into the conditions and impulses of the art experience of "horse in the flower garden." It is nothing more nor less than the total experience-meaning of "horse in the flower garden" as determined by the structured substantial form, and by the apprehensive capabilities and capacities of the audience modified by its will, inclination, or compulsion to submit to the art expression and to respond to its experience-meaning.

Man is much more than an impression-response receptor, however. Man is also a complicated, complex retainer of impression, an accumulator of experience, a storehouse of knowledge, a cache of meanings, and a generator-receptor charged with impulses. He may receive an impression of moon movement, retain the impression in his retentive functionality, associate that retained impression with another impression of the rise and fall of waters, and by affinitive association develop knowledge of tides, find an experience-meaning in Nature, and come to the comprehensive understanding of phenomena that is called wisdom. Man is the measure and the measurer of all conditions that touch him, and his garner of retained impressions is the device of comparison, the tool, the means by which he is measured and with which he measures. Without retentive function, man would be incapable of building, of making, of expressing impressions of associational response. It is his retentive faculty that allows man to accumulate and differentiate the impulses of his experience, to establish himself as the highest order in the hierarchy of Nature's parts. Retention of impression provides a standard for comparison, a means of establishing relative value, without which man would be a mechanically invariable responder to impulses, incapable of judgment, comprehension, or wisdom. The retentive nature of man is that which allows him to have for use that which his receptor nature makes him subject to. Without the ability to retain impressions of experience, conditions and impulses would flow through and around man without leaving impression. Man would be functionally static in a Nature of mechanistic behavior because he would be incapable of apprehending the functional significance of impressions and associational interpretation of the experience-meaning of conditions and impulses. But man is a dynamic quality of Nature, forming, shaping, structuring, doing and making, responding to impulses and apprehending the experience-meaning of impressions. And this dynamic quality is evidence of and evidenced by the retentive function of man's experiencing and experienceable nature. The ability to compare, to judge, to measure is dependent upon retention; retention provides the means and experience provides the object, material or nonmaterial, of comparison, judgment, measurement. It contains the conditions and the impulses through which, by comparison and judgment and measurement, man achieves an apprehensive grasp of the experience-meaning of impressions. Retention is the faculty which makes possible the fusing and merging of impressions which give rise to new meanings and experiences, to memory, to doing, to making, to art.

Retention of impressions makes possible the expositive function, a function that man alone evidences in any substantial degree among the functional orders of Nature's hierarchy. Man alone records his impressions in the substantial form of art to preserve his experience-meaning for posterity and to immortalize his participatory identity with Nature in his perpetuated memory, his art. This perpetuated memory, this art function in the structuring and ordering and solidifying of impressions for retention in a substantial form external to the retentive faculty of the physical, mental, emotional, spiritual, and behavioral man, is an evidential immortality of ego identity made possible only through the fusing and merging of impressions and the functioning of a retentive faculty that accumulates and stores impressions—through experiential impulses striking at all of man's responsive states—to provide a source of conditions and impulses for expressive impression of man's place in the Nature he represents. The internal or personally functioning retentive faculty, as differentiated from the more durable, external art memory, is a referential memory dependent on associational impressions to provide the impulses of impressive identification. It is a dynamic, functioning quality delimited only by birth and death in the sense of sentient participatory experience; by the bounds of spiritual involvement in the extraphysical sense; by the receptor capabilities in the emotional, intellectual, or behavioral sense; and by genetic structure or racial memory in the atavistic sense. It is the quality that for each man defines for him personally his grasp of truth and beauty and reality, that gives the peculiar, the particular, the uniquely individual qualities to that which each man "knows," and that allows him to describe, define, or explain his experience-meaning in expositive expression either through prosaic communication of thought or through supratopical, nontime limitable memory, art. This retentive faculty, this referential memory that is both personally topical and communally universal or universally personal and topically communal, is the basis for all of man's knowledge and the source for the man-centered focus of all relationships: man to god, man to Nature, man to man, man to idea. Referential memory or retentive faculty is not a function of mind alone either in the functional process of the impression's coming into the retainer through the receptive state, in the holding of the impression in the retentive state, or in the outgoing of the impression in the expressive state. Physical memory is operative whenever a genetic transmission occurs; behavioral memory is operative whenever behavioral conditioning causes a behavioral repetition of response to an initiating impulse; Nature memory is operative whenever reproductive process brings forth new beings; emotional memory is operative whenever conditions and impulses revive an emotional response. Degrees of referential memory, of retentive faculty, are operable in all of Nature's orders—even minerals retain particular cleavage characteristics; but it is in man that the most complexly variable—differentiated and subject to experience modification and qualification—impressions occur in the most highly specialized and differentiatable manner of reception, retention, and expression to be found in Nature. The degree of sophistication of referential memory provides the degree of difficulty in interpretation and analysis of man as man, of man as functional entity in Nature, of man as artist, and, in the complications resulting from the transforming of impressions into representational substantial form, of art as an expression of man's commitment to Nature—his nature and the nature of Nature.

Man the individual; man the unique; man the subject of birth, life, and death; man the sophisticated organ upon whom is played and who plays Nature's harmonies and disharmonies; man the creature of memory and with memory, memorable and remembering; man the victim of environment and the shaper of environments; man the delver into the filth of time and the developer of a sense of beauty; man the maker, the poet; and man the doer, the craftsman; man the timeserver and time consumer, the temporal consciousness of a time segment in his individual nature and the infinite memory through art of a universal time cycle; man the possessor of sentiment retentive faculty as well as of nonsentient retentive quality; man is the only form in Nature with obvious referential memory preserving that memory in art to immortalize himself and to record his nature in representational form outside himself for the enlightenment and entertainment of posterity. Man as man, as a form of Nature, is enveloped by Nature; but man as recorder of impressions, as creator of referential substantial forms representing Nature and the experience-meaning of Nature, envelops Nature. He is absorbed by Nature in his natural function as a form in Nature; he absorbs Nature through his receptive processes; he retains Nature in the form of impressions of Nature in his retentive faculties; and he becomes the voice of Nature in his function as expressor of impressions. Submerged in the nature of his own nature and deriving from within the conditions and impulses of internal experience to achieve the meaning of self, man is a subjective creature; elevated above or projected outside the nature of his own nature and deriving impressions from associational conditions and impulses of external experience to achieve the referential meaning relative to his self-functioning, man is an objective creature. When subjective man and objective man merge, when they fuse in functional responsiveness to the impressions of experience internal and external, and when that fusion is represented in referential memory, man becomes capable of the highest order of relative judgment and selectivity of representational conditions and impulses and tangential impressions. When the highest degree of such fusion occurs, man becomes a genius; and when the highest abilities to express such fusion are developed, man possesses the potential for genuine artistry, for expressing in substantial form the real experience-meaning of Nature, fancied, imagined, observed, felt, sensed, absorbed, intuited, dreamed, suffered, empathized, extracted, impelled, apprehended, and known.

Whether man the artist fashions his substantial form of impressions of experience-meaning consciously or unconsciously, whether he fashions it of stone or sound or color or word, whether he structures the conditions of his materials himself or whether they determine their own structural affinity and identity from the impulse he gives them and that they possess in their own right and by their own natures is immaterial to the experience-meaning inherent in the structured form of Nature that art is. Art is the brain, the organ that preserves, the self-perpetuating memory of the retentive faculty, the evidence of referential memory that survives the receptor-retainer-expressor of impressions. Art turns the transitory and the ephemeral into

231

the permanent and the substantial; it transforms the impression into substance for the creation of new impressions to be received, retained, and re-expressed in a new context to create new experience and new meaning and new knowledge in an infinite progression of evolutionary experience-meanings and expressive forms of referential memory. Without the art-memory, man would revert to artlessness, to animal nature, to meaninglessness.

Referential memory in its preservational state, in art, is dependent on the retentive faculty for its materials, for the fusion of impressions and the association of impulses that make it referential. Without reference, without corollary conditions or impressions, without relative experience, there would be no activation of impulse to memory or to thought; and consequently there would be no overt, representational expression, no art. The conditions in art are conditions of the retentive faculty, of memory in relation to or in reference to other conditions, setting in motion experiences that create meanings consequent upon the qualities of referential memory inherent in the initiating set of conditions and consistent with the response-provoking impulses occasioned by the qualifying structural affinities of the initiating conditions and the receptor-response faculties or states. Without time lapse, or duration of motion, or depth perception, there can be no sense of distance—distance is relative to one or another of the conditions that give it experience-meaning, and without the referential memory of time, motion, or depth with which to refer it, distance is non-existent as far as the response faculties are concerned; the meaning of distance, the experience of distance, the impression of distance is a nonquality, a negation of space, an unfelt and unsensed and unknown absence of meaning. Referential memory is the source of experience-meaning; it supplies the conditions essential to experience-evolution and meaning-evolution because it supplies the impulses to re-experience and to qualify the responses to experience impressions. It shapes and is shaped by the conditions relative to it and emanating from it as incorporable impressions of experience. Man as a retainer of impressions is the corporeal container of the incorporeal; man as an expressor of impressions in art incorporates those impressions into the substantial form that is the presentation for re-experience or reincarnation of the meaning inherent in them as an experience to be had relative to the referential memory of the audience.

Referential memory is not necessarily subject to time consideration; genetic memory, topical memory, and projectionable memory may occur simultaneously in the same being and be incorporated in the same impulse as part of the experience-meaning of an impression in a timeless contemporaneity of experience. All memory may be compassed in the no-time lapse between pre-lapse and post-lapse; it is the province of art to fix the continuum of experience and its referential memory-evoking impulses into a durable impression that holds in a timeless moment of expression, of substantial form without time relevance, the experience-meaning impression of experiential contemporaneity. Art is an assertion of experience-meaning contemporaneity dependent on referential memory in its structural formulation and in its impression-response evocation; but the "meaning" of an art expression or of an impression evoked by art is not necessarily an intellectual meaning, a mental comprehension. The meaning may well be the experience itself, the sense of order, the feeling of a responsive impulse relative to a referential memory. A modern painting may have as its "meaning" only the sense of harmony or disharmony emanating from the structural relationships of two colors or two lines or two forms, and one of the colors or lines or forms might even be external to the painting itself; the relative quality might be the space in which the picture is hung, the termination of the painting itself in relation to the nonpainting of its environmental position, or the color of the background on which it is imposed; but the meaning of the painting will be established as a response of experiential significance relating a referential memory congruent with the experiencing of the painting itself to a responsive impulse that may remain latent or that may evoke perceptive awareness. Meaning in such an instance would not be a meaning in the sense of a debatable proposition, but rather the meaning of coming into contact with, of feeling an impression of, of sensing a compatibility or incompatibility with the qualities of the object. The "meaning" a work of art has is the impression of experience it evokes by the structuring of its conditions and the impact its impulses have on the responsive natures of its audience; in fact, a work of art may have three distinct meanings: the meaning it has for the artist, the meaning it possesses in its own substance, and the meaning it evokes in its audience. Ideally, the three meanings will be identical; but, practically, total transmissibility between artist and audience through the medium of the work of art is subject to the fallibility of both artist and audience and of the functional capacity of the means of expression to convey a total, identical impression of experience-meaning. The essential meaning of a work of art, however, is the experience potential it possesses in relation to the referential memory of its audience. That the experience potential is unrealized because of audience ineptitude in submission and responsiveness, or because of artist ineptitude in structuring experience-provoking impulses into the work, is obvious. But the work of art remains, with its experience potential, the focus-perspective complex that is the real meaning of the work; it is its own meaning, not the meaning of the audience superimposed upon it, and not even the unrealized intent to meaning the artist might attempt to give it. Intent of artist and intent of audience are of no consequence if work of art does not itself, in and by itself, and of its own substance and accord permit and require and not disallow consentient intent.

234

For the artist art is the consolidation of substance—conditions, impulses, and impressions—of his experience into a substantial form that gives permanence to the experience-meaning he has of Nature as the qualities of that experience-meaning have been shaped by his receptive nature and modified in his retentive nature; his referential memory further qualifies the identification of the retained impressions and chooses the mode of expression, the forms, and the selected conditions of the transmissible expression of the experience-meaning. There is no implication here, however, that the choosing and selecting done by the artist are necessarily conscious activities, nor that the initial impulse to create an artistic expression, the will, inclination, or compulsion to do or make in artistic form, is a matter of deliberate response to any particular demand on any one particular quality of the artist's responsive natures. Quite possibly art results from impulses stirred by referential memory, in any of its characteristic qualities, to find expression out of the determining impulses of the memory itself functioning below or above the level of comprehension on the part of the artist. In this case, the artist receptor-retainer of impressions would be nothing other than the functional scribe of Nature herself, doing as Nature prompts and as Nature wills, with artistic submission to creative or re-creative impulses inherent in the experiences and the conditions of Nature finding reincarnate and permanent form in the expression of the artist. We do not mean to imply that such a condition is necessarily the only source of art, or even that it is a source of art. We are merely allowing for the possibility of such being the case without denying or affirming a Nature determinism as the source of art except as man the artist is himself an object of Nature. We would maintain, however, that whatever its source, whatever its impulses, whatever its motive, art, as expression using the materials of man's manipulation for the form the expression takes, is a matter of referential memory seeking and finding response-provoking form at the hands of man, and that the substantial form is what must be experienced by an audience to apprehend the experience-meaning embodied in the work of art. The impressions elicited by or compelled by the work may, in combination with other impressions in the receptor-retainer faculties of the audience, coincidentally create an experience-meaning that is not found in the initiating work of art or in the artist; but that coincidental impression of experience-meaning, though stirred by the work, is not the experience-meaning of the work; it is the experience-meaning of the audience within whom the experience-meaning is established and to whom it must be attributed. A peaceful cloud floating in the atmosphere is not the memory it evokes of a storm, and the previous experience of storm is not attributable to the existence of that one peaceful cloud. To so attribute referential memory and experience to an object which does not in itself carry the experience or the impression evoked imposes on the object qualities it does not possess and which must not be considered in the determining of its nature. To do so would be to deny the specific experience-meaning of the object and to create an experience-meaning peripheral to the nature of the object itself and additional to the whole meaning permitted and required and not disallowed by responsive fidelity and interpretive integrity. Such fidelity and integrity is requisite for genuine apprehension and valid comprehension of the experience-meaning of any object of experience. Inferential meanings are not attributable to experience unless the experience itself determines their entirety; inferential meaning is audience meaning, not art meaning, and though it is stirred by art, it is not an inherent quality of the work of art itself.

Inferential meaning, as contrasted with tangential impression, is a functional attribute of audience imposition upon or into the structured conditions and impulses of the work of art; it is audience oriented and audience initiated, and it is dependent on audience referential memory to establish it as an experience-meaning that, though the impulse activating it may reside in the work of art, is significant only outside the work of art. The significance of tangential impression, however, though it is also dependent on audience reference or audience relating to the conditions inherent in the work of art for the impulses which create responsive impressions, lies entirely within the structural identity of the work of art, and its function is to direct the focus-perspective impressions to the work of art rather than to the extra-art creative function of the audience. Inferences may be drawn from the work of art; and, indeed, particular conditions in a work of art isolated from the structural wholeness of all the conditions that make up the entire substantial form of the experience-meaning, may lead to implicational impressions from which inferences may be drawn to create an experience whose meaning is not substantiated by what the work permits, requires, and disallows. Such inferential meanings and inferential experiences may be valuable stimuli to audience knowledge and audience processes of thought, and so should not be discouraged as entertainment and enlightenment; but certainly, without total substantiation by all the qualifications inherent in the work, inferential meanings and experiences should not be allowed to alter or distort, add to or subtract from, the experience-meaning of the work itself.

Inferential meanings, by the very nature of their being audience initiated as peripherally responsive impressions with extra-art work relevance, range from impulsive caprice, usually associated with inadequately learned audience responder-receptors; self-expressive whimsy, often a gesture to attract attention to the responder through supererogatory imposition of personal whims; vagarious extravagance, a self-glorifying remaking of the work of art by interpretation into something that is the creation of the responder rather than of the artist; and crotchet, more often than not, a vainglorious setting up of an

237

almost completely unrelated set of conditions and attributing them to the work of art, or stubborn and eccentric insistence that the artist's intent was something other than what the work evidences and therefore the work itself is faulty. Audiences and critics alike are sometimes guilty of interpreting by inference, which results in implications detrimental to the nature of the art with which the interpretation is associated and does disservice to the entire functional complex of Nature, art, and audience by creating a distortion of the experience-meaning implicit in the work by subverting the structural entity of the experience-meaning that is the work expressing in substantial form the impressions which fix the experience-meaning of the work in the responsive receptor-retainer faculties of the audience.

Art is meaning put into apprehensible form; it is experience cleared of nonessentials; it is time immobilized for timeless re-experience; it is Nature reincarnated in another form; it is the breath of knowledge, the birth of wisdom, and the death of ignorance; it is the substance of the abstract made real; it is the transitory made permanent, the ephemeral made solid, the dark made light; it is the ebb and flow of human consciousness, the tide of human evolution, the surge of human meaning in the sea of human experience, and it must not be subverted by the inconsequentials of inference.

Inferential art, that vague, disassociational, alienatory, obscure expression that only seems like art because it imitates the substantial form of art and employs the tools of art without carrying the experience-meaning of art, is probably characteristic of the artistic pretenders and the "arty" of every age; quantitatively it amounts to a burden that staggers and clutters her figure with obscuring debris; qualitatively it accounts for most of the trash that bulges the walls of libraries and museums and provides the source of inconsequential tea-time blather for the less than first-rate affectors of artistic acumen for the pseudo-artistic professors of culture. Inferential criticism, likewise vague, disassociational, alienatory, and obscure, is negative rather than positive criticism; it finds its substance in what art is not rather than in what it is. It finds fault for what is not in a work, and carps on what is there. It is critic oriented rather than art oriented, and tends to give critical preferences rather than descriptive analysis and interpretation of a work of art. Perhaps the most that can be said for inferential criticism is that it provides employment for a host of mediocre teachers and commentators who would otherwise be incapable of finding time-consuming subsistence for the duration of their nonessential lives and that it does keep some few out of politics and preaching. The inferential critic would probably criticize the artist for putting a snake in Eden rather than describe the experience-meaning of the snake in Eden. Inferential criticism is presumptuous and arrogant; it is an affront to Nature, art, and artistry, and a supercilious imposition on audience consciousness; it puts a cataract on the aesthetic eye and a blight on artistic appreciation and understanding.

Parallel to inferential meaning, which has at best a dubious impulsive relationship to the work of art and which is dependent on the work of art as a prior condition for a basis of inference, is prevenient meaning, an anticipatory meaning dependent on expectation of experience-meaning to be found in the work of art and existing prior to the experiencing of the substance of the work of art. Both inferential meaning and prevenient meaning are audience oriented and both function as responsive impulses to make impressions that have little substantial or valid meaning unless the work of art explicitly permits, requires, and does not disallow impressions based in inference or prevenience. Prevenience, as well as inference, takes the form of caprice, whimsy, vagary, or crotchet; but in relation to a specific work of art, prevenience is suppositionally antecedent to direct experience with the work, whereas inference is coincidental with or postpositional in relation to experience with the work. Prevenience is pre-experiential; inference is post-experiential; of the two, prevenience is possibly the more detrimental to experience-meaning because it prefigures the experience and anticipates impressions rather than having the experience itself establish the impulses that command responsive impressions. Often prevenience is a negative or even a preventive attribute of experience; it negates when it disallows submission to the experience; it prevents when it disallows the experience. It is common for professors to hear: "I won't take that course. I live in the Twentieth Century; what can Eighteenth Century art say to me?" Here is prevenience at work preventively. Also commonplace is: "I don't like it; it isn't what I expected." Here is prevenience at work negatively. Audience expectation has nothing to do with the experience-meaning inherent in a work of art except as a prejudice predisposing impulses and presignifying responses, with the result that the experience-meaning is predetermined, often at extreme variance with the potential the work has for substantially valid experience-meaning.

Critically, prevenience implies judgment and analysis based on the prejudices of the critic rather than reliance on the experience of the work to be criticized for substance demanding description. An age that allows prevenient criticism has its art function, form, and experience-meaning determined by the critic; art becomes totally utilitarian, and its utility is only the substantiation of the critical bias that defines its function, form, and experience-meaning. Critical totalitarianism is artistically intolerable; it prohibits the freedom the artist must have if art is to evolve with Nature's evolution, and it inhibits the expression of impressions that are essential to the development and evolution of man's knowledge and wisdom. To prevail, art must maintain dominance over criticism; but prevenient criticism, by the nature of its before-the-fact speculative condition, supplants art as a creative expression and focuses interpretive attention on the critical criteria it expresses by determining for art the focal and perspective ranges to be allowed to art. It predetermines allowable impressions and predefines the values to be attributed to the work of art. It conditions audience expectation, and, in a sense, dictates the kind and quality of response to be permitted or disallowed without regard for the responsiveness that a work might itself require for apprehension of its potential experience-meaning. The experience-meaning will be the meaning of the critical criteria, not the meaning inherent in the art experience. Prevenient criticism precludes open-minded attention to the work of art because prejudgment is too difficult to set aside to allow submission to the experience of the work to occur in any other than the most astute of the geniuses among critics. Indeed, the genius among critics is not apt to be guilty of prevenient criticism, for critical genius would be too discerning of the inherent potential danger to artistic impulse and impression and freedom that prevenience induces to allow himself the liberty of employing prevenient criteria unless his intent were to mutilate and destroy the essence of art, the voiced conconscience and consciousness of Nature. It is just here, in the conscience of Nature, that prevenience affords the greatest of threats; for prevenience is arbitrary, and its arbitrary nature is most often directed toward value judgment of limited or topical application rather than toward values of universal or timeless applicability; it tends to judge "good" or "bad" in moral terms what may be conventions or customs in conditions disassociated from the predilections of the critic. Prevenient criticism is biased in that it establishes the values to be ascribed to the work of art rather than allowing the work of art to present the values that are in the nature of Nature and the nature of the conditions comprising the work of art. Art usually judges values only by the structuring of conditions to present the experience through which impressions of values may attain meaning; the predetermined values of prevenient criticism must find corroboration in the work of art, or the work is "bad" despite whatever experience-meaning of "good" or "bad" inheres in the work. Prevenience defines in the abstract, whereas art presents in the concrete; using the nature of the one to judge the experience of the other is a sin against Nature and art, and to qualify art under the terms of prevenience is to eliminate meaning from the experience of art and substitute arbitrary, biased, topically personal values for universal values, good or bad, exemplified in a work of art. Art is not good or bad, and its conditions are not good or bad, to accord with the preconceptions of a critical point of view; it is good or bad, and its conditions are good or bad, in relation to the integrity of the impressions of experience it evokes and the meaning it creates with fidelity to Nature. Here is no matter for "moral" judgment, only substance for descriptive analysis without the qualification of prevenient bias. By its insistence that the values of art, regardless of time, intent, or experience, be determined in accord with mores, conventions, and customs of a particular time, place, moral topicality, prevenience negates that sense of contemporaneity in event, experience, and meaning so essential to unbiased evaluation of art and so basic in the structural unity of the experience-meaning conditions in art and so elemental to the self-perpetuating qualities of art. Prevenience is not prevision nor clairvoyance as its practitioners would have one believe; it is strictly the establishing beforehand of the values that are to be considered in the evaluation and determination of the experience-meaning of art regardless of the qualities the art might possess outside the perspective of the prevenient criteria and the focus of the prevenient definition of art function. Prevenient critics are usually characterized by the priestly priggishness of their pronouncements, the unilateral prejudice of their attitudes, the holier-than-thou self-satisfaction with their abilities, and the biased moral certitude of their tone. Prevenience in operation in typical fashion might go something like this:

Administrative censor: No. You can't produce *Oedipus the King.*
Drama director: Why not?
Administrative censor: Because it's a dirty play.
Drama director: Have you read it?
Administrative censor: No.
Drama director: Will you read it before you give your final re-
    fusal?
Administrative censor: Certainly not.
Drama director: Why not?
Administrative censor: Because it's a dirty play.

Narrow-minded? Ignorant? Stupid? Irrational? Prejudiced? No.
Only prevenient.

Allied with, and usually derived from, prevenient approaches
to Nature and to art are triplet demons that feed on critical
vanity and ignorance and excrete on Nature and art: intervenient criticism, interpolative criticism, and interpositional
criticism. The three are additive in that they infuse into art
conditions that are not necessarily relevant to the function of
art and incite impulsive responses that are not derivative from
the particular work of art, but rather from the nature of the
infused conditions, themselves alien to the structurally related
conditions and impulses of the pristine original art expression.
Interposition, in this sense, is perhaps the least offensive of the
three because its function is merely suggestive of prescription
or definition. Interpositional approaches to art, by their suggestive natures, put forward prevenient suggestions and condition the responsive natures of the audience to expect particular
qualities or conditions in the work of art. A tendency is given
impulse to find justification in the work of art for the suggestion;
anything remotely suggestive of substantiation of the suggestion,
even, perhaps especially, out of context, is regarded as proof
positive of the validity of the interpositional point of view by
the interpositional critic, and the work is judged by its vindication of the critical attitude. If, however, the context of the work

243

reveals no parts or conditions to vindicate the interpositional attitude, the critical response to the work, no matter what the potential experience-meaning of the work itself might be, is negative. Interpositional criticism introduces speculative criteria, and because speculation requires validation and vindication in order to establish its authority, it defines preveniently what must be in art to justify its position as arbiter of art. What is implied here is not that an interpositional critical approach is invalid, but rather that the validity of the interpositional approach must be substantiated by the work of art, by the experience-meaning of the whole work of art, before the speculative theory may be considered as an appropriate means of arriving at the truth of the art experience. But the art experience that is fragmented, that is determined by prevenient interposition, that finds its meaning in parts that vindicate a particular point of view, or that is diffused by failure to find substantiation of the interpositional view, is not the truth of the potential experience-meaning of the work of art; and beauty that is suggested by interpositional definition is not the beauty to be found in the fidelity to Nature of the genuine art experience and the integrity of the work of art as an expressive impression of Nature. Interpositional truth and interpositional beauty are artifices of critical approach and critical self-focus rather than attributes of Nature and of art and art focus; and their perspectives are critical rather than artistic, definitive rather than experiential, prescriptive rather than descriptive, theoretical rather than actual and real. Suggestion is meritorious when it is soundly based in the entire substance of the experience-meaning of the whole substantial form, but it is deleterious when its aim is toward vindicating interpositional attitude rather than toward apprehension of the experience-meaning of the work of art. Interposition is a sort of critical promissory note with no real substance to serve as collateral when it is called for payment. It is indebted to art, but without subsidy by art it operates as an artistic deficit and as a drain on the substance of the Nature wherein art finds its resource.

Intervenience, though not as prevenient as interposition, is more obvious in its additive function. It uses the work of art or nature as collateral, but misrepresents the nature of its resources by causing irrelevant qualities of its nature to be interpreted as influencing conditions or impulses within art or Nature. Intervenience is impositionally interpretive, and it pleads its own cause rather than the cause of art or Nature. It attributes its own interpretive values to the work of art to inflate the abstract value of the work and thereby establish a paper capital disproportionate to the natural experience-meaning value of the work of art. Interpretive distortion of the experience-meaning value then becomes the interest-bearing capital of the intervenient critic, and he operates at a profit as long as the inflated value of his collateral remains unchallenged. But once discerning audit reveals the discrepancies between the real experience-meaning and the inflated experience-meaning the collapse of the intervenient structure of interpretive distortion is inevitable and the resulting depression of the over-all attributed values—the experience-meaning of the work combined with the irrelevancies of intervenient interpretation—leads to bankruptcy of the critical structure and a momentary, at best, deflation of the experience-meaning value of the work of art. This deflation is almost in itself a law of Nature as a reaction to the disenchantment brought about by the failure of a trusted institution. If the values of art itself were not the only substantially real values, the failure of the intervenient interpretation would be disastrous to art; but, happily, real art in the long run establishes its own real value despite the setbacks of additive or subtractive distortions of its experience-meaning and perpetuates itself to outlive any of the corruptive interpretive forces that attach themselves to it. Intervenience modifies, influences, and hinders valid interpretation of the inherent experience-meaning in a work of art by interfering with the fusion and merging of the conditions and impulses of that work of art as they combine to form the impressions that become the experience of the work made a response demanding meaning. The primary function of intervenient criticism or interpretation is the protection of its own interests and the satisfaction of its own arguments; as with all digressive modes of interpretive function, its values are focused on art as a tool of the interpreter rather than having the focal values of the work of art determine the nature and direction of the critical perspective. All additive or subtractive means of interpretation distort the experience-meaning of art and all are detrimental to the understanding of the function of art as an audience experience and the apprehension of the art experience as a meaning of Nature building through experience the comprehensive qualities of man's potential in the world that is his. Intervenience precludes the total submission to the experience that is an essential of uncorrupted knowing the experience because intervenience by its own "coming between" nature alters impressions of conditions and impulses that inhere in the substantial form of the experience expression and distorts the impressions as they emanate from the structural affinity of the conditions and impulses within the form of the experience. As the distortions merge with other impressions in the retentive faculties of the receptor, they further divorce themselves from the realities of the art experience and become the impulses generating fancies about art that have little or nothing to do with a particular art experience, and these fancies in turn become the criteria by which another work of art may be judged, thus moving the functions of response farther and farther from art and nearer and nearer to criticism as the initiator of experience-meaning. As art diminishes or is diminished by such practices, it becomes less and less an object of experience-meaning and more and more merely an esoteric cultural decoration functioning only for a precious effete; the vitality of art becomes exhausted, and its values become the subject of effete determinism, serving only to ornament sterility and create an affected façade of aesthetic appreciation and apprehension. Intervenience, together with other prevenient and additive or subtractive influences, is conducive to decadence in both response to Nature and response to art—in artist and critic and audience —and leads to ignorant pride in degeneracy, glorifying ego centered conceptions, values, and prejudices and creating a false sense of individual worth and ability in relation to Nature and art. In the hands of the degenerate and the decadent, the effetely sterile, art and Nature become baubles, playthings, in a sophisticated nonreality where art and Nature are disassociated from experience-meaning and make-believe becomes the standard of experiential response and judgment, where fanciful impression takes precedence over functional reality, where the ignorant teach the wise, and where aberrants become the standardizers of normalcy. In such an atmosphere art and Nature become impure, absorbing the corruption and the contamination of pretense and the putrescence of prejudice. Interpretation becomes a matter of privately individual conception: Shakespeare's *Hamlet* becomes Smith's *Hamlet*, Jones's *Hamlet*, Pupovitch's *Hamlet*; Shakespeare's *Hamlet* ceases to exist except as a tool to build the reputations of Smith, Jones, and Pupovitch; and the experience-meaning of *Hamlet* is whatever distortion capable of being popularized that Smith, Jones, or Pupovitch can make of it. May the Protector of Nature save us from Smith, Jones, and Pupovitch!

Interposition, intervenience, and interpolation are all inhibitors of natural evolution in the functional processes of reception, retention, response, and expression; they tend to establish artificial criteria both for the artist and for the audience by infiltrating into artist and audience consciousnesses qualities and concepts that emanate from inexperience and inadequately conceived speculation and to ingratiate themselves into the arbitrary

critical structures that become the inheritance of a new generation of artists and audiences. This process of regeneration of
inherited critical "truth" perpetuates functional ignorance; and
whenever the new generation uncritically venerates the traditions of its cultural heritage and qualifies its own experiences
with the errors of its ancestry, stagnation and regression are the
natural consequence. Artistic response to Nature, fidelity in expressing impressions of experience, integrity in reception and
retention of impressions, and freedom from erroneous interpretation of fused and merged impressions are requisite to natural,
functional evolution of the art process from experience to expression of impression to reception of impression to reincarnation of experience. Tradition may well serve as a guide in the
process, but it must not be the sole determiner of the entire
function, particularly when the traditional heritage is founded
in topical conditions of its own time and generates qualities that
even in its own time were error-ridden or were lacking in the
impulses that cause to evolve the contemporaneity of universal
truth which is the only tradition of cultural heritage meriting
functional application by another generation. Traditions are
meritorious when they harmonize with the experiences of another age, but they are deleterious when their influences inhibit
progressive evolution or when they become the arbitrary dicta-
tors of functional processes out of their own age.

Interposition and intervenience are insidious deterrents to
natural evolutionary processes because their effects are insinuative and therefore difficult to discern when they become part
of a body of inherited traditions; but those effects exercise a real
influence in determining the values to be ascribed to impression and expression out of the context of their own time because they create an intercurrent of response that seemingly
relates topicality, universality, and contemporaneity. This is
particularly true under conditions that permit the garnering of
so-called facts from the past and the acceptance of those "facts"

unquestioningly as contemporaneous truth. Smith's speculation in one generation becomes Jones's fact in another generation and Pupovitch's truth in another, and in each stage of development chronic acceptance of error or misinterpretation creates an aura of validity that is quite insusceptible to correction or emendation. Inveterate "truth," no matter how invalid, becomes the *status quo* of responsive fidelity; and, through nonskeptical immersion in "truth," the responder becomes confirmed in a perpetuating sequence of conditions and impulses that disorient both artistic and natural integrity. Fidelity and integrity cease to be functions of the truth of natural experience and become the mythical and superstitious truths of speculative and fanciful inexperience and ignorance. Beauty ceases to be in actuality and exists only in definition prescribed by inherited tradition whenever cultural heritage and its perpetuated errors take precedence over participation in the conditions of experience that describe the functional processes of natural evolution in both Nature and art. Prevenient approaches, when they become effectual "truth," create artificial rather than natural evolution, and their effects lead away from valid response rather than to the fidelity and integrity of natural experience and submission to the conditions and impulses that inhere in the substantial form or in Nature as the only valid bases for the impressions of experience that provide interpretive fidelity and integrity.

As an additive to functional experience, interposition interrupts the fusing and merging processes that combine the conditions and impulses of natural experience and that provide the relative "meaning" of the impressions creating experience-meaning for the responder to Nature and art. The suggestive nature of interposition interrupts the structural unity of the experiential conditions to create divergent or digressive impulses that may lead responsive faculties away from the particularities of the modifying and qualifying functions of fusion and merging and thereby establish both focuses and perspectives alien to,

249

extended from, or distorting of the focuses and perspectives of the uncontaminated experience. Intervenience, though also additive, is interpretive rather than interruptive. It distorts the fusing and merging processes most often by lifting conditions and impulses out of context and establishing their meaning in terms of theory or speculation or prejudice and reinserting conditions and impulses with their newly specified meaning back into the structure of the experience to alter the impressions generated by the fusion of the new meaning with the merged conditions of the original structure of experience-meaning. Hamlet, with an Oedipus Complex interveniently inserted into an interpretation of the "Hamlet conditions," alters the experience-meaning impressions of *Hamlet* and makes an Oedipal Hamlet quite a different experience from a Hamlet not subject to the Oedipus Complex. A "flaw in character" interposition becomes an inveterate "truth" as a suggestive requirement for tragedy and creates a need on the part of an audience to find a flaw in character where no such flaw need exist as a meaningful necessity of tragedy; and indeed the search for a flaw and the felt need of finding a flaw might lead both the artist and the audience to introduce interruptive speculation that would drastically alter the initial experience-meaning of a work of art or Nature and establish a focus or a perspective completely alien to the experience-meaning inhering in the experience.

Interposition and intervenience are both insinuative, and, in a sense, both are interpolative in that they add to the essential experience conditions of their own formulation, suggestive and interpretive. Interpolation, however, in its fittest sense, adds substance to the already total accumulation of conditions and impulses in the initial substantial form of art or experience of Nature. Even when interpolation has as its purpose the clarification of an experience or condition or impulse impression, its function is additive and its effect is distortive. If anything can be added to or subtracted from a total experience without altering that experience, the structural qualities of the conditions and impulses of the experience are either deficient or excessive, and the experience-meaning of the whole substantial form— particularly in art—is either inadequate or superfluous and therefore unworthy of the highest accolades of art. Critically, interpolation, by adding substance to a work, creates a new and different substantial form, a form alien to the original and containing conditions and impulses and creating impressions apart from the experience-meaning delineated by the original form; criticism of the new form cannot be transferred to the original form without attributing to the original form qualities that it does not possess, qualities that are uniquely those of the new form and not necessarily applicable or attributable to the original form of experience-meaning. Interpolation creates meanings of its own, meanings superfluous to the required experience-meaning of the original structure of conditions and impulses in the original substantial form. This is not to say that the new experience-meaning may not be superior in its own nature to the original experience-meaning, but that the new experience-meaning is not the experience-meaning of the original and that any critical interpretation of only the new experience-meaning impression is invalid interpretation of the original. Two lines added to the substance of *Hamlet*, the popularly accepted textual *Hamlet*, to substantiate a particular interpretation of *Hamlet* create a new *Hamlet*, a different *Hamlet* from the original, a *Hamlet* that must be criticized apart from Shakespeare's *Hamlet* and with qualifying and modifying conditions that can not be attributed to Shakespeare's *Hamlet* in an appraisal of Shakespeare's *Hamlet* that has fidelity and integrity.

Interpolation functions principally in critical scholarship dealing with works from the past and in contemporary performance arts. Scholarly interpolation is concerned primarily with restoration and emendation of faulty or mutilated works, and when it is done with integrity and fidelity to the principles of the work being interpolated, it is a meritorious service to art. When, however, the purpose of interpolation is to modernize or to popularize a work of art out of the artistic conditions of its own time or out of the context of its own experience-meaning, that purpose serves only to create a different piece of art and performs a disservice to the original work, although the new creation may be in itself a meritorious supplement to the field of art so long as its own qualities are not critically attributed to the original. Christian interpolations into non-Christian art change the experience-meaning of the non-Christian substantial form and create a new experience-meaning, perhaps worthwhile in its own right, but hardly conducive to fair analysis and interpretation of the original non-Christian expression and hardly evocative of the responses required to reincarnate the experience-meaning impressions of the original or to generate the submissive impulses of unbiased evaluation. A Christian *Beowulf* is not a non-Christian *Beowulf* even though a non-Christian *Beowulf* may establish an extremely worthy experience-meaning of its own. Interpolation hinders apprehension of the experience-meaning of the original work in its own contextual substance of conditions, impulses, and impressions; but it may aid in the comprehension of a new and different experience-meaning that results from a combination of the conditions of the original and the conditions supplied by interpolation. When interpolation has as its main purpose the enhancement of a particular interpretive point of view that is not essential to the experience-meaning of the noninterpolated work, interpolation is a subversion of the functions of Nature and art in relation to that work; but when it serves to correct transmitted errors of prior interpolation, interposition, or intervenience, or to restore impression evocative impulses and conditions lost or mutilated in transmission, it functions in service to Nature and art. Interpolation is never meritorious when its aim is to distort the impression impulses of an original, to disturb the experience-meaning of that original, or to create a new experience-meaning at the nonrecompensed expense of the original. Interpolation in performance arts is reprehensible when biased interpretation for popular appeal is its object and particularly when the presentation is made in such a manner as to attribute the interpolations to the original or to sanctify the interpolator by attributing to him the qualities of the original. Just as art is its own reason for being, its own justification, and its own perpetuator, so must its evaluation and its worth rest on its own merits; and so must interpolation rest on its own merits, not upon the reputation of that which has been the subject of interpolative addition. Just as with criticism, interpolation is secondary to art. It depends on the prior existence of art to provide the conditions of its function, and it cannot be allowed to usurp the position of art as the expression of Nature or the object of Nature representational impression. Interpolation may be an adherent of art, but it is not a peer of art; and when it is passed off as a functional component of the art experience its position is hypocritical at best.

Directly related to interpolation and other additive devices of art experience alteration are the practices of substitution and rearrangement to create a different form of impression from that inherent in the experience-meaning of the unconverted form. Though additive devices change structural relationships, usually they retain enough of the quality of the original to provide a significant identification with the original. Indeed, the additive critic or interpreter is most often dependent on identification with the merits of the original to qualify him for any recognition, and therefore it behooves him to identify as much as possible with the original unless his main purpose is to destroy the identity of the original and to establish a counterfeit in its place or to remove the original as a potential experience-meaning impulse to man's responsive natures. Substitution and rearrangement disorient the fusion process within the work of art; and by upsetting the functional relationships of the conditions structured into the substantial form, they establish impulses totally alien to the qualifying and modifying functions of the conditions which create the impressions that form the original experience-meaning of the work. Both substitution and rearrangement are devices employed by critics, interpreters, and audiences to make the experience of the work say what they want said, rather than to allow the work to say what it has to say. A degree of prevenience is usually present when substitution or rearrangement is operative, but these processes may come into being because of error or unconscious transposition of expressions or conditions.

Substitution is generally a device employed to make a work conform to a particular prevenient standard of taste or to a particular topical ideology determined by popular criteria or critical prejudice. It is usually deliberate in such instances, and its aim is to protect audience or critic from experiences contrary to its definitions of "right experience" or "right meaning." When it is deliberate, with such aims, substitution is a dastardly perversion of art function; and, no matter how well-meaning, it corrupts and distorts the communal memory of man and creates an arbitrarily one-sided limitation on man's potential for knowledge expansion and experiential evolution by establishing bias and prejudice as the determinants of "right function" in art. Substitution corrupts art by changing the conditions in the work of art so that a different fusion of impressions may result in a different responsive identification or so that an alienation from experience-meaning of the originally structured conditions and impulses may occur. Through substitution art becomes a vehicle for propaganda rather than an expression of experience-meaning. Practitioners of substitution have contempt for the integrity of art and its fidelity to Nature; they are bent on propagating their own views and do not hesitate to contaminate anything that may be used to serve their narrow-minded, usually fanatical, purposes. They are the litterbugs of art, driving through the ways of art with the tailgate of their garbage truck down, spewing pollution on anything beautiful or true that happens to be in the way. They unload their filth in the food bins of artistry and feed their mess to art consumers. They use a truckload of manure to fertilize one little violet and destroy it with their own excrement, deliberately, knowing full well that its natural perfume cannot penetrate their shoveled-on odor and that its fragile beauty cannot pierce the heavy muck they pile on it.

Substitution, as the term implies, denotes the putting of one thing in place of another—it is additive and subtractive at the same time. It subtracts conditions from the original experience-meaning structure, and it adds conditions that form a new experience-meaning structure more to the liking or inclination of whoever makes the substitution. For the substitutive interpreter art has no inviolability; it is there merely as an object on which he has license to operate in his own way for his own selfish ends to establish his own experience-meaning out of that which he was incapable of conceiving as an expression of his own origination. The substitutive interpreter is a cancer in the body of art, incapable of function outside art and destroying the organic wholeness of that which it inhabits. Pristine art ceases to exist when through substitution its experience-meaning has suffered alteration. Humpty Dumpty isn't Humpty Dumpty when a tennis ball is substituted for his egg body. Substitution changes conditions, and changed conditions in the art context change the experience-meaning that art is. Perhaps there are those who would prefer Humpty Dumpty with a tennis ball body, but what would be the experience of "all the King's horses and all the King's men" if the substitution were made? Substitution may improve upon a work of art, but the work of art that has been "improved" isn't what it was; the improved work of art is not conducive to the same responsive impression as was its source, and its experience-meaning is not the experience-meaning of the egg-bodied Humpty Dumpty. Shakespeare could put an ass's head in Fairyland; the substitutive interpreter puts it into everything he touches; the difference is that Shakespeare did it with art and wisdom, whereas the substitutive interpreter does it with a mirror showing his own likeness.

Substitution assumes that interpretation is superior to the art that it acts upon; it arrogates unto itself the function of art improvement, to bring art up to standards it sets, on the assumption that the non-artistic critic or audience knows better than the artist what is permissible or required in art function. The substitutive interpreter is of necessity an expurgator of art before he is an appender to art. He expunges what is objectionable to him or purges art of that which has the impulse to impress an experience-meaning contrary to the experience-meaning he wishes to have expressed. In this context he is a deletionary critic, a bowdlerizer, an art emasculator. He would geld Don Juan and spay Fanny Hill. He would take away the charms of Helen or the vivid frankness of the Wife of Bath. His Iago would not be malevolent, and his Juliet would be without innocence. His *Faerie Queene* would not be written in Spenserian stanzas, nor would his *Odyssey* be in epic form. As the substitutive interpreter interpolates to replace his expurgations, Don Juan would become an altar boy and Fanny would be the Mother Superior in a Cloister. Helen would be repulsive and the Wife of Bath would blush chastely whenever the Parson passed by. Iago would be a scoutmaster and Juliet a go-go dancer. The *Faerie Queene* would be in heroic couplets and the *Odyssey* would become a sonnet sequence. Substitution cannot leave art alone; it beats resistance out of its victim and rapes the defenseless form, impregnating it with the seed of monstrous distortion and causing it to give birth to a mutant, misshaped and malignant, a caricature of art and Nature. Snow White puts on blackface, Lear becomes an Eskimo chief, Uncle Tom goes into the bleach pot, and Pontius Pilate pardons a young Jew.

The substitutive assault on art mutilates form, corrupts experience, mutates impulses, contorts impressions, conditions responses, and makes meaning in art meaningless.

Deletionary or expurgatory functioning pillages art and Nature, loots them of their experience-meaning properties, and supplies them with a new order of conditions. It ravages and devastates. It despoils art, and it spoils what it doesn't totally destroy. Its function is not to preserve art but to preserve the biases of its practitioners and perpetuate in the communal consciousness and memory only those qualities supporting the topical prejudices of a particular critical perspective. Expurgative critical approach selects for retention in art those qualities and conditions of art that are complementary to its own point of view and purges art of those qualities and conditions that might propagate a contrary view or impression. In the processes of selecting, deleting, substituting, and adding, art undergoes a transformation that destroys the identity of its origins, the identification of its own experience-meaning, the natural fidelity of its structure, the complementary function of its form and tone, the integrity of the relationships of its conditions, the response evocative force of its impulses, and the effectiveness of its impressions; it no longer remains art but becomes merely a tool used unscrupulously to give semblance of artistic character to its user, artistic credence to propagandistic views, authority to topical opinion, grace to prosaic thought, image of natural fidelity and integrity to gelded, ornamented, mutant structure, and façade of validity to the distortion of impressions that it emits and evokes. Substitution, or any of the qualities that make up substitution, steals from art, exercises a sort of reverse plagiarism by inserting into art conditions and meanings contrary to those it lifts from art. The substitutive practitioner is an artistic pickpocket. He takes the valuables of art with one hand and dexterously replaces them with his own dross with the other. His only fidelity is to his craft of thievery; his only loyalty is to his own selfish prejudices; and the only integrity he has is relative to his nature as a looter of art. This is not to say that practices of substitution are always all bad. Individual cases of substitution may improve individual works of art even though the practice destroys the identity of the work as an original expression of experience-meaning; and certainly not all works of art are good art, nor do all works of art merit respectful consideration. But the practitioners of substitution rarely have the ability or the appreciation requisite to meritorious choice of the object upon which they will operate; and it were far better for hundreds of works of bad art to survive than for one work of good art to be mutilated. Putting fire to a forest to flush out one porcupine gnawing on a tree may save another tree from that porcupine, but perhaps the fire will do more to the forest than the porcupine would. Practitioners of substitution are arsonists of the whole of art to get at the one porcupine gnawing on one tree in the art forest.

Substitution is quite often less obvious than the foregoing would seem to indicate, and its practice is more often than not one of unconscious response rather than of deliberate intent to destroy or mutilate. Most substitution is to be discerned in audience response to impression impulses and takes the form of audience substitution of its prevenient meaning for the experience-meaning inhering in the structure of conditions in the substantial form. An audience may substitute its understanding of the meaning of a word for the meaning established by the context of the work. Ignorance of symbolic significance may allow the substitution of personal meaning for the purposed meaning of symbolic experience. Functional imbalance in responsive natures may occasion faulty reception of impulses and cause substitution of impressions in either the receptive or retentive faculties of the audience, and response imbalance may cause substitution of experience-meanings quite outside the awareness of the audience. Failure to comprehend the relationships of conditions in the process of merging and fusing might well cause a substitution of an unqualified or unmodified impression for one that should be quite another experience. Lack of apprehension of the complementary function of form and tone to meaning and experience could cause a substitution that would completely alter the potential intensity of the experience and thereby distort the meaning of the experience or even void the experience of any meaning. But lack of intent to do harm does not minimize the harm done to art as a whole by the practices of substitution or deletion. Perhaps there is even greater harm done by unconscious substitution than there is by deliberate substitution. Whether a hand is amputated by accident or by intentional surgery matters little in consideration of the loss of function of that hand. Indeed, accidental amputation probably will occasion greater danger of infection and mutilation than will deliberate amputation. Art can very well do without either deliberate or accidental amputation, and the substitution of prosthetic devices for the natural part will seldom restore the total function of the organically sound whole. A mechanical hand may do different things than will a sound natural hand, but it certainly will lack the qualities of dexterity and feeling that the natural hand has. And a glass eye seldom functions as efficiently as the natural eye. Glass-eyed, hand-amputated art is not the art that functions most effectively in the evolution of human experience or in the development of Nature comprehension.

Another device of critical interpretation, or misinterpretation, widely practiced by those who place their own sense of artistic fitness above their regard for the inviolability of art or the expression of the artist is rearrangement of the parts of the work of art to bring about a different sequence of conditions and a consequent difference in the modifying and qualifying fusion and merging within the substantial form to create an impression of experience-meaning not conveyed or given impulse by the original order of conditions. Rearrangement is often used to give credence to a particular critical point of view: using a particular order in the presentation of Shakespeare's sonnets to give semblance of a design that originates in the mind of the critic rather than as a function of the poet; playing with the possible relative positions of the poems in *In Memoriam* to establish a sequence that verifies a particular view of Tennyson's poetic development, or his philosophic evolution, or his intensity of grief; or the changing of positions of scenes in *Hamlet* to demonstrate a particular actor's interpretation of Hamlet as a valid portrayal of what Shakespeare "really meant." Rearrangement distorts the focus in art and creates a perspective at variance with that of the original structural order of conditions. The experience-meaning is altered because the structural relationships of conditions and impulses that establish impressions no longer function with the same harmony with the rest of the substance of the work as their original relative positions as modifiers and qualifiers of experience-meaning indicate they should if the work is an example of artistic fidelity and integrity. Rearrangement alters tone and mood, artistic complements of idea and experience inherent in the experience-meaning of the structurally unified substantial form and creators of the relative impressions that become the meaning of the work to an audience. When done deliberately, rearrangement is a rape of art function; when done inadvertently, as in the case of accidental transposing of words, it also impregnates the work of art with seed that will give birth to experience-meaning not native to the original nature of the work. In either case, rearrangement inhibits the projection of impulses true to the original structure and makes the reception of impressions and the apprehension of experience-meaning from the original work an impossibility for the audience. Barrymore becomes the creator of his own Hamlet even though the audience attributes Barrymore's Hamlet to Shakespeare, and Shakespeare is criticized for Barrymore's

260

handling of Hamlet—if Barrymore should presume to improve upon Shakespeare's interpretation of Hamlet.

Tonal substitution is quite often achieved by rearrangement, and the complementary function of tone as an adjunct to experience-meaning may then establish impressions out of keeping with the tonal impulses required by the previous arrangement. If art is to remain pristine, if it is to have any validity in the evolutionary processes of man's nature, if it is to maintain its position as the highest quality of man's communal memory and the record of his function in Nature, it must remain free from the contorters of its form, structure, tone, substance, conditions, impulses, and experience-meaning impressions. Nothing that is disallowed by the structural identity of a work of art should be allowed to a critic or interpreter or audience of art; nothing that is required by the work of art for total response to its experience-meaning should be deleted; nothing inhering in the conditions of the work should be altered in any way; and nothing permitted by the work should be disallowed if it is not in excess of what the work itself permits or requires; otherwise, art ceases to function as anything other than a base for critic-audience improvisation and innovative intrusion into its sense.

Experience, as a functional process in both the creative and the responsively re-creative base of art, is Nature in operation, stirring impulses to the surface of the conditions carrying the experience to create impressions that are the meaning of experience. To preserve fidelity to Nature and integrity in responsive interpretation of both Nature and the artistic voice of Nature, a relative affinity of art and Nature must be maintained; a balance between the order and structure of natural experience and the order and structure of the expressive impression of experience is requisite to responsive interpretation that is neither excessive in total responsive function nor deficient in the functional processes of reception, retention, and expression. Balance, then, is the principle that, growing out of functional relationships in Nature, becomes the functional principle in the structuring of conditions in art to maintain the natural fidelity and integrity of Nature as an expressive impression or reincarnation of natural experience in art. Without such relative balance in and with both natural experience and reincarnate experience in the substantial form of art re-creation, there can be no relative meaning; the experience-meaning of art then has no base, no originating condition or impulse, no functional identification with any experience to set in motion responsive impulses generating experience-meaning of human level significance, and art nullifies itself as a potential functional experience. But it is precisely here, in experience, in Nature, that art finds both its source of conditions, its impulses to being, its impressions requiring expression, its essence becoming manifest in the substantial form of art and through art becoming the apprehensible meaning of being in the nature of all experience to which man is susceptible. Consequently, if the substantial forms of impressions of experience do not correlate with natural experience, if expression of impressions is not contingent upon experience, if impulses are not emergent from experience in Nature, and if the apprehensive qualities of man's responsive nature do not receive, retain, and transmit the essence of natural experience and make it manifest in substantial form, there is no art; there is no record of truth; there is no communal, transmissible apprehension of beauty; and there is no evolutionary process in the nature of man or the nature of Nature to inform man of either his progression or his regression in relation to anything with which he is associated or with which he may compare his state for evaluation of his condition in Nature. Art is a corollary of Nature, of experience in Nature; it is the expression in substantial form of the experience-meaning of Nature, of the essence of Nature made manifest; it is the memory of experience, of functional processes in Nature that provide the meaning of being; it is the memory bank of experience to be drawn upon by all ages in the search for truth and beauty. Without art, experience passes without record, and meaning has no transmissible substance. Without art, time floats without direction, and Nature evolves without a conscious being's awareness of the occurrence of change. Without art, Prometheus' fire is extinguished, and the gods go unworshiped. Without art, knowledge is inert, and the earthworm and man are peers in wisdom, in conscious and conscientious formation of impressions, and in conscionable reliance on Nature as the impulsive source of all experience and of all meaning—the fire is out; the conscious memory is dead; the conscience is yet to be; the experience is meaningless; and the meaning is merely a mechanical, chemical, electrical process without thought, emotion, or intuition; there is no consciousness of a change in direction, no awareness of the meaning of experience, no impulse to create, no inspiration, and no aspiration. Prometheus taught all arts to all men and raised man, the image of the god, above the earthworm; and without the arts of Prometheus, man must return to the soil and perform with his brother beasts as a competitive equal; or he will perish, unable to function in the perpetuating processes of natural balance.

263

VIII

THE UNITY IMPULSE

OF ALL THE QUALITIES AND CONDITIONS AND IMPULSES OF Nature, Time alone possesses within itself the unique property of absolute ubiquity; for Time alone is the one common, totally universal principle within which all Nature's functions and evolutionary processes find setting. And Time by itself is without dimension; only by relation to other conditions of Nature may it be segmented or fragmented, and then only in terms of the duration of the condition or quality of the condition against which or toward which it imposes itself. Time envelops all of Nature and is involved in all the functions and processes of Nature. For this reason, perhaps the ancients were wrong who, in defining the limits of artistic imitation of Nature, supposed a unity of time as a finite principle that could be arbitrarily contained. In actuality, however, only the substance of conditions, the quality of impulses and consequent action show potential for finite limitation; and the complexity of natural fusion and assimilation of substances and impulses and the consequent variety of potential conditions and actions defy unconditional definition save by the inscrutable omniscience of Time and the irresistibly evolutionary omnipotence of Nature, to-

The Unity Impulse

gether and inseparably fused to form the one constant: the evolutionary continuum of self. Within the magnitude of the Time-Nature complex, all other conditions are minute, miniscule, measurable only in infinitesimal units of impulse impact on the evolutionary process and in terms of degrees of influence upon each other, but of no great consequence to the grand natural realm within which they move, the setting of all motive and action.

Time is the essence of all Nature, of all Nature's processes and functions, of the evolutionary principle in Nature's hegemonic ethic-aesthetic, and of the mean-tolerance in Nature's self-perpetuating identity. Time may and does limit substance, condition, and impulse (the materials and functions of natural process) and allows them a topical reference which provides a seeming validity to sequential but not necessarily natural or actual experience. But since Time is ubiquitous and all enveloping (and the one essential for the existence of Nature—the life force or spirit of Nature, so to speak) it is Time which determines durational quality of substance, condition, and impulse (and the impressional durability of finite experiential awareness and responsiveness); substance and condition and impulse are merely the tools of Time wielded by Nature to create a transitional experience-meaning impression of consequence-provoking potential, identifiable only by sentient beings capable of sequential memory-impression processes, by sentient or nonsentient beings capable of genetic transmission of experience, and of nonsentient nonbeings capable only of alteration through the mechanically transforming processes of natural evolution. Artistically, then, Time (in that imitation of Nature termed *Art*) is the prime limiter, and substance (the materials structured into the substantial form of impression-evoking qualities by the artist) is the limited. All action, impulse, or experience-meaning provocation is *in medias res* in terms of Time as an infinite principle of Nature, finitely determinable only through

265

arbitrary establishment of consequential relativity to topical conditions or by the realization of experience-meaning as an infinitesimal iota of apprehension finitely fixed as an impression provocative in the infinite ubiquity of Time. Only in such terms may there be a unity of time validly consequential to any action in Nature represented substantially in the translation of experience into form, the meaning of art.

The ubiquity of Time is naturally the one omnipresence wherein even Nature is at her least an indigenous quality and at most a coexistent, coeval entity, a manifest form of evident function, the natural and total habitat of all her separate parts assimilated by interrelatedness and interdependence into a determinable and self-determinative identity, recognizable in part through the efforts of her sentient parts and perpetuated in forms other than her own by the innovative functions of art substituting representational substances for the evanescent qualities of experience. Time delimits substance and experience, and Time mutates impressions of experience-meaning, the processes of sentient memory and genetic memory and nonorganic mechanical memory, just as she mutates the substances and materials forming the Nature of the natural universe. The *Unity of Time*, therefore, is prevalence of Time, and Time is the prevenient essence of all functions and processes, natural or imitative. Chronology and historicity are merely arbitrarily imposed adjuncts to Time, rational attempts sentiently devised to provide topical reference points for the fixing of event or memory or experience-meaning within the finite relativity of a minute fragment of sentient recall. As adjuncts of Time, attributive to rational sentience-seeking of referential focuses, chronology and authenticity of event sequence are only subserviently and topically relative to the temporal infinity of macrocosmic magnitude and perspective. The referential focuses, even of events of such duration as the perceivable history of man as a sentient creature, reflect at most microscopic experience-meanings; and the arts of man must, therefore, be viewed, not as microcosmic representations of the macrocosm, but rather as bits and pieces of impressions of the microcosm reflecting momentary experience in Time with conditions that in themselves have momentous implications only to the microcosmic nature of sentient beings whose affinity to macrocosmic Nature is so tenuous that it might be termed insignificant except in relation to the ego-defined importance of temporal topicality. Time, then, is a principle of duration, but not of measurable duration except by artificially imposed focuses establishing points of departure from which not Time, but duration is gauged, and gauged in terms of action or event occurring not with the ubiquity of Time, but rather with the ubiety of topical or environmental conditions.

Ubiety, contrary to ubiquity, may be fixed naturally and positionally within the framework of Nature. The "where" of an action or event has a natural physical quality that does not transcend sensory perception, but the "when" of the same action or event depends upon arbitrary and artificial delimitation referentially imposed and measured by the durability of that action or event relative to some rationally devised scheme of temporal or environmental fragmentational focus. The "when" transcends sensory perception in natural functional ubiquity, whereas the "where" depends upon the ubiety of natural function and is essentially a condition of local relation. Ubiety, though alterable by Time mutation of the relations of local conditions and locales, is the one state in Nature relatively stable in spite of evolutionary processes, environmental fluctuations, and artificial innovations; but this does not imply a stability that is static, for the "where" of a particular physical condition in Nature is subject to the same ultramundane laws as are all the other conditions of Nature, and the concept of place as a nonviolable "where" would defy the essential integrity of Nature as sole determiner of her own nature under the excess-

267

deficiency provision of her mean-tolerance fixation prerogative. Suffice it to say that though Nature may put a mountain
in a place once occupied by a sea, the "whereness" of a place
as opposed to the conditions occupying "where," the space-
occupancy condition aside, remains constant in relation to natural law. Even if man were to move the mountain, the physical
"where" of its former locale would not be altered; only the appearance of "where" would be changed. This, of course, in
the interrelatedness of all the conditions of Nature, would affect other conditions and effect alterations of their forms, substances, and impulses; but the result would not affect natural
ubiety, merely the physical characteristics of "where." Certainly
this does not imply an impediment to movement from place to
place, from physical to metaphysical or to nonphysical, from
local to universal, or from mundane to extra- or ultramundane.
Rather it implies that though appearance of place may have
many faces, its positional reality is constant; and, by sequential
extension of logic, seeming is not necessarily being, and physical
quality is not the essence of place, in the sense of natural ubiety.
Action must move conditions from place to place—otherwise
there is no dynamic function, no drama, no motion; and art,
as a translation of Nature, must show movement or represent
movement, at least as an evocation of response or an impulse
to sentient awareness, to be valid in terms of the natural ethic-
aesthetic transferred to substantial form expression of the
experience-meaning impression derived ultimately from apprehension of natural functional processes evolving within the context of Nature's Time-Place, ubiquity-ubiety, unity.

Viewed as inseparable parts of an integrated whole, Time
ubiquity and place ubiety provide only two of the essential conditions, universal perspective and local focus, for functional
processes, either in Nature or in art. The third essential, the
essence of functionality itself and of the evolutionary character
of Nature given impulse within her parts, must be the principle

of action, animating and modifying conditions within the fusion of Time and Place to create the impulses that give rise to motion and motive, the forces that provide identifiable characteristics and create the polarities of excess-deficiency among the conditions comprising the local relationships and the ubiquitous significances of natural movements and conflicts. Absolute staticity or absolute dynamism, in this sense, may only be viewed as hypothetical ultralimits of excess-deficiency, exceeding the tolerance endurance of the natural ethic-aesthetic and incapable of conformity to the mean of perpetuation and survival. The evidence of natural change and the presence of discernible Time-Place relationships provide irrefutable proof that the universe, at least as far as sentience will allow apprehension, is neither inertly static nor chaotically dynamic, but rather that it is in a mean-seeking state of mobility somewhere between Nature's tolerable limits of excess-deficiency, and that in terms of sensory perception its evolutionary mutability continues inexorably, neither in absolute excess nor in total deficiency of any of the qualities or conditions essential to its functional survival or perpetuation.

Ubiquity and ubiety, then, in their Time-Place relativity and in sentient apprehension of them in their relationship to the natural universe and its ethic-aesthetic impression translated into art, become the setting against which and in which all responsive faculties find their impulsive and impelling activations. Ubiquity and ubiety, however, as response generatives of both temporal and spatial impressions subject to the vagaries of responsive faculties and the re-creative potentials of fused and assimilated impressionalities of fallibly sentient imitation or translation of experience-meaning, may become distorted in their transition from reality into the new state of art; but even the distortion, if it is to be considered a valid work of art, must demonstrate, if not the reality of the natural ethic-aesthetic, at least the suggestive potentiality of the conditions and materials

269

of its structured substantial form to elicit responsive experience-meaning impressions that are credible possibilities under the mean-tolerance law affecting the substance of the work and effecting both impulse generation from within the work and responsive awareness from without. It is within Nature's Time-Place setting that the impulses inherent in the conditions of Nature generate and compel response, the essential ingredients for all change and motive, animate or inanimate, dynamic or static. We will call this generating and compelling impulse *action*, whether its force is impelling or expelling, implosive or explosive, moving toward or away from an object condition, internally derivative or externally derivative, so long as any change or activity is manifested as a result of its presence. Action, then, in both its Nature context and its form and structure translation into the context of a substantial form, is a contexture, derivative from and contingent upon the interplay of impulses between, among, and contiguous with the conditions comprising the major context of the Time-Place, ubiquity-ubiety, complex in Nature.

Time-Place comprises the conditions within which Action is germinated, nourished, and made to reach fruition; it is the soil without which the Action could not have inception and could not flourish because it is the base, the surface, from which Action derives its nature and on which it performs its function. Action is a consequence of the essential presence, at the same time universal and topical, of a generative impulse inherently fixed in and emergent from the fusion of Time and Place into the procreant unity of Time-Place, an eternal Phoenix whose self-perpetuating powers provide both the fuel and the fire for all other action, transient and permanent, as well as for its own regeneration. Time-Place provides its own unity and its own identity, unalterable save by its own admission and prerogative; Action, however, as a consequence of Time-Place and a derivative contexture of Time-Place, owes its being and its scope to

270

the exigencies of Time-Place. Because it is so constituted from the impulses it inherits and because its duration is determined by the nature of its procreation relative to the object conditions toward which or from which it is directed, Action may be arbitrarily fixed or segmented in relation to the particularities of conditions and impulses with which it is concerned, and it ceases as a tolerable force once it reaches the tolerance limits of Nature. Because it is relative to object conditions which are also subject to the Time-Place complex, Action is an attribute of the natural ethic-aesthetic, and as such it must function within the structure of the excess-mean-deficiency principle. This provides for a complex variety of motions and directions, expressions and impressions, impulses and responses, because each part of the excess-mean-deficiency principle demands, in relation to its object conditions, both action and reaction converging upon or diverging from the infinitely manifold combinations of object conditions.

There are six possible and basal motivational movements: excess to deficiency, deficiency to excess, excess to mean, mean to excess, deficiency to mean, and mean to deficiency. But because object conditions must be taken into account in each movement and because action begets reaction in causal relationships, a motivational movement might well result in an excess to excess, deficiency to deficiency, or mean to mean direction. And because of the multiplicity of combinations, each influencing and directing action relative to it in conjunction with action relative to another, without doubt there will be simultaneous and contrary movements and directions and motives contingent upon any one object condition's merits. Goneril's actions toward King Lear are both at the same time excessive and deficient and move in varying degrees of excess and deficiency relative to a complex variability of object conditions. Multiples of excesses and means and deficiencies are relative to the multiples of object conditions relevant to a given situation in the Time-Place setting, which in itself presents a qualifying multiplicity of infinitely variable potentialities for conditions and impulses. An excellent example from art would be the multitude of conditions, impulses, and events in *Paradise Lost* wherein chronological sequence is fused with omnipresence of being, contemporaneity of event, simultaneousness of actions, and vast translocations of physical properties in Time-Place conceptualism—a conceptualism involving a nonambiguous, complexly variable interrelationship functioning universally and topically, with ubiquity and ubiety, between the dualistic natures of Time-Place fused into one identifiable procreative entity, the fundamental essence of identification of all conditions, impulses, and actions (potential and actual) subject to the exigencies of Nature.

Nature, in her perpetuating function, is in a constant process of evolutionary movement emanating from the impulses generated by the counterbalancing variations from the mean of static order to strike a balance, the mean, between the extremes of excess and deficiency beyond which the tolerance of Nature will allow no continuation. The play between the tolerable extremes, muting and qualifying the one the other, creates the harmony of Nature as each motion of natural process affects every other functional substance in Nature through the interrelation of all those parts which in fusion constitute the whole of Nature. The disposition of one natural motion or substance toward another activates impulses which demand response from all motions and substances disposed to reception of impulses and response to them. It is then the impulse-reception-response equation of the natural ethic that elicits or excites conflict in the natural order which in turn involves the evolutionary processes of Nature in the dynamic interplay of creative energies disposed to establish both the aesthetic harmony and the ethical order of the natural universe. It follows that in the impulse-reception-response function there must be both a causal and an effectuated relationship, interrelated and interdependent, inherent in the nature of the impulses providing the dispositional reception between impulse and response and providing for the relative intensity of disposition that depends on the merit of the object of the impulse for the magnitude of the response required to provide the effect commensurate with the ethical mean variably focused between excess and deficiency in cause and effect or impulse and response. Where there is no cause or effect there is no motion, no function, no evolution; where the mean becomes fixed there is no dynamic interplay, no "music of the spheres," no creative process, and Nature becomes static, inert.

Inertia is not a dynamic quality, it goes without saying; and inert substance or condition can contain no more than a potential for function or evolutionary process. That which is static must become the recipient of motive generated from a causal condition or combination of conditions before the creative potential may be released to become the object of response, and, in the case of the sentient response, of impressions which vary with the infinitely conditioned faculties of each individual responder who, in a sense, dependent on the limits of his own responsive nature, creates within himself impressions which are uniquely his. Consequently, any change from the static to the dynamic, from the inert to the active, from the neutral to the involved, is a creative process because any change in quality or condition creates something that was not identifiable as the nature of the host quality or condition. In this sense, creativity or creative impulse may be either negative or positive, destructive or constructive, moral or immoral; but it cannot exist as the midpoint between the extremes of those contraries except as inertial potential. So long as functional processes continue there is no stopping of the impulse-reception-response continuum on a point of absolute balance; balance is achieved only between the allowable tolerances and depends on the variables meriting imbalance to counter the forces of contrary nature operating on the other side of the midpoint. The natural ethical mean is not then the midpoint between two extremes; it is rather what may be called a vibration about and in an inconstant condition wherein mutually antagonistic opposites may tolerate each other and wherein their natures respond to each other without destroying each other. This condition might well be called "comedy." A condition wherein the natures vibrate in such a manner as to cause one or the other or both of the natures to "suffer" loss of self-identifiable equanimity might then be called "tragedy."

Both comedy and tragedy are inherent as potential in any or all conditions that form the structure of experience; and either may become a function of the germinal condition when impulses generated from within or excited from without vitalize the ethical conditions of the impulse-reception-response formulation of impression. Their differentiation into qualities is not then to be based on the condition from which they originate (since either may originate in the same condition and may be identical before their potential becomes a reality), but rather on the manner of excitation of impulse, the nature of the reception, and the intensity and magnitude and kind of response elicited. It is not the condition itself which is the tragedy or the comedy; but rather the nature of the impulses emanating from the condition eliciting impression reception and responsive reaction provides the propensity toward tragedy or comedy. Sentience and the nature of sentient response, the Nature-conditioned qualities of sentient beings, determine (at the level of human awareness and human translation of experience into art) the experience-meaning impressions generated by the interplay of conditions, impulses, and responses and define those experience-meaning impressions in terms of topically limited absolutes, absolutes which have a simplifying utility in application but which tend to minimize perspective and falsify focus by exclusion of qualifying details and by generalization concerning interrelatedness of parts. Only when sentience ranges beyond topical formulaic absolutes may the totality of experience-meaning be apprehended and the comprehension of the natural ethic-aesthetic become an intrinsic functional quality of human awareness and responsiveness.

Tragedy, in the ethic-aesthetic of natural functionality, as well as in the valid translation of experience-meaning into substantial forms, is the adaptation or alteration of conditions resulting in the loss of identity and the consequent suffering involved in the process of identity loss; or it is the natural destruction, also involving suffering in the process, of a condition or conditions unable to evolve within the tolerances of excess-deficiency allowed by Nature. Nature establishes the excess-mean-deficiency ratios and she determines the tolerances relative to each condition within her total structural reference. Sentience, the unique particularity of one condition of Nature, provides not only means and manners of rational adaptation and evolution within the natural ethic, but it also provides will, curiosity, and imagination to attempt to challenge the limitations determined by the natural ethic. Such challenge, if it exceeds the allowable tolerances either of the natural ethic or of a topically constructed ethic, or if it is deficient in its function in relation to either the natural ethic or the topically constructed ethic, is bound to suffer destruction of its identifiable condition or to suffer the loss of identity of that condition; and that is tragedy. By the same token, a topically constructed ethic that exceeds the tolerances of the natural ethic or is deficient in its adherence to the conditions of the natural ethic is bound by its defiance of the natural ethic to suffer destruction or alteration, and that is tragedy to the adherent of the topically ethical condition. An implication here is that will may function at will within certain relatively dependent and interdependent mean-tolerance ratios, but aberrational function relative to the ratios, or defiance of them, will most certainly result in the imposition

275

by Nature of her inexorable law of self-perpetuation at the expense of sentient will. The will of Nature of necessity will take precedence over the will of even the strongest of her parts, and the result will be tragedy for the willfully defiant or aberrant part.

But there is also a form of tragedy that is not willful in its defiance of the natural mean-tolerance relativity, but rather the function of sentient error or misconception or ignorance of the natural ethic, and that is the tragedy of topical fallibility wherein suffering is imposed from without or is germinated within a condition that is determined not by the natural ethic but by the artificial construct of Time- or Place-limited utility and arbitrarily defined functionality. Claudius' topical definition of order and utility poses conditions at variance not only with the mean-tolerance ratio of Nature but also with the precepts of Hamlet's sentiently defined ethic. Since both are aberrations of topically defined order—Hamlet's ethic is not Claudius' ethic, and vice versa—both must suffer destruction or painful adaptation in order that a mean may be achieved even though neither is necessarily willful in other than his own definition and his desire to perpetuate that definition and his own identification with that definition. Ego, whether a condition of Nature's self-determination or of a sentient part of Nature, whether altruistic or selfish, tends to give impulse to conditions demanding definition in terms of self. When these conditions relate principally to sentient beings the proclivity is toward gratification of the appetites of only a part of Nature; when they relate principally to Nature herself the disposition is toward the preservation of the identifiable whole at the expense of the aberrant part. So we have natural ego founded in natural ethics and artificial ego founded in sentiently defined and topically limited ethics. The former is universal, the latter is transiently topical; and the universal will ultimately take precedence over the topical. In like manner, that which most accords with the natural mean-tolerance ratio will find essential preference to that which has lesser accordance with the natural mean-tolerance ratio both in natural functionality and in natural process. The topical process gravitates toward the natural function when Nature's ego exerts its pre-eminence over the topical ego, and the natural will exerts dominance over the topical will, but at the same time the will and ego of Nature leave the will and ego of Nature's parts free to destroy themselves if they defy the mean-tolerance ethic inherent in Nature's total function. Obviously, then, tragedy may be given impulse in either circumstance—as a condition of Nature's mean-seeking ethic or as a condition arising from the conflicts in sentient and topical associational qualities— whether it is grounded in the whole of Nature or in a part of Nature. But whatever its circumstance, tragedy and its concomitant, suffering, reside as potential within the conditions that make up Nature, and they are released for responsive function as tragic forces whenever the bounds of the mean-tolerance ethic are breached. Comedy, on the other hand, though arising from the same conditions as tragedy and often being generated by the same impulses, remains within the limits of the mean-tolerance. It is moved by the straying of a condition from the mean toward the tolerable limits on either side of the mean, but it never passes the bounds of tolerance limitation even though it may so nearly approach those limits as to be touched by the pains of adaptation or the suffering of destruction. Generally there is no loss of identity in comedy, but rather the transformation of identifiable parts from their uniquely differentiated entities into an amalgamation of conditions approaches the mean in such a manner as to insure perpetuation of identity even though that identity must be sought in a different context from that which was evidenced before the transformation. Comedy operates within the mean-tolerance law of Nature but accommodates a degree of nonconformity to the mean that does not exceed the tolerance allowance of the essential ethic. Tragedy operates outside the mean-tolerance law of Nature, and its nature is constituted by the suffering of such change or destruction as is necessary to bring conditions within the law to insure continuation of the substantial whole. In a sense, then, comedy is a mean-seeking motion conforming, though perhaps reluctantly, to the mean-tolerance law. Tragedy, on the other hand, confronts the tolerance limits of excess or deficiency and must produce suffering proportionate to the deserts of its degree of nonconformity to the mean-tolerance law. Conformity to the law is the fateful nostrum of comedy; tragedy has no panacea except its own suffering, and the excesses or deficiencies of its conditions must be destroyed as nonconforming excesses or deficiencies with uniquely identifiable natures before the natural integrity of the mean-tolerance law may be restored. Tragedy breaches the tolerance line; comedy does not.

Perhaps the most telling of examples from Nature herself to explicate the mean-tolerance rule governing the excess-deficiency ethics of Nature as a whole in relation to the conditions of one of her parts would be the condition of life itself as it is known to sentient beings. As a condition, life makes certain demands on Nature to supply other conditions essential to the sustenance and maintenance of the mean requirements of life perpetuation and consonant with the well-being of that condition. There is a considerable variation from the mean conditions necessary for the preservation of life, but whenever the tolerable limits of excess or deficiency in those conditions are exceeded, life ceases to function in its previously identifiable condition. A further example might well be the condition of an inflated balloon. A condition of excess atmospheric pressure (beyond tolerable limits) will cause the balloon to implode; a condition of deficient atmospheric pressure (beyond tolerable limits) will cause the balloon to explode. The tolerable limits will be established by the degree of inflation and the degree of excess or deficiency in relation to the ability of the balloon to tolerate excess or deficiency. Any variation from the mean of balloon well-being may be painful, but the implosion or explosion will occur only when the tolerances are exceeded. The resultant condition will be balloon tragedy.

Nature allows her parts unlimited freedom, total freedom to exercise will, determination, and inclination, the absolute freedom to attempt evolutionary adaptation of either self or of Nature herself, the freedom of self-destruction for violation of Nature's ethic-aesthetic of tolerance limitation. In this sense Nature is at the same time both benevolent and malevolent: benevolent and permissive and tolerant when the will of her parts plays freely within the bounds of her will, which is the will of her self-perpetuating ethical nature; malevolent and oppressive and intolerant when the will of her parts would in their freedom of exercise impose upon her either a destructive mutation of their identities or a malformation of her identity as the sole arbiter of her self-perpetuating ethical nature. Freedom, in the context of the natural formulation of a universal ethic-aesthetic, is essentially composed of the will and determination of a natural part to express its own identity within the confines of the will and determination of the whole to preserve and perpetuate its identity and maintain its supremacy as whole over the possible mutation of any of its parts attempting to transcend the ethic-aesthetic of the whole without precluding the evolutionary adaptation of the whole and its parts to the exigencies of functional constitution of new conditions created by realignment of parts, qualification of the natures of conditions by new combinations of parts, or by destruction of congruent conditions which had previously provided qualifying identification of either the whole or of any of its parts.

Nature, the essential entity which contains all things and of which all things in an infinity of variable and complex affinities and interrelated dependencies constitute the dynamically evolutionary structure, function, and identity, is the universal ubiquity self-contained, self-sufficient, self-forming, and self-regenerative. The parts, the dependencies and affinities of things constituting the whole, by chance or by manipulation by other parts, may seem to create phenomena outside the contextual tolerances sentiently attributed by the only part of Nature capable either of definitive analysis or definitive error, but in either case limited by the fallibility imposed by ignorance, an inadequacy of translation of experience into substantial form (the sentient memory of experience-meaning), and the very unfathomable nature of the total complexity of Nature herself. In topical comprehension these phenomena may seem to have universal significance, whereas in the actuality of universal functional ubiquity they may be merely manifestations of momentary aberrations from the mean-tolerance of Nature, and as such their significance will be meaningless except to those parts and conditions directly affected as Nature molds them into the context of her ethic or expels them from existence as parts of her entity. The complexity, then, of the whole natural universe and the infinitely variable combinations of its experienceable qualifying parts, poses monumental problems even to the analyst of only the structural cause-effect relationships between and among the parts of the natural universe (as differentiated from the artificial universe of sentient translation of experience into substantial forms), and consequently with the functional qualities of interrelated parts not only within themselves but with other interrelated combinations of parts and with the constitution of the whole from the qualifying conditions of influence, control, effect, and the substance-producing qualities of those parts. The problems become infinitely more monumental when the analyst, as the artist or as the critic, deals not only with the materials of the natural universe itself, but also becomes involved with the sentiently fallible translation of man's experiential meaning impression of those materials into substantial forms employing, as their material substance for impulse generation of response, materials and substances which have little in common with the native substance of experience and must rely on symbolic reconstitution and suggestive image of the initiating impulse to create impression-provoking substantial forms to perpetuate memory of any conditions or experiences not genetically transmissible.

The ethic-aesthetic of Nature is the cohesive quality, the truth-beauty principle and the universal law under which all things serve or die. The parts of Nature, particularly the sentient part, in rebellious divergence from the mean-tolerance norm of Nature's law, provide Nature's problems. And Nature solves them if her parts will not or can not, remorselessly and irrevocably, leaving in the wake of her inexorably dynamic evolution and her adamant adherence to her own survival and perpetuation principles the artifacts and fossils of all recalcitrant parts that fail to defer to the supremacy of the whole.

One of the fatal errors of man, particularly in his arts and his criticism, is to depend not upon the perpetual substance of Nature for the materials of his art or his critical machinery but upon the artifacts and fossils of Nature's rejected parts. An almost universal failure of sentience is to regard the artifact or fossil as an archetype to be reconstituted rather than as a pattern of failure in adherence to Nature's law to be restructured in conformity with that law: that man, as the sentient part of Nature, both in his functionally topical action and in his artistically functional role of memory retainer, is subject to the truth and beauty of Nature's evolution and to the topical aberration that creates only artifacts and fossils. When man develops his traditions on the processes and functions evolving within the law, he is sanctioned by the natural ethic, but not necessarily so by the topical ethic devised by sentience; when he develops his traditions on the foundation provided by the artifacts and fossils without their aberrant qualities, he may stand under the momentary aegis of topically sanctioned ethics but will be doomed by the same fate that overtook the artifacts and fossils upon which he built his traditions. Nature herself is the only true archetype and the only genuine source of universal models either of natural or of artistic perfection—the truth and beauty of the sages, and the ages. Traditions are fundamental to the safe and natural progression of man's nature within the context of the natural ethic, but they must be founded on the adamantine reality of natural law and the realization of the functional processes of that law; otherwise they lead only to catastrophic error. The validity of a tradition may be gauged only by its function within the natural ethic; its utility, no matter how transient or ephemeral, is most certain to be gauged within the definition of the topical ethic. Man, the artist and critic, must come to grips both with the intransigent natural ethic and the transient topical ethic; his short-term, utilitarian, activity will stem from the latter, but his long-term, perpetuating, activity will flower only from the soil of the former; and no matter how powerful may be the *isms* and gods in limited temporal or environmental context, they are only topically important unless by restructuring they may be made to range beyond the immediacy of Time and Place to remain within the mean-tolerance of the evolutionary natural ethic-aesthetic. Without a built-in, functional, impulse-generating adaptability and restructuring potential, *isms* and gods become artifacts, excretions of natural process fit only to fertilize a new order of conditions and impulses or to provide a wallow for those parts of Nature suited only for retrospective perception, sensitive only to the potency of Nature's ordure, and receptive only to relics of that which has grown functionless in Nature's evolution. Traditions that fertilize are essentially meritorious; they stimulate impulses for new growth and evolutionary potential; they provide the motive impulse for dynamically vital restructuring of conditions. Traditions that are inert, that are unadaptable to the evolutionary process, that play no role in the dynamics of the natural ethic-aesthetic, that provide only a wallow for the responsively static or retrograde—such traditions are futile detriments to those parts of Nature adhering to them in contravention of the progressive function of Nature. Thus Nature provides for a limited perpetuation of death and destruction and statics as well as for a limited perpetuation of life and construction and dynamics within the focus of her mean and the perspective of her tolerance, all contained within her ethic-aesthetic and bound to existence solely by the affinities of conditions co-relating among the parts to make up the structural entity, identity, unity, and entirety of the whole cohesively structured masterpiece of component parts.

Identification of artistic impulse, process, and function (as well as of critical impulse, process, and function) with the mean-tolerance law of Nature's ethic-aesthetic may well provide the only consistent tradition capable of providing a base not only for the making of a work of art with both topical and universal validity but also for a valid principle of critical analysis indigenously associative of topical context with extratopical substance, form, style, and structure. Art, that is, great art, is relevant not only to the topical conditions temporally and environmentally imposed upon it, but also it is relevant to the grander orchestration of the infinitely variable combinations of tones, structures, substances, and conditions pulsing through the substantial form of Nature herself, the primal genesis of all impulses and motive forces giving and receiving response, the elemental source of experience-meaning.

In this context tradition and its near relatives, myth and legend, are not at all nonessentials in the formulation of values (either topical or universal) that have an immediacy of effect in Nature-Art substantialism; and, indeed, if they transcend topical relevance to become (whether by Art-memory propagation or Nature-memory perpetuation) inviolable adjuncts of the natural ethic-aesthetic, they fuse into the grand complexity

283

of natural progressive evolutionary principle and function naturally within the limits of Nature's mean-tolerance relativity. However, if mythopoeism is merely topical in its context and applicability, or if legend or tradition is limited only to momentarily dynamic temporal or environmental conditions, their ubiquity is never attained, and they become functionless aberrants outside the immediacy of their own topical context, subsistently effectual only as they qualify and intensify the generative impulses of their immediate temporal utility. That is not to say that temporal affinities are without their own immediate values—that would be patently false—but rather that the cause of naturally ubiquitous progression has not been served. Essentially, then, mythopoeism, if it is capable of metamorphic evolution (or if it be grounded in the essential substance of the natural ethic-aesthetic), may be the most profound of the art-impulse motives, subliminal only to Nature's perpetual motives and motions; and, at the level of human nature (man's experience-meaning sentience), it may well be the seminal impulse not only of man's functional participation within the whole of Nature's being but also of his re-creative or reincarnative impulses toward artistic perpetuation of his experience-meaning impressions. Certainly primitive animism and atavism, because of their nearness to Nature in her most pristine form, may well be sentient man's most essential bases for the development of a fundamental ethic-aesthetic soil in which to germinate the seeds of myth and grow the fruits of a genuinely valid mythopoeic art. Myth that is uncluttered by the vagaries and artificialities of pseudo-sophisticated aberrance probably maintains man's primal memory record; and, consequently, such natal myth may be the ultimate in sentient cognizance of man's natural place in the universe and his recognition of himself as a functional part of Nature and the potential he has in the natural processes of Nature's evolutionary exuberance.

The things of Nature, all things, are natural correlatives of sentient awareness, the cosmic generation of all response, and the basal substances to be translated into the substantial forms of art. Just as the essential integrity of Nature is dependent on the fidelity of her parts, so too is the integrity of art dependent upon the fidelity of the sentiently derived impressions of experience to the natural ethic-aesthetic harmony orchestrated by Nature. None of the godsmiths, artistic or critical, of parts (moral, political, social, scientific, or other) can do more than pretend to create or analyze a system explicative of either the entirety of Nature or of the translation of the experience of Nature into substantial form.

All sentient beings are, in a sense, interpretive analysts of Nature, for they function as integral parts of the natural whole wherein their very existences as responsively sentient beings require that they interpret relationships and positions and establish roles in terms of those interpretations as part of the topical process, positive and negative, conventionally and often superficially imposed or superimposed upon Nature and her ubiquity-ubiety-action principles. These finitely topical interpretations form the experience-meanings, the impressions, gathered and sieved through all the responsive faculties, that provide man with the beliefs, laws, consciousness, and conscience that direct his activities within any generalized topical context. The artist puts those experience-meanings into substantial form to perpetuate their "truth"; and the critic, if he functions properly, judges the efficacy of the substantial form to present with fidelity and integrity those experience-meanings required or allowed, but not disallowed, by the ethic-aesthetic of Nature.

285

INDEX

Index

Antigone, 126–27

Apprehension, experiential and sentient: of tragedy, 22; functional: of artistic impulse, 108–109; of meaning: form of art, 238; range of impression, 216; reality of conditions, 18–19; sensation and, 201; validity determination: causal identification in, 174–75

Arbiters of artistic impulse, 93–97

Archetype, 281–82

Arrogance, critical impulse, 129–34

Art, apprehensible form of, 238; artifice, 168–69; assertion of experience-meaning contemporaneity, 233–34; corollary of Nature, 262–63; creation of new worlds, 84–89; creation of order, 107–109; critical mutilation of, 141–46; dependence on Nature, 283–85; derivative of Nature, 199–207; dissonance in, 183–84; establishing order, 226; evidence of artistic impulse, 96–97; evidential judgment of, 97–98; experience, 137–41; experience-meaning from Nature, 146–48; experience-meaning of, 218–20; experience potential, 185; expression of experience-meaning, 208–63 *passim*; fixation of experience, 233–34; focal form, 95; functional representation, 171–72; function of, 160–62, 218–19, 231–32; ignorance the enemy of, 138; imposition of audience experience on, 219–20; impression, 160–62; inferential, negative nature of, 238–39; inherent functions, 102; intermediary function of, 217–18; interpolation as disservice to, 251–53; judge of artist, audience, critic, 96–97; lessoner, 137–41; limitation of criticism by permitting, requiring, disallowing, 111–15; man-nature impression, 172–77; mediary between experience and substantial form, 111; myth and legend, 283–84; natural compulsion, 154–55; Nature the source of, 262–63; origin of, 131; permanence of experience-meaning, 235–38; perpetuated memory, 228–30; potential actuality of, 82–83; preservation of referential memory, 231–36; prevalence of prevenience over, 239–43; prostitution of, 92–93; referential memory in, 230–31; relation to criticism, 136–37; retainer of experience-meaning, 262–63; retentive faculty a condition in, 232–33; revelation, 86; self-determination of materials in, 231; self-sufficiency of, 217–20; source of experience-meaning, 141; status symbol, 144–46; subservience of, 103–105; substantial form, 116; substantial form of impression, 213, 221–24; substitutive contempt for, 254–55; superimposed values, 96; supplanted by prevenience as creative expression, 240–43; teacher, 139–41; Time its limiter, 265–66; topical relevance of, 283; translation of experience, 175–76; universal bases of, 82–83; "value," 142–46; variety of views, 98–99

Art and audience, relative experience of, 233

Art and Nature, ethic-aesthetic of, 153; ethic-aesthetic relativity in, 156–207 *passim*; excess and deficiency in, 153–60; experience-meaning fusion in, 167–207 *passim*; interpolation a subversion of, 252–53; relative affinity of, 261–63; relativity of, 153

Art and peripheral knowledge, 219–20

Art creation vs. audience creation, 218–20

Art diminishing, intervenience and, 246–47

Art experience, interposition as diffusion of, 244

Art fragmentation, interposition as, 244

Art function, 131–32; perceptual unification, 226

Artifice, art as, 168–69; critical, interpositional criteria as, 244

Index

Artificial judgment criteria, 247–48
Artist, artistic impulse test of, 99–100; art judge of, 96–98; as critic, 93–95; detachment of, 218–19; fidelity of re-creation by, 81–82; integrity of response, 82; man as, 182–207; milieu of, 93; obligations of, critical impulse, 117–18; re-creative ability, 81–82
Artist-audience, function: artistic impulse of, 94–95; participation: artistic impulse of, 93–95
Artistic, abstraction, 80; awareness, 80; beauty: 179–81; adherence to natural ethic-aesthetic, 180–81; function of ethic-aesthetic in, 179–81; cognizance of implications, 80–81; complements, rearrangement an alteration of, 259–63; degrees: of perceptivity, 81–83; of receptivity, 81–83; of sensitivity, 81–83; discernment, 80–81; empathy, 80; focus and perspective: determined by prevenience, 240–43; fusion of, 89–90; foresight, 111; freedom, 89–93; genius, function of, 181–82; imagination, 80–81; importance, limitations on, 90–109
Artistic impulse, 80–109; arbiters of, 93–97; artist-audience function, 94–95; artist-audience participation, 93–95; art, the evidence of, 96–97; audience determination, 90–95; contemporary experience-meaning, 104–109; creative nature of, 82–83; experiential nature of, 84–90; explicit and implicit functions, 107–109; focuses of, 87–89; freedom and order, 87–98; functional apprehension, 108–109; identification of, 283–85; integrity of artist, 97–98; manner of re-creation, 87–88; means of creativity, 87; nature of, 81–83; perspectives of, 89; qualities of, 83–86; responsive limitations to, 105–106; retention of experiences and meanings, 106–109; self-perpetuation of, 98–99; sentient: condition, 80–86; differentiation, 80–109; structure of substance, 84–85; substance of, 86–87; test of artist, audience, 100–101; topical reference, 105–106; tradition, 80
Artistic, insight, 80; integrity, 179–81
Artistic limitation, audience criteria, 90–92; critical imposition, 90–92; topical formula, 91
Artistic, loyalty, 93; nature, 134–36; perpetuation, universality, 100–109, potential, 230–32; selectivity, 83–85; synthesis, in creative process, 84–109; truth, 179–81
Artistry, materials of, 163–66
Art loyalty, 146–47
Art-memory: 231–38; critical impulse, 138–41
Art-Nature affinity, 157–207 *passim*
Ascription, ethic-aesthetic, 188–89; of value, comparison-contrast, 198–99
Assertion of experience-meaning contemporaneity in art, 233–34
Assimilation, creative process, 84–88; synthesis, contemporaneity, 210–11
Association, affinitive: development of knowledge, 227–28; impression to experience, 216–17; complementary, 178; correlatives of impression, 214–16; guilt in, 29–30; referential, experience to impression, 216–17; integrity of tangential impression, 223–24
Assumptions of substitution, negative nature, 256–57
Atavism, 76, 284
Attributions to referential memory, 236–37
Attributory natures, 220–21
Audience, artistic impulse test of, 100–101; art judge of, 96–100; as critic,

288

Index

93–95; art, relative experience of, 232–33; determination of artistic criteria, 90–93; experience of, imposition on art, 218–20; function of, in experience-meaning reincarnation, 176–79; its creation vs. art creation, 218–20; its imposition of inferential meaning, 236–39; obligations to critical impulse, 117–22; orientation by prevenience, 239–40; receptor of experience-meaning impression, 221–27

Avoidance of tragedy, 19–20

Awareness, alienatory capability, 29; artistic, 80–109 *passim*; conditions of, subconscious, conscious, unconscious, 7–9; essence of tragedy, 24–25; intensity of, 11–12; magnitude of, 11–23; of tragic pain, 32–79 *passim*; qualification of identification, 29–79 *passim*; sources of, 28–29; tragic, 10–23

Balance, adaptability in the ethic-aesthetic, 149–207; ecological, 151–52; ethic-aesthetic integrity of, 155–207 *passim*; excess-deficiency, 150–52, 198–207; functional, 150–207 *passim*; in conditions, 16–17

Balance vs. imbalance, evolution, 195

Barrymore, 260–61

Beauty, artistic: 179–81; adherence to natural ethic-aesthetic, 180–81; ethic-aesthetic perseverance, 182

Beauty, fidelity in representational function, 180–81; function of ethic-aesthetic in, 179–81

Beauty, intrinsic: 175; and tangential impression, 223

Beauty, nontopical, 179; structural genius, 180–82; suitability of manner of art, 180–81; the "Good" in Nature, 189–91, 196–99

Behavioral state, artificial inducement, 69; memory, 229–30; responsiveness, 11; tragic pain, 67–72

Beowulf, 252

Bias, prevenient, 241–43; prevenient substantiation of, 240–44; topical criticism, 123–26

Caprice, type of prevenience, 239

Causal-effectual relativity, 272–73

Causal identification, determination of apprehensive validity, 174; in art and Nature, 174–75

Cause-effect, complexity, 174–75; ethic-aesthetic, 157–60; experience-meaning of, 174–75; harmony of, 175; identification, 174–75

Celebrity vs. scholarship in criticism, 142–46

Cézanne, 219

Choice and consequence, tragedy, 12–14

Claudius, 150, 276

Claudius-Gertrude relationship, 192–93

Cognition, Nature's memory responsiveness, 205–206

Cognizance of implications, artistic, 80

Coincidence, of inference, 239–40; of impression, 236

Comedy, conformity, 278; inherence potential of, 273–78; mean-seeking of, 278; mean-tolerance within, 278; tragedy differentiation from, 274–76

Communal, comprehension, 154–55; identification through racial memory, in tragedy, 76–78; identity of tragedy, 75–78; norms, 73–75; tragedy, 74–79

Index

290

Index

substance forms, interpolation as, 250–51; of new worlds, art, 80–109; process of, 80–109; process of, artistic synthesis, 80–109; process of, imaginative assimilation, 83–109; of order, art, 106–109

Creativity, action processes of, 273–74; artistic impulse a means of, 86–87; sentience, 8–9; sentient impulse to, 8–9

Criteria, critical, experience-meaning, 241; critical, prevenient, 241; interpositional, critical artifice, 244; judgmental, artificial, 247–48

Critic, artist as, 93–96; artifice of, interpositional criteria as, 244; art judge of, 96–97; audience as, 93–95; deficiency of, 116–17, 127–35, 141–45; dilution of art by, 142; excess by, 141–45; expurgation by, 255–58; faddist, 118–20; fetishist, 130–33; genius of, 119–21; hindsight by, 111–12; imposition of standards by, 90–92; obligations of, critical impulse, 117–19; qualities of differentiation of, 127–37

Critical impulse: 110–48; arrogance, 129–34; art as memory, 138–41; craft of, 141–44; demands of, 120–23; description of, 137–41; determination of experience-meaning, 113; doctrinal prescription, 123–34; errors of deficiency, 139–41; function of, 135–48; identification of, 138–39; integrity, 123–48; limitations of, 113–14, 124–35; mythopoeic, 133–34; nature of, 110–48; obligations of artist, critic, audience, 117–19; prescriptive formula, 114–15; "flaw in character," 115; purpose of, 114; re-creation, 121–22; schools of, 127–44; selflessness of, 146–47; specialization by critics: 127–44; ambiguists, 128; enigmaticists, 128; moralists, 128; prosodists, 127–28; semasiologists, 128; stylisticists, 128; thematicists-messagists, 128; tonalists, 128; submission to experience-meaning, 148; substantial form as art, 115–16; topical degeneration, 144–48; topical prescription, 123–27

Critical, *isms*, 119–24; license and substitution, 255–57; limitations by what art permits, requires, disallows, 111–15; mutilation of art, 140–48; prescription, 114, 121–33; rearrangement, 259–61; specialists, 127–44; vagaries, 141–44; vanity, 243–61

Criticism, additive, 243–53; celebrity vs. scholarship in, 142–44; deletionary, nature of, 257; expedience as experience in, 142–43; experience-meaning criteria of, 241; expurgatory, 257; impulse to determine effectiveness, 110–13; inferential, negative nature of, 238–39; institutional view, 122–34; integrity in, 144–48; interpolative, 250–53; interpositional, 243–45; interpositional, speculative nature of, 244; nature of, 132–33; prevenient, nature of, 239–43; psychological, 126–27; relation of art to, 137; specialist authority, 127–29; speculative, 119–21, 140, 244, 250; substitutive, 254–57; substitutive, negative nature of, 250–51; test of, 114; topical bias, 123–32

Crotchet, type of inferential meaning, 237–38; type of prevenience, 239–40

Curiosity, tragic, 13

Curse of Nature, man's tragedy, 206

"Death wish," 92–93

Decadence, responsive: intervenience as, 247

Deficiency, critical, 116–17, 126–35, 141–46; errors of, critical impulse, 140–42; excess and, 150–207 *passim*

Deficiency and excess, aesthetics, 157, 188–89; function of, 156–57; in Nature and art, 152–60; topical, 202–203; 275–76

Definitive, rather than experiential, nature of interposition, 244

Index

Deflative nature of intervenience, 245
Degeneration, topical: critical impulse, 144–48
Degrees, of response, 81–83; of artistic perceptivity, 81–82; of artistic sensitivity, 81–82; of tragedy, 24–79
Deletionary criticism, nature of, 257–61
Derivation of ethics from Nature, 153–56
Derivative contexture of ubiquity-ubiety, action as, 268–73
Descriptive, ethic-aesthetic, 189–92; structure, ethic-aesthetic, 171–207; synthesis, 114–17
Destruction, tragic, 150
Detachment, of artist from work, 218–20
Determination, of apprehensive validity, causal identification in, 174–75; of artistic focus and perspective by prevenience, 240–41; of experience-meaning, critical impulse, 113–15; of experience-meaning, intangible, 216–18; of experience-meaning, tangible, 216–18; of Time, durational quality, 264–67
Devices, contextuality of, 178–79
Dichotomy, tragic, 206–207
Differentiation, and retention, 227–30; complexity of in art, 171–74; of impression, 224–28; of "meanings," 234; of referential memory, 229–30; of tragic pain, 32–79 *passim*
Diffusion of art experience, interposition as, 244
Dilution of art by criticism, 142
Dimension of Time, 264
Diminishing of art, intervenience and, 246–47
Disallowance, natural, 204–205
Discernment, artistic, 80–81
Discordance, topical, 183–84
Disharmony, tragedy as, 204–207
Disservice to art, interpolation as, 252–53
Dissonance in art, 183–84
Distortion, rearrangement of experience-meaning, 259–61; of focus and perspective, interposition a, 249–50; nature of intervenience, 245–47; nature of substitution, 256–57
Divergent conditions, interplay of, 196–99
Doctrinal prescription, 123–27
Don Juan, 127
Don Juan, 256
Drama, human, in Nature, 1–285 *passim*
Durational quality, determiner of Time, 264–67
Duration of tragedy, 79
Dynamic function of retention, 227–30
Dynamics of Nature, 199–207
Dynamism and staticity, excess-deficiency limit of, 268–69

Ecological, balance, 150–52; ethic, 56–57
Effect, total, of substantial art form, 116
Effectiveness, criticism, impulse to determine, 110–13
Ego, 276–78
Elemental state, contractual obligation, 7

Index

Emotional, memory, 229; state: range of, 52–67; responsiveness, 11; tragic pain, 51–67; tragic pain, differentiation of, 58–62
Emotional suffering, presentient, sentient, postsentient, 53–67; nature of, 54–67; relativity of, 53–67
Emotional vulnerability, 54–55
Emotive response, direction of, 54–62
Empathy, artistic, 80; associative, 27–29; projection of, 113–14
Endurance, tragic, 12–13, 34–35
Enemy of art, ignorance, 138
Enigmaticist, critical specialist, 128
Entity of Nature, the essential, 279–81
Epimetheus, 111
Epitome of Nature's achievement, man, 203
Error, sentient: tragedy and, 276
Error and deficiency, critical impulse, 139–46
Essential, entity of Nature, 279–81; mean divergence, 195–99
Ethic, ecological, 56
Ethic-aesthetic, 149–207; action the attribute of, 269–74; adherence to, and artistic beauty, 180–81; ascriptive, 188–89; balance adaptability of, 149–207 *passim*; balance and integrity, 155–207 *passim*; cause-effect in, 157–60; contemporaneity of process, 158; descriptive structure, 171–207 *passim*; evolutionary identity, 152–207 *passim*; experience, meaning derived from, 172–76; experience-meaning, province of art, 187–94; experience-meaning, reincarnate experience, 162–207 *passim*; focus and perspective of, 194; function in artistic beauty, 179–81; fusion, 195; integrity as morality, 152–207 *passim*; internal qualities of, 191–92; movement of, basal motives, 271–72; natural mean, 149–54; natural phenomena, its seminal principle for experience, experience-meaning, 95; Nature's stamina, 203–205; order of integrity, 195–99; perseverance of, 182; reincarnative experience in, 171–207; relativity of in Nature and art, 157–207 *passim*; violation of, interpolation, 193
Ethic-aesthetic impulse, 149–207; integrity of Nature, 149–207 *passim*; natural law, 151–207 *passim*
Ethic-aesthetic of Nature, beauty an adherence to, 180–81; man subject to, 184–207 *passim*; and art, 153–207 *passim*; and tragedy, 22–23
Ethical balance, and tragedy, 22–23
Ethics, functional derivative of Nature, 156; natural, intransigence of, 281–82; universality and topicality, 40–42
Ethics and aesthetics, aesthetic of integrity, 156; intrinsic qualities of Nature, 159–60; relation of in art and Nature, 156
Ethics of Nature, derivation of, 154–56
Euphues, 221
Evaluation, functional, inhibitors of, 247–48
Evaluative response, 178–79
Evanescence of Time, 265–66
Evidential judgment of art, 97–98
Evocation of response, variability of, 225–27
Evolution, balance vs. imbalance, 195–96; contingent artistic, 87–91; identity of, ethic-aesthetic, 152–207 *passim*; mean-seeking action, 272–73; nature

293

Index

of action, 272–73; rational principle, 204–207; synthesis of, in retrospective tragic recognition, 64–65

Excess, critical, 141–44

Excess and deficiency, 150–207 *passim*, 171; aesthetics, 156–57; function of, 156–57, 196–207; topical, 202–203, 275–76; in Nature, tragedy, 275–83; in Nature and art, 153–59

Excess-deficiency, balance, 198–207; interpolation as, 250–51; limits of staticity and dynamism, 268–69; tolerance, tragedy and comedy a confrontation of, 277–78

Excess-mean-deficiency ratio, Nature established in tragedy and comedy, 275–83

Expedience, as experience in criticism, 142–43; topical, 206–207

Experience, additive, negative value of, 253–57; and wisdom, 140; antecedent, 191–94; antecedent of prevenience, 239–40; art as, 137–39; as meaning, 165–67; associational affinity to impression, 217–27; associational reference to impression, 216–17; as substance of meaning, 165–67; expedience as, in criticism, 142–43; fixation by art, 232–34; function of response, 169–70; impression, associational reference, 217; impressions of, 211–63 *passim*; inherent meaning, 218–20; interpolative, nature of, 250–53; intervenient, nature of, 245–47; Nature in operation, 261–63; of art, interposition as diffusion of, 244; of art and audience, relative, 232–33; of continuum and referential memory, 233–34; potential, art as, 185–86; potential, relative to referential memory, 234; prior, and tangential impression, 220–23; psychic, generation of intangible impression, 214–15; reincarnate, 161–64; reincarnative, ethic-aesthetic in, 171–207 *passim*; sentience the essence of, 205–207; significance of, 208–263 *passim*; source of impression, 213–14; substitutive, negative value of, 253–57; variability of, 204–205

Experience-meaning, art as, 218–20; art as a retainer of, 262–63; art modification of, 184–94; contemporaneity, assertion of in art, 233–34; contemporary, of artistic impulse, 104–106; criteria of criticism, 241; critical impulse determination of, 113; determination of, tangible and intangible, 216–17; ethic-aesthetic reincarnate experience, 162–207 *passim*; expression in art, 208–11; from Nature, art, 146–48; fusion in art and Nature, 167–207 *passim*; generation, Nature, 158–59; impression and audience receptor, 221–23; impulse of, 208–63 *passim*; impulse to respond, 208–63 *passim*; *in medias res*, 265–66; intrinsic quality, 177–79; meaning of, 233–34; means, complement of, 175; nature of, 208–63 *passim*; of cause and effect, 174–75; of tragedy, 22–23; permanence of in art, 235–38; prescriptive, 189–90; rearrangement and distortion of, 259–61; referential memory, qualifier of, 235; referential memory, the source of, 232–33; reincarnate, 216; reincarnate, audience function, 176–77; reincarnation of tangential impression, 223–24; relativeity of, 261–63; seminal principle for artist and audience, 95; source in art, 141–42; tangential impression, complement of, 220–23; transmission of, 174–78, 199–202

Experiential, conditioning, 201–202; conditions, susceptibility to, 212–16; fidelity of tangential impression, 223–24; nature of artistic impulse, 85–87; significance, 214–16; significance, congruence with referential memory, 233–34; significance, of tangential impression, 222–23

Explicit contract with life, 27–28

294

Index

Expositive function of retention, 228–30
Expression, creative, art supplanted by prevenience in, 240–41; of experience-meaning, art, 270
Expurgation, critical, 257–58
External condition, sentience, 6–7
Extra-art function of inference, 237–38

Faddist, critical formula, 90–91; critics, 119–20; popularity, 143–44
Faerie Queene, 256
Fallibility, human, 280–83; of response, 173–74; tragic, 19–20; transmissible, 234
Fanny Hill, 256
Faulkner, "The Bear," 125
Feelings, 58–63
Fetishists, 130–34
Fidelity, and integrity, compatability of, 170–207 *passim*; experiential, of tangential impression, 223–24; in representational function, Beauty, 180–81; of re-creation by artist, 82; representational, 162–63
Figurative externalization of natural principle, 184–85
Finite principle, unity of Time as, 264
Fixation of experience by art, 233–34
"Flaw in character," prescriptive formula and critical impulse, 115
Focal form, art, 95
Focus, of artistic impulse, 87–89; of tragedy, man as, 20–22; referential, Time as, 266; tragic impulse, 18–19
Focus and perspective, artistic, determined by prevenience, 240–43; artistic fusion of, 89–90; in tangential impression, 226–27; interposition a distortion of, 249–50; of ethic-aesthetic, 194
Focus-perspective complex, 234
Foresight, artistic, 111
Form, apprehensible, of art, 238; focal, of art, 95; substantial, impression put into, 161–207 *passim*; substantial, in art impression, 221–23; substantial, materials of, 231–32; tone and, complementary function of, 259
Formula, topical, 91
Fragmentation of art, interposition as, 244
Freedom, and order, artistic impulse to, 91–92; of artistic expression, 91–96
Free will in Nature, 279
Function, art as, 160–62; artistic impulse, artist-audience, 94–96; as interpolative additive, 250–53; dynamic, of retention, 227–30; explicit, of artistic impulse, 107–109; expositive, of retention, 228–30; extra-art, of inference, 237; generative, of ubiquity-ubiety, 269–71; implicit, of artistic impulse, 108–109; in institutional contract, 6–9; of art, 131–32, 218–20, 231–32; inherent, of art, 102; of art, perceptual unification, 226–27; of artistic genius, 181–82; of audience in experience-meaning reincarnation, 176–77; of critical impulse, 135–48; of ethic-aesthetic in artistic beauty, 179–81; of excess and deficiency, 156–57, 196–207; of form and tone, complementary, 259; of man in Nature, 173–74; of response, experience as, 169–70; of tangential impressions, 220–21

Index

Functional, balance, 151–52; evaluation, inhibitors of, 247–49; quality of tangential impression, 223–24; representation, art, 171–72
Functionality, action the essence of, 268–69
Fusion, ethic-aesthetic, 194–95; experience-meaning, in art and Nature, 167–207 *passim*; of artistic focus and perspective, 89–91; of objective and subjective man, 231; of tragic conditions, 18

Generation, of experience-meaning, Nature, 158–60; of intangible impression through psychic experience, 214–15
Generative function of ubiquity-ubiety, 269–71
Genesis of impulse, Nature, 283–85
Genetic memory, 201–202
Genius, artistic, function of, 181–82; critical, 119–21; imaginative quality of, 185–87; structural, artistic beauty, 180–81
Goneril, 271
Guide, tradition as, 248
Guilt, associative, 29–30

Habitat of man, Time as, 266
Hamlet, 192–93, 219–20, 247, 250, 251, 260; experience-meaning, 192–93
Hamlet, 150, 192, 193, 219–20, 250, 260–61, 276
Happenstance of intangible impression, 217
Harmony, of cause-effect, 174–75; man-Nature, 182–85; natural, 182–84, 195
Hindsight, critical, 111–13
Human fallibility, 173–74, 234, 280–83
Helen, 256

Iago, 256
Identification, awareness of qualification, 29; causal, in art and Nature, 174–75; cause and effect, 174; of critical impulse, 138–39; of tangential impression, 223–24; with Nature, universality, 190–92
Identity, evolutionary ethic-aesthetic, 152–207 *passim*; natural, 172–73; relational, 224; tragedy as loss of, 275–76
Imagination, 184–87; artistic, 80–81; function in Nature, 186–87
Imaginative assimilation, in creative process, 84–86
Imbalance, ethic-aesthetic, 149–207 *passim*; critical, 124–26; impulse to action, 17–18; in conditions, 16; in Nature and art, 196–97; natural impulse, 195; responsive state, 214–15
Immanence, tragic, 62
Immediacy of tragedy, 66
Imminence, tragic, 62
Impasse, tragic, 60–62
Implicational impression, 237
Implicit contract with life, 27
Impression, affiliate, 220–21; apprehensive range of, 213–16; art as, 160–62; associational affinity to experience, 217; associational correlatives of, 214–16; associational reference to experience, 216; coincidental, 235–36; complexity of response to, 217–21; differentiated, sophistication of, differenti-

Index

Index

Interpolative, criticism, 251–53; experience, nature of, 250–53
Interposition, additive nature of, 249–50; critical, 243–45; critical criteria, artifice, 244; critical, speculative nature of, 244; definitive rather than experiential, 244; diffusion of art experience, 244; distortion of focus and perspective, 249–50; fragmentation of art, 244; interruptive nature of, 249–50; intervenience and, as qualities of tradition, 248–49; prescriptive, 244; theoretical, 244
Interpretation, license and tangential impression, 223; nature of intervenience, 250
Interrelation, of responsive states, tragic pain, 38–42; of topical and natural order, 197–99
Interruptive nature of interposition, 249–50
Intervenience, corruptive, 245–46; deflative, 245; diminishing of art, 246–47; distortive, 245, 246–47; experience, nature of, 245–47; interposition and, as qualities of tradition, 248–50; impositionally interpretive, 245; interpretive nature of, 249–50; misrepresentation, 245; preclusion of submission to art, 246; responsive decadence, 247; self-attributing, 245; self-protective, 246–47; sterility of, 247
Intrinsic beauty, 175; and tangential impression, 222–23
Invalidation of tangential impression, 223–27

Janus, 111
Jeffers, Robinson, 122
Jones, Ernest, 219
Judgment, artificial criteria, 247–48; evidential, art as, 98; relative, 231
Juliet, 256
Jungian speculation, 122

Kama Sutra, 146
King Lear, 256, 271
Knowledge, development of through affinitive association, 227–30; peripheral, and art, 219–20; requirements of audience, 218–20

Latent tragic impulse, 15, 47
Law, natural, ethic-aesthetic impulse, 149–207 *passim*
Lessoner, art as a, 137–40
License, critical, and substitution, 255–56; interpretive, and tangential impression, 223–24
Limitations, of critical impulse, 113–14, 124–35; responsive, to artistic impulse, 105–106
Limiter in art, Time as, 265
Limiting qualities of Time, 265–67
Loss of identity, tragedy as, 275–76
Loyalty, artistic, 93; to art, 146–47
"Lycidas," 211

Macrocosm vs. microcosm, 267
Magnitude, of awareness, 11; of response, 11

Index

Man, as artist, 182–207 *passim*; epitome of Nature's achievement, 203; focus of tragedy, 20–22; in Nature, 1; in Nature, integral function of, 173–74; nature of, in referential memory, 229–31; objective, 231; objective-subjective fusion, 231; part of Nature, 1; subjective, 231; subject to ethic-aesthetic of Nature, 184–207 *passim*; superiority of, 184–87; test of Nature's tolerance, 203–204

Man-nature, a Nature-nature identity, 172–73; impression, art as, 172–77

Man-Nature, complex, 230–31; harmony, 182–85

Manner of art, suitability of, 179–80

Materials, of artistry, 163–66; of substantial form, 231–32; self-determination of in art, 231

Mean, natural, the ethic-aesthetic, 149–54; divergence, essential, 195–99

Mean-seeking, action, evolution, 272–73; comedy as, 278; mobility, 269; natural, 277–78

Mean-tolerance, 274–79; comedy within, 277–78; explication of, 277–79; tragedy outside, 277–78; variability of, 274

Meaning, derived from ethic-aesthetic experiences, 172–75; experience as, 165–67; experience as substance of, 165–66; inferential, 236–39; audience imposition of, 236–39; peripheral relevance of, 237–38; types of, 237–38; inherence in experience, 218–20; prevenient, nature of, 239–43

"Meaning of art," 170–207 *passim*

"Meaning" of experience-meaning, 233–34

Meanings, different, interpolation creation of, 250–51

"Meanings," differentiation of, 234

Means, complement of experience-meaning, 175

Memory, art, 231–40; art as, critical impulse, 138–41; behavioral, 229; emotional, 229; genetic, 201–202; mental, 229–30; natural, 229–30; perpetuated by art, 228–30; physical, 229; referential: 229–34; art as preservation of, 232–36; attributions to, 235–36; complications of, 229–30; congruence of experiential significance with, 233–34; differentiation of, 229–30; experience of continuum, 233–34; experience potential relativity to, 234; in art, 230–31; man nature, 230–31; qualifier of experience-meaning, 235; qualifier of impressions, 235; range outside the conscious, 235–36; source of experience-meaning, 232–33

Mental memory, 229–30

Mental state, of responsiveness, 11; tragic pain, 35–42

Mental suffering, types of, 37–38

Metamorphic evolution of myth, 284

Michelangelo, 145

Microcism vs. macrocosm, 266–67

Milieu, artist's, 93–97

Milton, John, 209–10

Misrepresentation, intervenience a, 245–47

Mobility, mean-seeking, 269

Modification of experience-meaning, art, 185–86

Mona Lisa, 144

Moral and ethical nature of tragic pain, 40–42, 47–51

Moralists, critical nonspecialists, 128

Morality, integrity as, Nature's ethic-aesthetic, 152–207 *passim*

Index

Motives of ethic-aesthetic movement, 271–72
Mutant, tragic, 149–50
Mutant order, and tragedy, 206–207
Mutilation of art, by criticism, 141–42
Myth, as memory record, 284
Myth and legend, relevance of, 283–84
Mythopoeic, critical impulse, 133–34
Mythopoeism, metamorphic evolution of, 284–85; values of, 284–85

Natural, compulsion, art, 153–55; contract or condition, 4–6; contract, pre-sentience, 4–5; contract, sentience, 5–6; ethic-aesthetic, beauty an adherence to, 180–81; ethics, intransigence of, 282; excess and deficiency, and tragedy, 275–76; harmony, 149, 182–84, 195–96, 197–98, 205; hierarchy, 200; identities, 172–73; integrity, 150–207; law, ethic-aesthetic impulse, 151–207; law, truth-beauty cohesion in, 281; law, universal supremacy of, 207; mean, the ethic-aesthetic, 149–54; mean-seeking, 276–78; permission, requirement, disallowance, 205; phenomena, seminal principle of ethic-aesthetic, 95, 205; principle, prevalence of, 204–205; qualities, confusion of, 172–73; sentience, 200–207; stamina, 203–204; will, and tragedy, 275
Nature, achievement of, man the epitome, 203; affinitive relationship of man in, 173–74; analysis, ability of sentience, 285; and art: ethic-aesthetic of, 153; ethic-aesthetic relativity in, 157–207; excess and deficiency in, 152–59; experience-meaning fusion in, 167–207; integrity the essence of, 152–56; interpolation a subversion of, 252–53; relativity of, 152–53; archetype, 282; art as corollary of, 262–63; art as derivative of, 199–207; art dependence on, 284–85; dynamics of, 199–207; essential entity of, 279–81; ethic-aesthetic, man subject to, 230–31; ethic-aesthetic of, and tragedy, 22–23; ethics and aesthetics, intrinsic qualities of, 159–60; ethics of, derivation of, 153–55; experience-meaning generation, 158–59; free will in, 279; function of imagination in, 186–87; "good" and "beautiful" synonymous with, 189–91; habitat of sentience, 1; identification with, universality, 189–91; integrity of ethic-aesthetic impulse, 149–207; memory, 229–30; of experience-meaning, 208–63; of inferential art, negative, 238; of man, 1–9, 10–23 *passim*, 24–79 *passim*, 80–109; of prevenience: inhibitory, 240; substitutive, 242; totalitarian, 240–41; utilitarian, 240; of prevenient criticism, 240–43; of prevenient meaning, 239–43; of tangential impression, 220–26; operation of, as experience, 261–63; principal genesis of impulse, 283–85; relative affinity to art, 261–63; source of art, 204–205, 262–63; source of art experience-meaning, 147–48; Time the essence of, 265–66; tolerance, man the test of, 203–204; topical conversion of, 203–204; tragedy of, 78; tragedy the curse of, 206; uniqueness of man in, 1; vs. topicality, 155
Nature-Art affinity, 158–207
Nature-man complex, 230–31
Nature-nature identity, man-nature a, 172–73
Nature-Time complex, 265
Natures, affinitive, 220–21; attributory, 220–21
Negative, asumptions of substitution, 256–57; nature: of inferential art, 238–39; of inferential criticism, 238–39; of substitutive criticism, 253–57
Nonchronological contemporaneity, 211

301

Index

Nonconformity, tragedy, 278
Nonintellectual structuring, 209–11
Nonsequential contemporaneity, 211
Normalcy, institutional, and the tragic condition, 72–76; societal or communal, 72–76
Nostalgia, 104–105

Objective, and subjective man, fusion of, 231; correlatives of impression, 214; man, 231
Odyssey, 256
"Oedipus complex," 250
Omnipresence of Time, 266–67
Operation of Nature, experience as, 261–63
Order, corrective, 196–98; creative, art, 107–109; derivative of natural ethic-aesthetic, 186; establishing of in art, 226; inherent, 20; interrelation of topical and natural, 196–99
Oresteia, 147
Orientation, audience, of prevenience, 239

Pain, antagonism to, 31–32; physical, 32–35; tragic: 31–35; awareness of, 32–35; behavioral state of, 67–72; differentiation of, 32–79; emotional state, 51–67; emotional state, differentiation of, 58–62; interfusion of states of, 42–43; interrelation of responsive states, 38–42; mental state, 35–42; moral and ethical nature of, 40–42, 47–51; physical state, 32–34; pre-sentient contract, 35–36; psychic nature, 44–45; relativity of, 34; resistance an impulse to, 47; sentient contract, 36–37; spiritual state, 42–45; states of, 31–32; types of, 44–45
Paradise Lost, 112, 210, 272
Participation, artist audience, artistic impulse, 93–95
Passions, 59–61
Perceptivity, 2, 5–6, 10ff., 24–79, 80–109, 113–14, 123, 134–35, 137–38, 171, 182, 211–12, 215, 282–83; artistic degrees of, 81, 215, 282–83; sensitivity and, 2, 5–9, 10–23, 24–79, 80–109, 113–14, 123, 134–35, 137–38, 171, 182, 211–12, 215, 282–83
Perceptual unification, function of in art, 226–27
Peripheral, knowledge and art, 219–20; relevance of inferential meaning, 237–38
Permanence of experience-meaning in art, 235–38
Permission, natural, 205
Perpetuation, of memory, art function in, 228–30; of self, artistic, universality of, 101–104
Perseverance of ethic-aesthetic, in art, 182–83
Perspective and focus, artistic, determined by prevenience, 240–41; artistic fusion of, 89–90; in tangential impression, 226–27; interposition a distortion of, 249–50; of ethic-aesthetic, 194–95
Perspective-focus complex, 234
Perspectives of artistic impulse, 88–90
Physical, memory, 229; pain, 32–35; states of responsiveness, 11

302

Index

Place, Time exigencies, 270–71
Pleasure, impulse to, 16–17
Polarities of tragic impulse, 18–19
Pontius Pilate, 256
Postexperiential nature of inference, 240
Postsentient state, 4, 6–7; conjectural, 6–7; reality of, 7; supernatural contract, 7; unconscious, 7
Potential, artistic, 231–32; of reality in art, 82–83; of responsiveness, 117–18
Pre-art prevenience, prejudice, 240–41
Preclusion of submission to art, intervenience a, 246–47
Pre-determination of values, prevenience, 241–42
Pre-experiential nature of prevenience, 240
Prejudice, pre-art prevenience, 240–41
Premonitory impression, 216
Prescience, artistic, 200
Prescription, critical, 114–15; 121; doctrinal, 124–27; topical, critical impulse, 123–27
Prescriptive, experience-meaning, 189–90; formula, critical impulse of "flaw in character," 115; nature of interposition, 244–45; standards, 99
Presentience, 4–9, 10–23 *passim*, 24–79 *passim*; contract and tragic pain, 35–36; outside consciousness, 5
Preservation of referential memory, art as, 232–36
Prevalence, of natural principle, 204–205; of prevenience over art, 240–41
Prevenience, antecedent to experience, 239–40; anticipatory nature of, 239; audience orientation of, 239; bias, 241–43; caprice, 239; criticism, nature of, 240–43; crotchet, 239; determination of artistic focus and perspective, 240–41; inhibitory nature of, 240; in substitution, 254; meaning, nature of, 239–43; negative qualities of, 240–41; pre-art prejudice, 240–41; predetermination of values, 241–43; preexperiential nature of, 240; prevalence over art, 240–41; substantiation of bias, 240; substitution as, 258–59; substitutive nature of, 242; supplanting art as creative expression, 240–41; suppositional nature of, 239–40; topicality of, 241–43; totalitarian nature of, 240; utilitarian nature of, 240; vagary, 239; whimsy, 239
Principle of finitude, Time as, 264–65
Prometheus, 111, 263
Prosodist, critical specialist, 127–28
Prospective recognition of tragedy, 65–67
Prostitution of art, 92–93
Province of art, ethic-aesthetic experience-meaning, 187–94
Psychic experience, generation of intangible impression, 214–16
Psychic nature, tragic pain, 44–45
Psychological, conditioning, 70–72; criticism, 126–27
"Publish or perish," 119

Qualification of awareness of identification, 29
Qualifier, of experience-meaning, referential memory, 235–36; of impressions, referential memory, 235
Quality, functional, of tangential impression, 223–24
Qualities, negative, of prevenience, 240–41; of critics, differentiation, 129–37

Index

Racial memory, and contemporaneity, 76–77; and presentient state, 4–5, 71, 76–77; in communal identification, tragedy, 76–77

Range of referential memory outside the conscious, 235–36

Rational principles, evolution of, 204–205

Reality, of postsentient state, 7; potential, of art, 82–83

"Real world," sentience, 8–12

Rearrangement, alteration of artistic complements, 259–61; critical, 259–61; distortion of experience-meaning, 260–61

Recall, nature of, 64–65

Receptivity, 2, 5–9, 10–23, 24–79 *passim*, 80–109, 113–14, 123, 134–35, 137–38, 171, 182, 211–12, 215, 282–83; of tragic impulses, 11–12

Receptor, acumen of, 201; audience, and experience-meaning impression, 171, 221–23; of impression, 180–81

Recognition, Nature's memory responsiveness, 205–206; of tragedy: 63–67; prospection, 65–67; retrospection, 63–66; of tragic consequence, 35

Re-creation, ability of artist, 81–82; artistic contingent evolution, 87–89; artistic impulse a manner of, 87–88; congruency of impulses, 88–89; contemporaneity in, 210–11; critical impulse to, 121–22; fidelity of artist, 81–83; focuses of artistic impulses, 88–91; function, tangential impression, 221–24; perspectives of artistic impulses, 89; tangential impression, 223–24

Reference, associational, experience to impression, 216

Referential, focus, time as, 266–67; memory: 229–34; and experience of continuum, 233–34; art as preservation of, 232–36; attributions to, 236; communal, 229–34; complications of, 230; congruence of experiential significance with, 233–34; differentiation of, 230; experience potential relativity to, 234; in art, 230; man nature, 230–31; personal, 229–34; qualifier of experience-meaning, 235; qualifier of impressions, 235; range outside the conscious, 235–36; source of experience-meaning, 232–33; topical, 229–34; universal, 229–34

Regeneration of critical ignorance, 248

Reincarnation, experience: 162–64, 216; ethic-aesthetic in, 171–207; experience-meaning: 216; audience function, 176–77; ethic-aesthetic, 162–207; tangential impression, 224

Relation, affinity, validation of in tangential impression, 224–27; condition of man's world, 1–9; identity, 224–27; significance, of tangential impression, 223–24

Relativity, affinity, art to Nature, 261–63; causal-effectual, 272–73; in Nature and art, ethic-aesthetic, 157–207; judgment, 231; of emotional suffering, 53–56; of experience-meaning, 261–63; of experience, of art and audience, 233; of experience potential to referential memory, 234; of natural principles, 197–98; of Nature and art, 153; of Time-Place, 269–79; of tragic pain, 34–35

Relevance, peripheral, of inferential meaning, 237–38

Repository of impressions, sentience, 8–9

Representation, beauty as fidelity of, 180–81; fidelity as, 136, 163; functional, art as, 171–73; impression as, 136–38; selectivity as, 231

Requirement, natural, 205

Resistance, impulse to action, 17–19; impulse to tragic pain, 45–48; to tragic impulse, 12–14

Response, artist's integrity of, 11–23, 24–79 *passim*, 80–109 *passim*, 110–48 *passim*, 149–207, 208–63 *passim*, 264–85 *passim*; emotive, direction of, 54–55; evaluative, 178–179; evocation, variability of, 225–27; experience as function of, 134–41, 169–70, 208–63 *passim*; fallibility of, 19–23, 110–48 *passim*, 173–74; imagination as adjunct to, 186–87; impulse to experience-meaning, 80–109 *passim*, 208–63; nature of, 10–23 *passim*, 24–79 *passim*, 80–109, 132–41, 149–207 *passim*, 208–63 *passim*; to impression, complexity of, 217–21; universality of, 11–12; variability of impression, 215–16, 274–85

Responsiveness, 10–23, 24–79 *passim*, 80–109, 132–41, 149–207 *passim*, 208–63 *passim*, 274ff.; acuity, 201; awareness, 10–23, 24–79 *passim*, 80–109 *passim*, 149–207 *passim*, 208–63 *passim*; capacity for, 11–23, 24–79 *passim*, 80–109 *passim*; complexity, 17–23, 24–79; decadence, intervenience, 247; endurance of tragedy, 12–23, 24–79 *passim*; essential of tragedy, 10–23, 24–79; individuality of natures, 21–22; integrity of, 11–23, 24–79 *passim*, 80–109 *passim*, 110–48 *passim*, 149–207, 208–63 *passim*, 264–85 *passim*; intensity of, 11–23, 24–79 *passim*; magnitude of, 11–23; potential of, 10–23 *passim*, 24–79 *passim*; states: behavioral, emotional, mental, physical, spiritual, 11–23, 24–79, 80–109; to tragedy, 10–23, 24–79, 80–109 *passim*, 110–48 *passim*, 149–207 *passim*, 208–63 *passim*, 274–85 *passim*; will and inclination to, 10–23, 24–79, 80–109

Retainer of experience-meaning, art as, 80–109 *passim*, 184–85, 208–63 *passim*

Retention, and differentiation, 227–28; dynamic function of, 227–28; expositive function of, 227–28; faculty of, condition in art, 232–33; of experiences and meanings, artistic impulse, 106–109, 235–37; of impression, 227–30

Retrospective nature of recall, 64–65

Retrospective recognition of tragedy, 63–64

Revelation, art, 86

Revelatory impressions, 57–58

Samson Agonistes, 211

Scholarly service of interpolation, 251–52

Schools of critical impulse, 142–44

Scylla and Charybdis, tragedy, 12

Segmentation of action, 270–71

Selectivity, artistic, 83–84; representational, 231

Self-attributing nature of intervenience, 245

Self-determination of materials, 231–32

Selflessness of critical impulse, 146–47

Self-perpetuation of artistic impulse, 98–99

Self-protective nature of intervenience, 246

Self-sufficiency of art, 217–18

Semasiologist, critical specialist, 128

Semblance of actuality, 136–37

Seminal principle, experience-meaning of, 95

Sensation and apprehension, 201–202

Sensitivity, 2, 5–9, 10–23, 24–79 *passim*, 80–109, 113–14, 123, 134–35,

137–38, 171, 182, 211–12, 215, 282–83; and perceptivity, ability, 10–23 *passim*, 24–79 *passim*; and perceptivity, capacity for, 10–23 *passim*, 24–79 *passim*; and perceptivity, will to, 10–23 *passim*, 24–79 *passim*; artistic degrees of, 80–109

Sentience, 1, 4–9, 10–23 *passim*, 24–79 *passim*, 80–109 *passim*, 201–207, 208, 284–85; ability to analyze Nature, 285; apprehension of tragedy, 1–2, 10–23 *passim*, 24–79 *passim*, 80–109, 201–207, 284–85; awareness, 1–9, 10–23 *passim*, 24–79 *passim*, 80–109 *passim*, 284–85; consciousness, 5, 21; contract, and tragic pain, 35–43; creative condition, 5–9; creativity, 8–9; error, and tragedy, 19–20, 30, 276; essence of experience-meaning, 205–207; external condition, 6; function in institutional contract, 5–9; impulse, 1–9, 10–23 *passim*, 24–79 *passim*, 201–207 *passim*, 284; impulse to creativity, 8–9; institutional contract, 5–9; natural, 199–207; perceptivity, 2, 5–6, 10–23, 24–79, 80–109, 201–207; receptivity, 2, 5–7, 10–23, 24–79, 80–109, 201–207; repository of impressions, 9; sensitivity, 5–6, 10–23, 24–79, 80–109, 201–207; speculative condition, 5; the "real" world, 8–9; unconsciousness, 5, 21

Sensory impression, transmutation of, 172

Sequence, impression, 177

Setting, ubiquity-ubiety nature of, 269–71

Shakespeare, 193, 219–20, 256, 260

Significance, experiential: congruence with referential memory, 234; of tangential impression, 222–23; significance of experience, 208–63; of tangential impression, 237; relational, of tangential impression, 223–24

Skinner, albino rats, 122

Snow White, 256

Societal norms, 73–74

Sophisticated utility, 202–203

Sophistication of differentiated impression, 225–27

Source, of art, Nature as, 262–63; of impression, experience, 213

Spatial impression, 269–70

Specialist authority, criticism, 128–29

Specialization, critical impulse, 127–29

Speculative criticism, 120–21

Speculative nature of interpositional criticism, 244

Spiritual state, of responsiveness, 10–23 *passim*, 24–79 *passim*; tragic pain, 10–23 *passim*, 24–79 *passim*

Stamina, of Nature's ethic-aesthetic, 203–204

Standards, prescriptive, 99, 115, 121

State, awareness of conditions, 7; conditions of: natural, sophisticated, supernatural, 7; contractual obligations: conjectural, elemental, institutional, 3–9; evolution process of progression, 7–8; man's world: postsentient, presentient, sentient, 7; natural, condition of, 3–9; of man: postsentient, presentient, sentient, 4–9; of tragic pain, 31–32; progression of, 7–8; sophisticated, condition of, 7; supernatural, condition of, 7

Staticity and dynamism, excess-deficiency limits, 269

Status symbol, art as, 144–45

Sterility of intervenience, 247–48

Structural affinity of conditions, 231–32

Index

Structure, descriptive, ethic-aesthetic, 171–207; nonintellectual activity in, 209–10; of substance, artistic impulse in, 84–110 *passim*
Stylisticist, critical specialist, 128
Subconscious state of awareness, 7
Subjective man, 231
Submission, to art, intervenience a preclusion of, 246; to experience-meaning, critical impulse, 148
Subservience of art, 103–106
Substance, artistic impulse, 80–109; structure and artistic impulse, 80–109
Substantial form, critical impulse of art to, 115–18; impression put into, 161–207, 208–63 *passim*; materials of, 86–109 *passim*, 208–63; of impression, art, 154–207; 208–63 *passim*
Substantial forms, interpolation as creation of different, 243, 247, 250–57
Substantiation, of bias, prevenience, 240; suggestive, 243–44
Substitution, and critical license, 255; contempt for art, 254; critical, nature of, 253–59; distortive nature of, 256–57; dual nature of, 254–56; experience, negative value of, 26, 253–57; nature of prevenience, 242; negative assumptions of, 256–57; prevenience as, 258–59; prevenience in, 254; tonal, 261
Substitutive tragedy, 26, 61–62
Subversion of Nature and art, interpolation a, 252–53
Suffering, emotional: nature of, 38–79; relativity of, 53–79
Suffering, states of, natural conditions, 10–23, 24–79; tragic, 10–23, 24–79; tragic awareness of, 10–23, 24–79; tragic: behavioral, 38–79; interfusion of states, 32–79; physical pain, 32–35; mental, 35ff.; moral and ethical nature, 40–42; spiritual, 42–79 *passim*
Suggestive substantiation, 243–44
Suitability of manner, art, 180–81
Superimposed values, art, 96–97
Supernatural contract, postsentient state, 6–8
Supplantation of art, by prevenience as creative expression, 240–41
Suppositional nature of prevenience, 239–40
Supranatural world of man, 2
Susceptibility to experiential conditions, 213–14
Stylisticist, critical specialist, 128
Symbolic, devices, 110; significance, 71–72
Synthesis, and assimilation, contemporaneity, 210–11; descriptive, 114–17; in creative process, 84; test of criticism, 114

Tangential impression: 211, 214, 220–27, 237; and interpretive license, 223–24; and intrinsic beauty, 223; and prior experience, 221; associational integrity of, 223–24; complement to experience-meaning, 220–23; experiential fidelity of, 223–25; experiential significance of, 221–23; focus and perspective of, 226–27; functional quality, 223–24; function of, 220–21; identification of, 223–27; invalidation of, 224; nature of, 220–27; re-creative, 220; re-creative function of, 221–24; reincarnation of experience-meaning, 220; relational significance of, 224–27; significance of, 237; validation of relational affinity in, 224–27
Tangibility, determiner of experience-meaning, 216; impression, 211–22

307

Index

Teacher, art as, 139–41
Temporal impression, 269–70
Temporal topicality, 267
Test of criticism, 114–15
The Divine Comedy, 122
Thematicist-messagist, critical specialist, 128
Theoretical nature of interposition, 224
"The Roan Stallion," 122
Time, 264–79; adjuncts, 266–67; determiner of, durational quality, 265–66; dimension of, 264; evanescence of, 266–67; habitat, 266; limiting qualities of, 265–66; mutation of experience-meaning, 265–67; mutation of ubiety, 267–68; natural essence, 265–66; omnipresence of, 266–67; referential focus, 266–67; ubiquity, 264–72; unity of, as finite principle, 264
Time-Nature complex, 265
Time-Place, exigencies, 267–72; relativity, 269–79
Tiresias, 111
Tolerance, excess-deficiency, 149–207 *passim*, 271–85; excess-deficiency, tragedy confrontation of, 277–79; of mean, variability of, 271–72; of Nature, man the test, 203
Tonalist, critical specialist, 128
Tonal substitution, 261
Tone and form, complementary function of, 259
Topical, absolutes, 274–75; allusion, 192–93; bias, criticism, 123–24; conversion of Nature, 203–204; degeneration, critical impulse, 144–48; discordance, 183; disorientation, 196–97; ethics, transience of, 282–83; excess and deficiency, 203–204, 275–76; expediency, 206–207; formula, 91; justification, 198–99; law, vs. universal law, 206–207; order, and natural order, interrelation of, 198–99; prescription, critical impulse, 123–27; reference, artistic impulse, 105–106; relevance of art, 283–84; will, and tragedy, 275–76
Topicality, ethics, 40–41; prevenience, 241–43; temporal, 267; vs. Nature, 155–56
Total effect, substantial form, art, 116
Total experience, 112
Totalitarian nature of prevenience, 240
Tradition, 281–85; a guide, 248; and artistic impulse, 102–105; aura of validity, 249; deleterious nature of, 248–49, 282–83; fundamental to man's progression, 282–83; insinuative nature of, 248–50; interposition and intervenience as qualities of, 248–50; meritorious nature of, 248, 282–83; natural ethics and, 281–82; uncritical veneration of, 248; values of, 248–85
Tragedy, 1–285; aberrancy, 206–207; avoidance of, 12–14, 20; awareness its essence, 24–25; awareness of, 20–23, 24–79, 80–109 *passim*; choice and consequence, 12–14; comedy differentiation, 274–76; communal identification, racial memory, 76–77; communal identity of, 75–100; condition of, 10–23, 24–79; conditions of man's existence and, 6; confrontation of excess-deficiency tolerance, 278; contemporaneity of event, and, 76–77; degrees of, 24–25; disharmony, 205–207; endurance of, 12–13, 34–35; essential form, 10; ethic-aesthetic of Nature, 23, 149–207 *passim*; ethical

308

Index

balances and, 22–23; experience-meaning of, 23; "flaw in character" interposition, 250; human fallibility, 19–20; immediacy of, 66; impulse to, 10–23, 24–79, 80–109 passim, 110–48 passim, 149–207 passim, 208–63 passim, 274–85 passim; individual and communal, 74–79; individuality of, 25–28; inevitability qualified, 19; inherence potential, 273–78; latency of, 62–63, 78; loss of identity, 275–76; man focus, 20–22; manifestation of, 22–23; natural excess and deficiency, 275–76; natural will, 276; Nature travestied, 78; Nature's curse, 206; nonconformity, 278; nonnormal, 68–70; outside mean-tolerance, 277–78; receptivity of impulses, 10–23, 24–79 passim, 80–109 passim; recognition of, 63–67; response, resistance, and endurance, 12–13; responsive natures, 21–23; responsiveness its essential, 24–25; responsiveness to, 45–47; responsive states, 11; result of sentience, 13; Scylla and Charybdis, 12; sentient apprehension of, 22–23; sentient error, 276; sentient requirements of, 10–11; substitutive, 61–62; the mutant in, 206; topical will, 275–76; universal will, 275–76

Tragic condition, 10–23 passim, 24–79 passim, 80–109 passim; institutional normalcy, 72–73; conditions, fusion of, 18; curiosity, 13–14; destruction, 150; dichotomy, 206–207; duration, 79; focus, external focus of, 19; immanence, 62–63; imminence, 62–63; impasse, 60–62; impulse: 10–23; activation, 10; active, 15–16; counter forces, 16–17; creating impression, 22–23; elucidation of, 58–62; focus of, 19; inherence in conditions, 14–23; inner focus of, 19; latency of, 15, 47; nature of conditions, 15–16; particularities of, 14–15; polarities of, 19; universality of, 14; impulses, ambiguity of, 30; magnitude, 79; mutant, 149–50; pain: awareness of, 32–35; behavioral state of, 67–73; differentiation of, 32–79; emotional state, differentiation of, 58–62; emotional state of, 51–67; inherence in condition, 31–32; interfusion of states of, 41–44; interrelation of responsive states, 38–42; mental state, 35–42; moral and ethical nature of, 40–42, 47–51; physical state, 31–34; presentient contract, 35–36; psychic nature, 44–45; relativity of, 34; resistance an impulse to, 47–48; sentient contract, 35–43; spiritual state, 42–51; states of, 31–32; types of, 44–45; recognition, consequences of, 35; prospection, 65–67; retrospection, 63–66; states, complexities of, 39–42, 77–79; suffering: 13–14; alienatory capability, 29; qualification of identification with, 29

Transience of topical ethics, 282
Translation, art as, 175–76
Transmissible fallibility, 234
Transmission of experience-meaning, 174–77
Transmutation of sensory impression, 172
Truth, artistic, 179
Truth-beauty cohesion in natural law, 281
Types of inferential meaning, 237–38

Ubiety, alterable by Time, 267–68; nature of, 267–68
Ubiety-ubiquity unity, 268
Ubiquity, Time, 264–67
Ubiquity-ubiety, action the derivative contexture of, 270–72; generative function of, 269–71; nature of setting, 269–71; unity, 268
Uncle Tom, 256

309

LT   .   R/N SITSD

Pollard